Teacher's Guide
Year 1
Individual and Group Keep-up

William Collins' dream of knowledge for all began with the publication of his first book in 1819.
A self-educated mill worker, he not only enriched millions of lives, but also founded a flourishing publishing house.
Today, staying true to this spirit, Collins books are packed with inspiration, innovation and practical expertise.
They place you at the centre of a world of possibility and give you exactly what you need to explore it.

Published by Collins

An imprint of HarperCollins Publishers
The News Building, 1 London Bridge Street, London, SE1 9GF, UK

HarperCollins Publishers
1st Floor, Watermarque Building, Ringsend Road, Dublin 4, Ireland

lettersandsounds.org.uk

Browse the complete Collins catalogue at
www.collins.co.uk

10 9 8 7 6 5 4 3

ISBN 978-0-00-850613-1

British Library Cataloguing-in-Publication Data
A catalogue record for this publication is available from the British Library.

Author: Charlotte Raby
Copyeditor: Carole Sunderland
Proofreader: Faye Cheeseman
Cover designer: Steve Evans
Typesetter: Pascal Don
Production controller: Katharine Willard
Printed and Bound in the UK using 100% Renewable Electricity at Martins the Printers Ltd.

MIX
Paper from
responsible sources
FSC™ C007454

This book is produced from independently certified FSC™ paper to ensure responsible forest management.

For more information visit:
www.harpercollins.co.uk/green

Wandle Learning Trust and Little Sutton Primary School have partnered with HarperCollins Publishers to provide teachers with a full systematic synthetic phonics programme, Little Wandle Letters and Sounds Revised, and accompanying Collins Big Cat readers. Full details of the programme, including CPD training, can be found at lettersandsounds.org.uk.

Contents

Short five-minute daily sessions

- Secure blending and fluent recognition of all the Phase 5 GPCs are crucial skills for Year 1 children so that they can become fluent readers.

- Use these one-to-one sessions to ensure all children can read words independently.

- Do not stop teaching children new GPCs in class – to do so risks these children falling further behind their peers.

- Do not stop these daily individual support sessions until the child can read words independently and has them firmly in their orthographic store.

For support, you will find the 'How to' videos in the keep-up section of the website, and easy-to-follow **Prompt cards** in this Teacher's guide covering:

- Phase 5: Teaching a new GPC and reading words

- All phases: Precision teaching

- Phase 3: Reading words

- All phases: Reading words with speedy digraph recognition

- Phase 4: Reading words with adjacent consonants

- All phases: Reading words without overt blending

- Phases 3, 4 and 5: Reading longer words

- Phase 5: Reading words with GPCs that have more than one sound, e.g. 'ow' /ow/ /oa/

- All phases: Reading tricky words.

Prompt cards

Phase 5: Teaching a new GPC and reading words

You will need:

- grapheme card for the GPC you are teaching
- Phase 5 grapheme mat
- grapheme cards that the child can read with confidence for **Win it!**
- words with the new grapheme – use the sound button side
- sticker to write the grapheme on for the child after the session.

What to do	Notes
Teach: New phoneme • Introduce the new phoneme. • Model the correct enunciation a few times. Ensure the child can see how you make the sound. • Use the **copy me method** to get the child to practise saying the sound after you several times.	• Ensure you use a clear voice. • Observe children and check all children are enunciating correctly.
Teach: New grapheme • Show the child the previously taught graphemes for the new sound. • Point to the new grapheme on the Phase 5 grapheme mat. Ask the child to point to the other linked graphemes that they know. • Show the new grapheme card. • Ask the child to read the grapheme as you hide it and then show it several times. • If it is a digraph, use the mantra *'two letters, one sound'*.	• Take note of all previous linked graphemes, which can be found on pages 21–22. There may be more than one.
Win it! • Add the new grapheme card to the review pack. • Play **Win it!** Add the new grapheme into a selection of graphemes that the child can securely read. • Shuffle and repeat. • When the child reads the new grapheme correctly, they can 'win' the card. Then ask the child to give you the card back to see if they can win it again.	• Choose graphemes that the child can read securely for **Win it!** If they don't read a grapheme easily, put that grapheme to the side and teach it in the next session. • Play **Win it!** a few times, putting the new grapheme back several cards each time in the review pack, to ensure the child has lots of practice. This will help move the grapheme into their long-term memory. • Make a sticker with the new grapheme written on it, and stick it upside down on the child's top or right way up on their sleeve so they can look down and read it. • Make sure the class teacher and parent/carer are told which graphemes they are learning with you so that they can practise them with the child at other times.
Read words **Child** • Put the word with the new grapheme in front of the child. • Ask if they can point to the new grapheme in the word. • Ask the child to sound-talk each grapheme and then blend to read the word aloud. • Ask them to point to each grapheme and then sweep beneath as they blend. Do **not** help the child. **Together** • Ask the child to join in and point to each grapheme, then say its phoneme, sweep and blend the word.	

All phases: Precision teaching

- Use this activity to give children repeated practice, which will help them gain fluency and aid automatic recall of GPCs.
- You can also use this **precision teaching method** with words and tricky words – just set up the grid with the appropriate words that need additional practice.

You will need:
- grapheme card for the GPC you are teaching
- photocopy of the blank grapheme grid:
  - Write the focus grapheme at least twice in each row in random places.
  - Write three other graphemes that the child knows fluently in the other spaces on the grid.

What to do	Notes
Focus grapheme - Show the child the grapheme side of the grapheme card. Draw the letter formation over the grapheme as you say the sound. - Repeat a few times using the **copy me method**. - The child can draw the letter formation over the grapheme as you say the sound together.	- You can also use the Phase 2 and 3 grapheme mat or Phase 5 grapheme mat to point to graphemes that the child needs to practise to gain fluency. - Choose up to four graphemes to practise, point to them in random order on the grid.
Grapheme grid - Put the filled-in grapheme grid in front of the child. - Model pointing to the focus grapheme on the grid and reading it aloud. - Point to the focus grapheme on the grid and ask the child to read it. - Ask the child to find the focus grapheme, point to it and read it. - Now ask the child to read all the graphemes in each line as you point. - If the child doesn't recognise a grapheme, tell them the sound and get the child to repeat and continue. - Repeat, building on fluency.	- This method can be used with words as well as GPCs.

Phase 3: Reading words

You will need:
- Phase 3 grapheme cards for a quick review
- Phase 3 word cards
- sticker to write the word on for the child after the session.

What to do	Notes

Start the session with a quick review of Phase 3 GPCs using the grapheme cards.
 	
Independent reading
Use the word cards showing the sound buttons.
 	
For each word:
• Put the word card (sound button side showing) in front of the child.
• Ask if they can see any digraphs in the word.
 	
Child
• Ask the child to sound-talk each grapheme and then blend to read the word aloud.
• Ask them to point to each grapheme and then sweep beneath as they blend. Do **not** help the child.
 	
Together
• Ask the child to join in and point to each grapheme, then say its phoneme, sweep and blend the word.
 	
Assess
• If the child is successful, read another word with this method.
• If the child is confident, challenge them to read without overt blending – blending in their head to read the word aloud.
• If the child is not successful, ask them to read the word with you, then go back to the **whisper method*** to support them.
	• Only use words with the GPCs that the child can read with ease. Do not make words with any GPCs that are not secure.
	• Choose 4–6 words to read in the session.
	
	***Whisper method**
	• For each word:
	  • Put out the cards to make the word.
	  • Model reading. Whisper and point to each grapheme. Sweep and blend.
	
	Child
	• Ask the child to have a go at reading.
	• Ask them to say each phoneme as you point to each grapheme.
	• Ask them to blend as you sweep beneath the word.
	
	Together
	• Ask the child to join in and point to each grapheme , then say its phoneme, sweep and blend the word.

Win it! • Use the side of the card without sound buttons for this activity. • Add one of the new word cards to the review pack. Make sure it is close to the top of the pack. • Each time the child reads the new word, stop the game, reshuffle the cards and move the card back a bit. • Shuffle and repeat, incrementally moving the new card back. • Each time the child reads the new word correctly, they 'win' the card. Then ask the child to give you the card back to see if they can win it again. • You can add another word to the pack, if time.	• Have a pack of 4–6 words the child can read with confidence as the review pack words for **Win it!** • Make a sticker with one word from the session written on it, and stick it upside down on the child's top or right way up on their sleeve so they can look down and read it. • Make sure the class teacher and parent/carer are told which words they are reading in these sessions, so that they can practise them with the child at other times.

All phases: Reading words with speedy digraph recognition

You will need:
- Phase 3 or Phase 5 grapheme cards for a quick review – whichever is appropriate
- Phase 3, 4 or 5 word cards – whichever is appropriate
- sticker to write the word on for the child after the session.

What to do	Notes
- Start the session with a quick review of GPCs using the Phase 3 or Phase 5 grapheme cards. - For each grapheme, show the side of the card without the sound button. **Child** - Put the word card in front of the child. - Ask if they can see any digraphs in the word. - If they cannot, show them the appropriate grapheme card. Remind them what it says and point to the matching grapheme in the word. - Ask the child to sound-talk each grapheme and then blend to read the word aloud. - Ask them to point to each grapheme and then sweep beneath as they blend. Do **not** help the child. **Together** - Ask the child to join in and point to each grapheme , then say its phoneme, sweep and blend the word. **Assess** - If the child is successful, read another word with this method. - If they continue to find it difficult to identify the digraphs/ trigraphs, model the process using the **whisper method**.	- Only use words with Phase 3 or Phase 5 digraphs/ trigraphs that the child can read with ease. - Use words with one digraph only to start with, e.g. 'seed', or 'treat'. Build up to words with more than one digraph once these words are secure, e.g. 'sheep' or 'each'. - Choose 4–6 words to read in the session. - Put aside any GPCs that the child cannot read automatically. Ensure these GPCs are taught in the next session using **Phase 5: Teaching a new GPC and reading words** and/or **All phases: Precision teaching**. - Do not stop teaching these GPCs until they are all automatic.
Win it! Use the side of the card without sound buttons for this activity. - Add one of the new word cards to the review pack. Make sure it is close to the top of the pack. - Each time the child reads the new word, stop the game, reshuffle the cards and move the card back a bit. - Shuffle and repeat incrementally moving the new card back. - Each time the child reads the new word correctly, they 'win' the card. Then ask the child to give you the card back to see if they can win it again. - You can add another word to the pack, if time.	- Have a pack of 4–6 words the child can read with confidence as the review pack words for **Win it!** - Make a sticker with the one word from the session written on it, and stick it upside down on the child's top or right way up on their sleeve so they can look down and read it. - Make sure the class teacher and parent/carer are told which words they are reading in these sessions – so that they can practise them with the child at other times.

Phase 4: Reading words with adjacent consonants

You will need:
- Phase 2 and 3 grapheme cards to make the words the child will read
- Phase 4 word cards, if the child progresses to independent reading
- sticker to write the word on for the child after the session.

What to do	Notes
Use the grapheme cards and check which GPCs the child can read fluently. Use these GPCs to make up the words for this session.	• Start making words with adjacent consonants and short vowel sounds. Words with two adjacent consonants at the end such as 'went' or 'help' are easier to start with.
Whisper method	• Move to two adjacent consonants at the beginning of words, such as 'drum' or 'smell', before reading words with three adjacent consonants, such as 'strap' or 'strong'.
• For each word:	• You can find a full list of Phase 4 words on page 20.
• Put out the cards to make the word.	• If needed, repeat the process with adjacent consonants and long vowel sounds.
• Model reading. Whisper and point to each grapheme. Sweep and blend.	
Child	
• Ask the child to have a go at reading.	
• Ask them to say each phoneme as you point to each grapheme.	
• Ask them to blend as you sweep beneath the word.	
Together	
• Ask the child to join in and point to each grapheme , then say its phoneme, sweep and blend the word.	
Assess	
• If the child is successful, read another word with this method – this time without whisper blending – and then try **independent reading** with word cards.	
• If the child is not successful, ask them to read the word with you. Then repeat the whole process for a few other words.	
Assess: Mix it up	
• Choose two words you have already read.	• Choose one word from the session to make a sticker, and stick it upside down on the child's top or right way up on their sleeve so they can look down and read it.
For each word:	• Make sure the class teacher and parent/carer are told which words they are reading in these sessions – so that they can practise them with the child at other times.
• Mix up the grapheme cards. Put them in the correct order to make the word.	
• Model reading. Read and point to each grapheme. Sweep and blend.	
• Mix up the cards and give them to the child.	
Child	
• Ask the child to put the cards into the correct order to make the word.	
• Ask them to point to each grapheme and say each phoneme.	
• Ask them to sweep beneath the word and blend to read the word.	

All phases: Reading words without overt blending

You will need:
- word cards that the child can read but for which they continue to use overt blending when reading
- sticker to write the word on for the child after the session.

What to do	Notes
Reading with overt blending For each word: • Put the word card in front of the child. • Ask if they can see any digraphs in the word. **Child** • Ask the child to sound-talk each grapheme and then blend to read the word aloud. • Ask them to point to each grapheme and then sweep beneath as they blend. Do **not** help the child. **Together** • Ask the child to join in and read the word, blending in their head. Sweep beneath the word as you read. **Assess** • If the child is successful, read another word with this method. • If the child is confident, move on to reading without overt blending – blending in their head to read the word aloud. **Reading without overt blending** For each word: • Put the word card in front of the child. • Ask them to point to any digraphs in the word and say what they are. • Tell the child to read the words on the cards without sounding out. • Ask them to sweep beneath the word as they read. • Repeat. **Assess** • If the child is successful, read another word with this method. • If the child is still blending aloud, go back to **Reading with overt blending**.	Use the cards without the sound buttons. • Choose one word from the session to make a sticker, and stick it upside down on the child's top or right way up on their sleeve so they can look down and read it. • Make sure the class teacher and parent/carer are told which words they are reading in these sessions – so that they can practise them with the child at other times.

Phases 3, 4 and 5: Reading longer words

You will need:
- Phase 3, 4 or 5 word cards of words with more than one syllable
- sticker to write the word on for the child after the session.

What to do	Notes

• Model chunking the first word, e.g. 'rescue'.
  • Cover the second part of the word (so the card shows 'res').
  • Sound-talk the first part of the word using the actions: point and sweep: r-e-s, 'res'.
  • Reveal the second part of the word and repeat the step above: c-ue c-yoo.
  • Blend as you sweep under the whole word: 'rescue'.
 	
Child
• Put the card in front of the child and cover the second part of the word.
• Ask the child to sound-talk each grapheme and then blend the first part of the word aloud.
• Reveal the second part of the word and repeat the step above.
• Ask them to point to each grapheme and then sweep beneath as they blend the whole word. Do **not** help the child.
 	
Together
• Ask the child to join in and read the word all the way through. Point to each grapheme and sweep beneath the word as you read.
 	
For each subsequent word:
• Put the word card in front of the child.
• Ask the child to identify the digraphs/trigraphs.
• Cover the second part of the word.
• Ask the child to sound-talk each grapheme and then blend the first part of the word aloud.
• Reveal the second part of the word and repeat the step above.
• Ask them to point to each grapheme and then sweep beneath as they blend the whole word. Do **not** help the child.
 	
Win it!
Use the side of the card without the sound buttons for this activity.
• Add one of the new longer word cards to the review pack. Make sure it is close to the top of the pack.
• Each time the child reads the new word, stop the game, reshuffle the cards and move the card back a bit.
• Shuffle and repeat incrementally, moving the new card back.
• Each time the child reads the new word correctly, they 'win' the card. Then ask the child to give you the card back to see if they can win it again.
• You can add another word to the pack, if time.
	• Model the procedure for the first word, to ensure the child knows what to do.
	• For each word, only reveal one syllable at a time for the child as they won't be able to work these out for themselves.
	• Choose four or five words to read in a session.
	• Include some single-syllable words to play **Win it!** at the end.
	• Choose one word from the session to make a sticker, and stick it upside down on the child's top or right way up on their sleeve so they can look down and read it.
	• Make sure the class teacher and parent/carer are told which words they are reading in these sessions – so that they can practise them with the child at other times.

Phase 5: Reading words with GPCs that have more than one sound, e.g. 'ow' /ow/ /oa/

You will need:
- Phase 3 catchphrase card
- Phase 5 grapheme card for the same grapheme
- images to sort the words under (see **Phase 5 GPCs with more than one sound** on page 22)
- Phase 3, 4 and 5 word cards with the grapheme you are teaching
- stickers to write the words on – one for each sound the grapheme makes – for the child after the session.

What to do	Notes
• Explain that the grapheme makes more than one sound. • Display the picture side of the catchphrase card and an image that matches the other sound the grapheme makes, e.g. /ow/ 'ow': 'wow', 'owl' and /oa/ 'snow'. • Point to each card. Say the catchphrase, e.g. /ow/ wow owl and the word 'snow', to help the child really 'hear' the two different phonemes. • Tell the child to say the correct sound as you point to the images.	• This activity is for children who **can** identify the digraphs but find attributing the correct phoneme difficult. • If children cannot identify the digraphs with ease, then they need: **Reading words with speedy digraph recognition**.
Sort the words by phoneme • Tell the child they will now read words and work out which image they should go under, according to the sound the grapheme makes. For each word: • Put the word card in front of the child. • Ask them to identify the digraph. • Read each word. • Ask them to help you sort the word to the appropriate sound.	• Please see the list of **Phase 5 GPCs with more than one sound** on page 22. • Use 6–8 words for this activity. Use word cards without sound buttons. • Some words have more than one pronunciation, e.g. 'read', 'wind'. Discuss these with the child and use them in contextualising sentences.
Assess • If the child is successful, read and sort another word. • If the child reads the word with the incorrect pronunciation for the grapheme, model the correct pronunciation for the grapheme and return the word to the pack of words for the child to try later.	• Make a sticker with two words from the session, one for each sound the grapheme makes written on it, and stick it upside down on the child's top or right way up on their sleeve so they can look down and read it. • Make sure the class teacher and parent/carer are told which words they are reading in these sessions, so that they can practise them with the child at other times.

All phases: Reading tricky words

You will need:
- tricky word cards to learn and tricky words for **Win it!**
- sticker to write the tricky word on for the child after the session.

What to do	Notes
• Show the tricky word on a card. • Read the decodable parts of the word. Point to the 'tricky bit' and tell the children the sound that this grapheme makes. • Model reading the word. • Ask the children to read the word a few times independently. **Win it!** • Add the new tricky word card to the review pack. Make sure it is close to the top of the pack. • Each time the child reads the new tricky word, stop the game, reshuffle the cards and move the card back a bit. • Shuffle and repeat incrementally, moving the new tricky word card back. • Each time the child reads the new word correctly, they 'win' the card. Then ask the child to give you the card back to see if they can win it again.	• Have a pack of 4-6 tricky words the child can read with confidence as the review pack words for **Win it!** • Make a sticker with one word from the session written on it, and stick it upside down on the child's top or right way up on their sleeve so they can look down and read it. • Make sure the class teacher and parent/carer are told which words they are reading in these sessions so that they can practise them with the child at other times.

Precision teaching grid

Phase 3: Ten-minute daily additional blending practice

- These children urgently need additional support, so they do not fall behind. Without immediate support, the gap between them and the class will widen over time.

- Focus on these children – make sure they get extra informal practice and sit close to you (in your eye-line) during teaching, so you can make sure they are fully participating.

- Some children find it hard to recognise digraphs and take longer to learn to read these in words. If the children in Reception are not reading words with digraphs with ease in class, they need to join the Phase 3 daily additional blending practice group.

- There are five weeks of Phase 3 daily additional blending practice lessons and they build cumulatively, so that the children who complete the full five weeks will be able to read words with all the Phase 3 GPCs. The Phase 2 digraphs are reviewed in week 1 to ensure every child starts from a secure base.

- Children do not need to complete the full five weeks if they become confident at reading words with digraphs and are keeping up in class.

- Although this group is devised for keep-up in Reception, it should also be used for the children in Year 1 who find it hard to recognise digraphs and take longer to learn to read these in words.

Lesson template

You will need:
- Phase 3 grapheme cards and Phase 2 cards to review and make the words
- word cards as listed in the lesson
- flip chart to model spelling
- writing materials for the children.

Review GPCs	Review focus grapheme	Teacher-led blending and Independent reading	Spelling

Quick review
• Ask the children to read speedy sounds.
• Use all the cards – grapheme side only. (Only show mnemonic side if the children are unsure.)
• Do **not** continue if the children cannot read these GPCs.
• If the GPCs are not secure, teach them as a matter of urgency.
• Do **NOT** attempt to teach blending with GPCs that the children cannot read.
	• Use the **copy me method** to practise pronunciation of focus grapheme. Repeat.
	• Show the mnemonic side of the grapheme card – make a connection between the image and the sound.
	• Review the catchphrase.
	• Repeat several times.
	• Use the **copy me method**. Show the grapheme. Trace over it as you say its sound. Repeat.
	• Use the mantra 'two letters, one sound'. Then say the sound.
	
	• Play the **Grapheme game**. Show alternate sides of the card as the children call out the object or the grapheme. Repeat several times.
	
	• Remind the children of the catchphrase!
	
	• Add the new grapheme card to the review pack. Play **Grapheme spotter** with the new GPC.
		Teacher-led blending
		• Use the grapheme cards to make the words.
		
		Supported method
		• Put out the cards to make the word.
		• Model reading. Read and point to each grapheme. Sweep and blend.
		• Use the **copy me method** to repeat the process with the children.
		• Read the word together – giving less support. Watch and assess the children.
		
		Whisper method
		• Put out the cards to make the word.
		• Model reading. Whisper and point to each grapheme. Sweep and blend.
		• Use the **copy me method** to repeat the process with the children.
		• Read the word together – giving less support. Watch and assess the children.
		
		Independent reading
		• Use the word cards.
		• Show the word.
		• Point to each grapheme and then sweep to indicate blending.
		• Do not help the children. Look at the children and not the card.
		• Model reading the word.
		• Use pictures, props and simple definitions to ensure the children understand the meaning of each new word.
		
		Quick review
		• Shuffle the word cards. Ask the children to read without blending.
		
		Weeks 3–5, lesson 5: Sort the words activity
		• Display the catchphrase side of the grapheme cards that you want the children to look out for.
		• Hold up each word and ask the children to:
		  • identify the digraphs
		  • read the word
		  • help you sort the word to the appropriate phoneme/grapheme.
			• Spell two words.
			
			• Use the grapheme cards to spell each word.
			• Display these and extra grapheme cards as distractors.
			• Use the **copy me** method to:
			  • say the word (e.g. 'hug')
			  • segment it (e.g. h-u-g)
			  • segment and count the sounds (e.g. h-u-g – three sounds).
			
			Model spelling the word with the grapheme cards:
			• Say the word (e.g. 'hug') and how many sounds you need to spell it (e.g. three sounds for 'hug').
			• Say each sound as you get the letters you need (e.g. h-u-g).
			• Repeat above, writing the letters.
			
			• Ask the children to spell the word and check it together.
			• Show the word and check the children's spelling together.
			• Ask the children to check and correct their spelling.
			• Repeat for the second word.

Week 1

Lesson focus	Revisit and review		Teach and practise		Practise and apply
	GPCs	Focus GPC/ catchphrase	Oral blending	Teacher-led blending words Independent reading	Spelling
qu **queen**	a i e o u j g b h ck	qu Quick it's the queen.	qu-a-ck qu-i-t qu-i-z	**Teacher-led:** quack quit quiz quick **Independent:** jug bat hen hop	quack quick
ch **cherries**	a i e o u v ff ck qu	ch Chew the cherries, children.	ch-i-p ch-i-ck r-i-ch	**Teacher-led:** chip chick rich much **Independent:** van vet off cap	rich chip
sh **shell**	a i e o u w ll x ck qu ch	sh Share the shells.	sh-o-p sh-e-ll f-i-sh	**Teacher-led:** shop shell fish wish **Independent:** win wig box bell	shop wish
th **thumb**	a i e o u qu ck ch sh ll z	th Thumbs up we're having fun.	m-o-th w-i-th th-i-ck	**Teacher-led:** moth with thick this **Independent:** duck shell zip wag	with this
Review	a i e o u qu ck ch sh ll w		qu-a-ck s-o-ck m-o-th	**Teacher-led:** quack rich sock fish shop moth **Independent:** wig cap van bell	fish sock

Week 2

Lesson focus	Revisit and review		Teach and practise		Practise and apply
	GPCs	Focus GPC/ catchphrase	Oral blending	Teacher-led blending words Independent reading	Spelling
ng **ring**	a i e o u qu ck ch sh th ss	ng Bling on a ring.	th-i-ng b-a-ng s-i-ng	**Teacher-led:** ring sing bang thing **Independent:** quack chat mess hat	ring bang
nk **pink**	a i e o u qu ck ch sh th ss ng	nk I think I am pink.	p-i-nk w-i-nk th-a-nk	**Teacher-led:** pink sink wink thank **Independent**: wet shut mum dad	pink sink
ai **tail**	y x w ck qu ch sh th ng	ai Tail in the rain.	t-ai-l w-ai-t m-ai-n	**Teacher-led:** rain wait tail sail main **Independent:** thin wing yes fox	tail rain
ee **sheep**	ai qu ch sh th ng zz	ee Sheep on a jeep.	f-ee-t w-ee-p d-ee-p	**Teacher-led:** feet meet weep deep **Independent:** with rain sing buzz	deep meet
Review	ai ee qu ch sh th ng		r-i-ng r-ai-n th-i-nk	**Teacher-led:** ring feet rain think song deep **Independent:** fox zip shell wing	shell wing

Week 3

Lesson focus	Revisit and review		Teach and practise		Practise and apply
	GPCs	Focus GPC/catchphrase	Oral blending	Teacher-led blending words / Independent reading	Spelling
igh **light**	ai ee qu ch sh th ng w	igh A light in the night.	l-igh-t n-igh-t r-igh-t	**Teacher-led:** high light night right **Independent:** web king feet wait	high night
oa **goat**	ai ee igh qu ch sh th ng	oa Soap that goat.	s-oa-p g-oa-t r-oa-d	**Teacher-led:** soap goat road boat **Independent:** night deep sail fill	soap goat
oo **book**	ai ee igh oa ch ll zz qu sh th ng	**oo** Hook a book.	l-oo-k w-oo-d f-oo-t	**Teacher-led:** look book foot wood **Independent:** chill fizz road tight	book look
oo **moon**	ai ee igh oa **oo** ch qu sh th ng	oo Zoom to the moon.	f-oo-d m-oo-n b-oo-t	**Teacher-led:** boot food moon zoom **Independent:** coat look boat high	moon zoom
Review	ai ee igh oa **oo** oo ch qu sh th ng		f-ee-t l-igh-t g-oa-t	**Teacher-led:** feet goat light tail soap night **Independent:** Word sort **oo**/oo – moon look food foot	cool right

Week 4

Lesson focus	Revisit and review		Teach and practise		Practise and apply
	GPCs	Focus GPC/catchphrase	Oral blending	Teacher-led blending words / Independent reading	Spelling
ar **dark**	ai ee igh oa **oo** oo	ar March in the dark.	b-ar-k h-ar-d c-ar-d	**Teacher-led:** bark hard park farm card **Independent:** cool wood mix kick	card park
or **horn**	ai ee igh oa **oo** oo ar	or Born with a horn.	f-or-k s-or-t w-or-n	**Teacher-led:** fork sort born worn **Independent:** quick car goat rain	sort fork
ow **owl**	ai ee igh oa **oo** oo ar or ur	ow Wow owl.	d-ow-n c-ow h-ow	**Teacher-led:** down cow town how **Independent:** feet turn shell fork	cow town
Review	ai ee igh oa **oo** oo ar or ur ow		sh-e-ll c-ow p-ar-k	**Teacher-led:** shell goat park cow down hurt **Independent:** Word sort ar/or – farm worn sort park	down dark

Week 5

| Lesson focus | Revisit and review | | Teach and practise | | | Practise and apply |
	GPCs	Focus GPC/ catchphrase	Oral blending	Teacher-led blending words Independent reading		Spelling
oi **boing**	ai ee igh oa **oo** oo ar or ur ow	oi Boing boing.	c-oi-l s-oi-l j-oi-n	**Teacher-led:** coil coin soil oil join boil **Independent:** town fur sort park		join boil
ear **hear**	ai ee igh oa **oo** oo ar or ur ow oi	ear Get near to hear.	n-ear b-ear-d f-ear	**Teacher-led:** ear beard fear hear near tear **Independent:** down join for with		hear near
air **chair**	ai ee igh oa **oo** oo ar or ur ow oi ear	air Chair in the air.	h-air p-air ch-air	**Teacher-led:** air fair hair pair chair **Independent:** hurt boil hear light		hair pair
er **digger**	ai ee igh oa **oo** oo ar or ur ow oi ear air	er A bigger digger.	l-a-dd-er h-a-mm-er l-e-tt-er	**Teacher-led:** ladder hammer letter boxer better summer **Independent:** bark hair near look		better letter
Review	ai ee igh oa **oo** oo ar or ur ow oi ear air er		c-oi-n f-ear t-ow-n	**Teacher-led:** coin chair fear hair town boxer **Independent:** Word sort ur/er – turn hammer better curl		fair turn

List of Phase 4 words

Adjacent consonant and short vowel sounds

CVCC

went help tent wind hand land
hump lamp jump band lump lift
best gift nest soft just lost
thump tenth belt sixth fact pond
champ chimp chest punch bench munch
shift shelf hunt cost melt milk

CCVC

shrink crack smash frog smell swim
drum dress plug drink bring truck

CCVCC

stamp spend crept twist trust swift
crisp blend crunch crust grand squelch

CCCVCC

script scrunch strand strict sprint

Adjacent consonant and long vowel sounds

CVCC

toast joint burnt paint boast

CCVC

bleed growl smart spark groan speech bright
sport steep float train start flight
green brown gloom spoon storm broom
sweet sleep slight croak crown clown

CCCVC

street screech sprain strain screen

CCV

stair smear star clear tree free

Phase 5 linked graphemes in order

Autumn 1

Phase 3 GPC	Phase 5 GPCs
ai	ay play
ow	ou cloud
ee	ea each

Autumn 2

Phase 3 GPC	Phase 5 GPCs			
ur er	ir bird			
oi	oy joy			
igh	ie pie	i tiger	i-e time	
oo yoo	ue blue rescue	u unicorn	u-e rude cute	
oa	o go	o-e home		
ai	ay play	a paper	a-e shake	
ee	ea each	e he	e-e these	ie shield
or	aw claw			

Spring 1

Phase 2/3 GPC	Phase 5 GPCs				
ee	ea each	e he	e-e these	ie shield	y funny	ey donkey
e	ea head				
w	wh wheel				
igh	ie pie	i tiger	i-e time	y fly	
oo yoo	ue blue rescue	u unicorn	u-e rude cute	ui fruit	ou soup
oa	o go	o-e home	oe toe	ou shoulder	ow snow
j	g giant				
f	ph phone				
l	le apple	al metal			
s	c ice	se mouse	ce fence		
v	ve give				
u	o-e some	o mother	ou young		
z	se please				

Spring 2

Phase 2/3 GPC	Phase 5 GPCs				
ur er	ir bird	or word	ear learn			
oo	u awful	oul would				
air	are share	ear bear	ere there			
or	aw claw	au author	aur dinosaur	al walk	oor floor	a water
ch	tch match	ture adventure				
ar	al half	a father				
o	a want					
r	wr wrist					
s	c ice	se mouse	ce fence	st whistle	sc science	
sh	ch chef					
c	ch school					
z	se please	ze freeze				

About the reviewers

Thomas Naunheim is a cybersecurity architect at glueckkanja AG and a Microsoft MVP, from Koblenz, Germany. His principal focus is on identity and security solutions in Microsoft Azure and Microsoft Entra. Thomas shares his experience and research with the community as a blogger at `cloud-architekt.net`, and he is a speaker at conferences and co-author of *Entra ID Attack and Defense Playbook*. He is a member of the *Azure Meetup Bonn* and *Cloud Identity Summit* organization teams and is also co-host of the podcast *Cloud Inspires*.

Harri Jaakkonen is a Nordic security practice lead at Avanade and Microsoft Security MVP who lives in Finland. His principal focus is on identity and security solutions in Microsoft Azure and Microsoft Entra. He has over 28 years of experience in the field in various areas. Harri writes study guides and previews deep dives for the community at `cloudpartner.fi`.

Content contributors

Sakari Pajulampi: A review of the MDO and MDE sections in *Chapter 3*

Joosua Santasalo: Attack scenario simulation in *Chapter 5*

Armando Penumuri: A contribution to *Chapter 10*

Table of Contents

Part 1 – Zero Trust, XDR, and SIEM Basics and Unlocking Microsoft's XDR and SIEM Solution

1

2

Introduction to XDR and SIEM 15

3

Microsoft's Unified XDR and SIEM Solution 31

Part 2 – Microsoft's Unified Approach to Threat Detection and Response

4

Power of Investigation with Microsoft Unified XDR and SIEM Solution   93

5

Defend Attacks with Microsoft XDR and SIEM   133

6

Security Misconfigurations and Vulnerability Management   163

7

Understanding Microsoft Secure Score   183

Part 3 – Mastering Microsoft's Unified XDR and SIEM Solution – Strategies, Roadmap, and the Basics of Managed Solutions

8

9

10

Preface

This book unlocks the basics and importance of Zero Trust, XDR, and SIEM, and dives deep into Microsoft's unified XDR and SIEM solution. You will learn about its powerful capabilities, holistic benefits, and real-world use cases. Plus, you will learn about individual defenders such as MDI, MDO, MDE, MDA, MDC, and Microsoft Sentinel.

Let's level up your security architecture! By the end of this book, you'll be a Microsoft XDR and SIEM pro, understanding Microsoft's unified approach and its power to break down silos and strengthen your defenses. This book is your one-stop guide to improving your security posture with ease. From early adopters to major players, the list of organizations embracing Microsoft's unified XDR and SIEM solution is growing rapidly.

In this book, you will learn about the following:

- The concepts of Zero Trust, XDR, and SIEM, and the importance of considering them to improve your security posture

- Microsoft's unified XDR and SIEM solution and the importance of adopting this unified solution and its holistic benefits

- How to elevate your security posture with the Microsoft Defender tools MDI, MDE, MDO, MDA, MDC, Sentinel SIEM, and SOAR

- The true capabilities of Zero Trust, XDR, and SIEM, and real-world use cases to improve your security posture with case-study-based learning

- How Microsoft's unified XDR and SIEM solution auto-disrupts some attacks

- How to adopt Microsoft's unified XDR and SIEM solution and some of the assessments and strategies worth considering

- How managed XDR and managed SOC services work and the importance of considering those managed services

Who this book is for

This comprehensive book is your one-stop guide to mastering Microsoft's unified XDR and SIEM solution.

This book is ideal for the following people:

- CISOs and IT executives, to help you make informed decisions about your security posture and streamline your security stack.

- Cloud security architects, to help you build a unified security strategy with Microsoft's powerful tools.

- Anyone struggling with fragmented security solutions, as it helps to eliminate siloed architectures and achieve better security faster.

- This book is especially relevant in today's remote work world. Many companies wrestling with a patchwork of security tools post-pandemic will find this guide invaluable. You will discover whether Microsoft's unified solution offers the perfect fit for your organization, especially with the added incentive of bundled tools with licenses such as E5, A5, and so on. You will also enhance your ROI and build a robust, unified security architecture with confidence.

- Aspiring SOC analysts and Microsoft Security enthusiasts, this guide is for you! Fast-track your SOC career or dive into Microsoft Security with this comprehensive Microsoft unified XDR and SIEM solution book.

What this book covers

Chapter 1, Introduction to Zero Trust, lays the groundwork for understanding why XDR and SIEM solutions are crucial by delving into the concept of Zero Trust: its importance, principles, architecture, implementation considerations, and significance for security operations. We'll explore these topics in detail with practical recommendations, building a solid foundation for your decision-making.

Chapter 2, Introduction to XDR and SIEM, dives deep into the world of XDR and SIEM, explaining their core functions and why they're essential for modern cybersecurity. It explores their true capabilities, practical use cases, and implementation strategies, untangling buzzwords such as EDR, MDR, NDR, and SIEM along the way. Ultimately, it proposes a solution to break down siloed security architectures and streamline SOC operations, empowering analysts with improved triaging, investigation, and threat-hunting tools.

Chapter 3, Microsoft's Unified XDR and SIEM Solution, dives deep into Microsoft's unified XDR and SIEM solution, showcasing its seamless integration and benefits. It then explores each defender within Microsoft Defender XDR (MDE, MDI, MDO, MDA, and MDC) and Microsoft Sentinel, the SIEM and SOAR solution. Finally, it makes a compelling case for why adopting this unified approach can break down siloed security tools and propel your enterprise to a whole new level of protection.

Chapter 4, Power of Investigation with Microsoft's Unified XDR and SIEM Solution, delves into how Microsoft's unified XDR and SIEM solution empowers enterprises to revamp their SOC, streamlining daily operations and life cycle management. It explores the critical benefits this integration offers over traditional siloed technologies, enabling faster threat response and enhanced triaging, investigation, and remediation workflows.

Chapter 5, Defend Attacks with Microsoft's Unified XDR and SIEM, examines the application of Microsoft's unified XDR and SIEM solution in safeguarding organizations against cyber threats such as identity-based supply chain attacks in cloud, **human-operated ransomware** (**HumOR**), and **business email compromise** (**BEC**) attacks. Beyond a thorough analysis of the threat landscape, practical demonstrations of these tools' effectiveness will be covered.

Chapter 6, Security Misconfigurations and Vulnerability Management, delves into the critical nature of security misconfigurations and vulnerabilities, outlining a high-level vulnerability management process and showcasing how Microsoft's unified XDR and SIEM solution tackles these challenges head-on.

Chapter 7, Understanding Microsoft Secure Score, empowers you to strengthen your organization's security posture by navigating effective strategies to boost your Secure Score and understanding the reasoning behind each recommendation.

Chapter 8, Microsoft XDR and SIEM Implementation Strategy, Approach, and Roadmap, guides you through successfully implementing Microsoft's unified XDR and SIEM solution, highlighting crucial topics such as assessments, strategic considerations, and best practices for effective adoption and deployment.

Chapter 9, Managed XDR and SIEM Services, dives into the fundamentals and advantages of managed XDR and SIEM services, revealing how their effective management can shield you against a vast spectrum of cyber threats.

Chapter 10, Useful Resources, offers valuable resources to sharpen your skills in Microsoft's unified XDR and SIEM solution, empowering you to defend your organization against evolving threats with confidence.

Conventions used

There are a number of text conventions used throughout this book.

`Code in text`: Indicates code words in text, database table names, folder names, filenames, file extensions, pathnames, dummy URLs, user input, and Twitter handles. Here is an example: "All alerts, incidents, and relevant data are synced between the solutions, and data is populated in Sentinel to the **SecurityAlert** and **SecurityIncident** tables."

Bold: Indicates a new term, an important word, or words that you see onscreen. For instance, words in menus or dialog boxes appear in **bold**. Here is an example: "If you need to verify the MSSP's permissions, they can be accessed from the **Service providers** blade in the Azure portal."

> **Tips or important notes**
> Appear like this.

> *Note*
> *This book includes numerous figures with text formatted to fit the page width. As a result, the text in these figures may appear small and difficult to read. For an enhanced viewing experience, we recommend accessing the color PDF, which is provided with every purchase. Please refer to the Download the color images section in the Preface for detailed instructions.*

Get in touch

Feedback from our readers is always welcome.

General feedback: If you have questions about any aspect of this book, email us at `customercare@packtpub.com` and mention the book title in the subject of your message.

Errata: Although we have taken every care to ensure the accuracy of our content, mistakes do happen. If you have found a mistake in this book, we would be grateful if you would report this to us. Please visit `www.packtpub.com/support/errata` and fill in the form.

Piracy: If you come across any illegal copies of our works in any form on the internet, we would be grateful if you would provide us with the location address or website name. Please contact us at `copyright@packt.com` with a link to the material.

If you are interested in becoming an author: If there is a topic that you have expertise in and you are interested in either writing or contributing to a book, please visit `authors.packtpub.com`.

Share Your Thoughts

Once you've read *Microsoft Unified XDR and SIEM Solution Handbook*, we'd love to hear your thoughts! Scan the QR code below to go straight to the Amazon review page for this book and share your feedback.

`https://packt.link/r/1835086853`

Your review is important to us and the tech community and will help us make sure we're delivering excellent quality content.

Download a free PDF copy of this book

Thanks for purchasing this book!

Do you like to read on the go but are unable to carry your print books everywhere?

Is your eBook purchase not compatible with the device of your choice?

Don't worry, now with every Packt book you get a DRM-free PDF version of that book at no cost.

Read anywhere, any place, on any device. Search, copy, and paste code from your favorite technical books directly into your application.

The perks don't stop there, you can get exclusive access to discounts, newsletters, and great free content in your inbox daily

Follow these simple steps to get the benefits:

1. Scan the QR code or visit the link below

https://packt.link/free-ebook/9781835086858

2. Submit your proof of purchase
3. That's it! We'll send your free PDF and other benefits to your email directly

Case Study – High Tech Rapid Solutions Corporation

In this book we will consider a scenario of driving digital transformation and security enhancement at High Tech Rapid Solutions Corp (a fictional company name we will use throughout this book).

Introduction

High Tech Rapid Solutions Corp, a global leader in manufacturing and distribution, has 60,000 employees spread across multiple office locations on three continents. The company management understands the need to modernize their security operations, leverage modern cloud-based technologies, and enhance current security measures. Before the COVID-19 pandemic, they had a more traditional approach and had been less attracted toward remote work. However, the COVID-19 pandemic forced the company to quickly adapt remote work practices, leading to major improvements needs in the company security practices and technologies. This new situation led to a reevaluation of High Tech Rapid Solutions Corp security measures, prompting the organization to consideration of a security monitoring strategy and architecture to address their security needs and tackle the challenges caused by their siloed architecture.

Alongside the security landscape changes, High Tech Rapid Solutions Corp faces challenges in driving its new technology initiatives. The adoption of modern cloud-based technologies requires careful planning, time, dedicated resources, and a workforce equipped with the necessary skills. The organization understands how important it is to find new and retaining existing professionals who can effectively implement and manage their planned transformation initiatives. The company does manage its **Security Operations Center (SOC)** by itself and does not leverage any service provider's managed services in this area, even though it has been under consideration.

Furthermore, the pandemic presented unique challenges to High Tech Rapid Solutions Corp, accelerating the need for a **cloud-first strategy**. The company appointed a new **Chief Information Security Officer (CISO)** to the management team in order to guarantee the secure adoption of modern cloud-based technologies. CISO, who provides extensive experience in the cloud security domain, plays a key role in supporting the company's strategy, security teams, and business to maintain security as the top priority.

The current environment

High Tech Rapid Solutions Corp operates in a dynamic environment, characterized by diverse technologies and platforms. The key aspects of its current environment are as follows.

A cloud environment

Currently the company is operating in a multi-cloud environment, leveraging both Azure and AWS for its cloud infrastructure and business needs. This strategic adoption allows the company to benefit from the unique security features and capabilities offered by each cloud provider, while ensuring strong data protection across its operations.

A hybrid cloud architecture

Currently the company maintains a hybrid cloud architecture, combining on-premises infrastructure with cloud resources. This approach enables this company to maximize security controls and compliance requirements, while capitalizing on the scalability, agility, and cost-effectiveness of the cloud.

User entities

They have a hybrid identity architecture in place that allows seamless authentication and authorization for employees, granting them secure access to resources and applications across the hybrid cloud environment.

Collaboration with partners

High Tech Rapid Solutions Corp collaborates with external partners to drive business growth and innovation. To establish secure collaboration, the company extends its identity management capabilities to partners by leveraging Entra ID External ID (former Azure Active Directory) B2B collaboration and cross-tenant capabilities, enabling partners to access specific resources and collaborate within designated workflows.

End user devices

High Tech Rapid Solutions Corp operates in a diverse device landscape that supports both Windows and macOS platforms. The following aspects outline the current device environment:

- **Windows devices**: Windows devices form the majority of the organization's device ecosystem. Approximately 80% of the devices within the organization run on Windows operating systems.

- **macOS devices**: The company recognizes the need to take care user preferences and are having macOS devices in its device catalog as well These devices, comprising approximately 20% of the overall device inventory, are equipped with security features and management tools to maintain consistent security standards across platforms.

- **Mobile phones**: The company operates on diverse platforms such as iOS and Android.

Server infrastructure

High Tech Rapid Solutions Corp maintains a diverse server infrastructure to support its operations. The server landscape includes a mix of Windows and Linux servers, with the majority being Windows-based.

An application landscape

High Tech Rapid Solutions Corp's applications are distributed across both on-premises and cloud environments. While legacy applications may still reside on-premises, they prefer modern technologies and cloud-native architectures for new application development, incorporating strong security measures to protect sensitive data and protect against cyber threats.

An IoT/OT environment

In the company's IoT/OT environment, **Internet of Things (IoT)** devices are integrated with traditional **Operational Technology (OT)** to optimize operations. Interconnected sensors and machines collect real-time data from production to supply chain, feeding into centralized analytics for quick decision-making. The main challenge with IoT/OT environment is that it is lacking proper security monitoring and visibility to the environment from monitoring point if view is limited.

Security challenges

High Tech Rapid Solutions Corp has identified the following security-related challenges for their multi-cloud environment:

- **Siloed security architecture**: High Tech Rapid Solutions Corp's existing security infrastructure consists of disparate products that operate in isolation, resulting in limited visibility, missing threat intelligence, and inefficient incident response capabilities.

- **Incomplete security insights**: The lack of centralized security monitoring and analytics hinders the ability to correlate and analyze security events, making it difficult to identify security threats and vulnerabilities promptly.

- **Inefficient threat response**: The absence of a unified security platform and standardized processes undermines the effectiveness and agility of High Tech Rapid Solutions Corp's incident response, leading to delays in containing and mitigating security incidents. Currently, they use a legacy **Security and Information Management System (SIEM)** and is keen to modernize SIEM with a cloud-based solution.

- **Regulatory compliance**: High Tech Rapid Solutions Corp must adhere to industry-specific regulations and compliance frameworks. Ensuring continuous compliance with standards presents challenges in terms of data protection, access controls, and security audits.

Management concerns

Management is especially concerned about the following specific areas and several possible attack scenarios, based on the history they have had with breaches:

- **Lack of visibility and control in an IoT/OT environment**: High Tech Rapid Solutions Corp's IoT/OT environment includes a wide range of devices and systems with varying security controls. This lack of standardized visibility and control makes the environment difficult to monitor and they are lacking of managing potential security vulnerabilities and incidents effectively.

- **Lack of visibility on internet-exposed digital assets**: High Tech Rapid Solutions Corp doesn't have a clear understanding of its digital assets that are reachable from the internet, as well as the possible weak configurations on them. Their digital assets includes domains, subdomains, web applications, cloud services, APIs, and IoT devices. The compliance and regulatory requirements that the organization must adhere to in different regions and industries mandate strict security standards and best practices, protecting customer data and intellectual property.

- **A Threat Intelligence (TI) data (feed) does not exist**: High Tech Rapid Solutions Corp's security teams don't have TI data available, which can lead to a situation where they don't have full visibility of potential attack vectors, and they are incapable of prioritizing the most critical threats and vulnerabilities. In addition, the company wasting valuable time and resources on false positives and irrelevant alerts, often missing key indicators of compromise and early warning signs of breaches. As it struggles to keep up with constantly developing security threats, High Tech Rapid Solutions Corp risks losing reputation, customer trust, and revenue due to data breaches and downtime.

Challenges emphasized by security teams

High Tech Rapid Solutions Corp's security team raised some concerns and challenges that they faced during the last year:

- The finance department noticed some suspicious activities in their mailboxes, the creation of suspicious mail rules, and a few confidential emails leaking outside their department.

- The SOC team noticed many incidents, and they are confident that handling certain vulnerabilities would fix these incidents and reduce the number of incidents/alerts, but they struggling to gain visibility on the vulnerabilities.

- The SOC team has limited resources, which leads to triage, investigation, and remediation challenges, and these delays cause escalations to senior management (i.e., lack of auto-remediation and mitigations).

- The SOC team spends long hours fulfilling management ad hoc reporting needs.

- Management is concerned about the SOC team's inability to promptly address vulnerabilities and misconfigurations, which is attributed to the absence of a defined process and a dedicated vulnerability management team.

- The HR department raised concerns to the security team about unauthorized users accessing their apps or servers.

- Management initiated cost reduction strategies across the organization and allocated limited funds to the security team, asking them to reduce their cost, reduce the headcount, and submit **Return on Investment (ROI)** for any proposals, while simultaneously enhancing their security.

- The existing security team is not ready to adopt new technologies and needs training and guidance for new initiatives.

- The security team noticed too many users responding to spam messages and noticed URL clicks, and management asked the team to control these activities and train end users.

- Management asked the security team to keep an extra eye on certain assets, as well as terminate employees and contractors/vendors.

- The security team noticed too many false positives and spent a lot of time addressing these.

- The SecOps team struggles to track apps in the organization and control them.

- The SecOps team don't have enough knowledge about the Entra ID application consent framework and on how new and existing application registrations and permissions should be evaluated.

- The SOC team doesn't have active security monitoring for on-premises identities.

- The SecOps team doesn't have active security posture management for their cloud or on-premises resources

- High Tech Rapid Solutions Corp operations runs in three different continents, and some employees travel between office locations, factories, and so on. For the SOC team, it's complicated to identify false/positive and true/positive logins with the current security monitoring solutions.

- In a multi-cloud environment, High Tech Rapid Solutions Corp has been struggling to deploy agents on all servers.

- High Tech Rapid Solutions Corp's SecOps team has been failing to identify possible attack paths to cloud resources.

Concerns raised by CISO

The following are the concerns raised by the CISO:

- **Attacks on M365 collaboration workloads (BEC)**: As High Tech Rapid Solutions Corp extensively use various collaboration tools, such as Microsoft Teams and SharePoint Online, it needs to address potential data leaks, phishing attempts, and other security risks associated with cloud-based collaboration. Additionally, the organization is concerned about the growing threat of **Business Email Compromise (BEC)** attacks, where cybercriminals target employees through email communications to compromise sensitive data, initiate fraudulent financial transactions, or gain unauthorized access to company resources. Mitigating the risks posed by BEC attacks has become one of the top priorities for the company, as these attacks can lead to severe financial and reputational consequences.

- **Ransomware attacks**: High Tech Rapid Solutions Corp is increasingly concerned about the rising threat of ransomware attacks. The potential impact of a successful ransomware attack on its critical data and operations is a major risk. The organization seeks robust security measures and proactive incident response capabilities to prevent, detect, and respond effectively to ransomware incidents. Ransomware attacks, combined with the potential threat of BEC attacks, have emphasized the need for a comprehensive and layered security approach. High Tech Rapid Solutions Corp aims to implement advanced threat detection and prevention solutions, conduct regular security awareness training for employees, and enforce strict access controls to minimize the risk of ransomware and BEC attacks.

A recent incident response case

The company faced a targeted BEC attack six months ago that had a financial impact on business, and they want to detect and prevent similar attacks from happening in the future.

The BEC attack on High Tech Rapid Solutions Corp contained the following phases:

- **Initial reconnaissance**:

    The attacker gained information about the company and identified key personnel through company's websites and LinkedIn.

- **A phishing email**:

    The attacker needed credentials to get access to the environment, and one of the most common ways is to do so is by some form of phishing email. On this occasion, they used a spearphishing attachment (T1566.001 in MITRE ATT&CK `https://packt.link/eOJcm`) that included a malicious attachment. By clicking the link, the user believed that they were logging into a Microsoft sign-in page and entered their credentials.

- **Persistence and exfiltration**:

    After gaining access to the target user's mailbox, the attacker created a forwarding rule to the mailbox for data exfiltration.

- **Financial fraud**:

    The actual victim of this attack was a procurement manager who believed that the email (marked as **Important** and **Confidential**) urging for immediate payment came from CFO.

- **Impact**:

    As a result of the successful BEC attack, the following occurred:

    - The financial team transferred a significant sum of money to the attacker's account, thinking it was a legitimate payment.

    - The real vendor who should have received this payment but did not receive it, contacted the company to inquire about the overdue invoice.

- The financial team realized it had been scammed, but it was too late to recover the funds, as they had already been transferred to an overseas account.

- The company suffered a financial loss, damage to its reputation, and potential legal consequences for failing to secure sensitive financial transactions.

To prevent such attacks in the future, the company is committed to strengthening its security environment security posture, focusing on implementing robust email security measures, employee training, and verification protocols for financial transactions.

Summary

This case study will be explored throughout the book in the different chapters, focusing on how High Tech Rapid Solutions Corp can benefit from leveraging Microsoft's unified XDR and SIEM solution to address security challenges.

Part 1 – Zero Trust, XDR, and SIEM Basics and Unlocking Microsoft's XDR and SIEM Solution

This part breaks down the basics of Zero Trust, XDR, and SIEM, and explains why you should think about using both XDR and SIEM together, especially Microsoft's unified XDR and SIEM solution. It's like having a security toolbox with all the right tools for the job, making it easier to protect yourself from cyber threats.

This part has the following chapters:

- *Chapter 1, Introduction to Zero Trust*
- *Chapter 2, Introduction to XDR and SIEM*
- *Chapter 3, Microsoft's Unified XDR and SIEM Solution*

1

Introduction to Zero Trust

In this chapter, the goal is to understand what **Zero Trust** is and the history behind it. In today's rapidly evolving digital landscape, the adoption of Zero Trust has become imperative. Its role in bolstering security operations cannot be overstated as it introduces a proactive and layered approach to cybersecurity. Various Zero Trust architectures and principles have emerged in the cybersecurity realm, emphasizing continuous verification and restricted access. We will consider a compelling case study that will further exemplify the transformative power of Zero Trust, showcasing how it effectively addresses complex security challenges, providing organizations with a resilient and adaptable defense against modern threats.

This chapter will cover the following main topics:

- Zero Trust and its history
- Why do we need Zero Trust?
- Zero Trust in security operations
- Zero Trust principles and architectures
- Real-life examples
- Case study analysis

Zero Trust and its history

When we hear Zero Trust for the very first time, it sounds interesting, right? It's very common for many to start thinking the following:

- What is Zero Trust? Is this a product we need to implement?
- How soon can we install and configure it?
- Does Zero Trust mean don't trust anything or anyone? Then what about our daily work routine? Will there be any impact on the business?
- What about the tools/products we have in place? Is it compatible with other products in place? Do we need to replace these tools?

- Do we need special skill set resources? Is any training needed?

- Why is almost everyone talking about Zero Trust? Is this something that just started or is it gaining momentum?

To start with, Zero Trust is not a product; it's a security framework and a strategic approach to secure an organization and harden its attack surface. This model assumes that no user or device is inherently trusted, irrespective of the origination (an external or internal network). Before we get into the details, let's look at the history (see *Figure 1.1*).

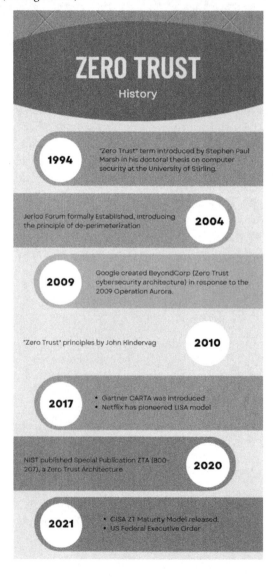

Figure 1.1 – Zero Trust history

So, looking at the history, it's very clear that when Zero Trust started a long way back, a few companies initiated their Zero Trust journey when some of their workloads started shifting outside of the traditional network perimeter. Then, with **bring your own device (BYOD)** and **software as a service (SaaS)** gaining momentum due to the Covid-19 pandemic as remote working increased, threats expanded along with other factors, such as technology advances and situations forcing organizations to shift from a traditional environment to a modern one.

Why do we need Zero Trust?

The Covid-19 pandemic has been a game changer. The Covid-19 outbreak forced almost all companies to adopt remote working aggressively (whether they liked it or not) and that changed the threat landscape, such as the nature of attacks, types of attacks, frequency, and exposure. Few companies thought they would expose only some of their sensitive digital estates beyond the firewall. This fast-phased transition to remote working has left many organizations struggling to implement the needed infrastructure and they have ended up with siloed architecture.

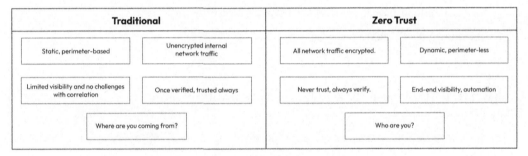

Figure 1.2 – Traditional versus Zero Trust comparison

At one point, there were clear boundaries for the **virtual private network (VPN)** where more focus was on the external side of it, but things have changed with the Covid-19 pandemic; threat risk has expanded to pretty much all of the enterprise, including **operational technology (OT)** and the **Internet of Things (IoT)**. With that, almost all organizations started thinking about implementing remote work for their employees for business continuity, and honestly, we were personally impressed with how quickly things changed. Many start-ups, small- to mid-sized companies, took this seriously (probably as a lifetime opportunity), invested heavily, and benefited from this.

During the pandemic, organizations tried adopting security tools quickly to protect their digital estates. In most cases, they ended up with **siloed architecture**, and that led to conflicts in the architecture and design. For example, collaboration and productivity teams prefer open/unrestricted guest management with self services, identity and access teams preferred managed identities with a governance model, network and infrastructure teams preferred established remote access and remote desktop solutions, while collaboration teams used video conference solutions with a direct connection and SaaS-based solutions.

They invested a lot of money and time in implementing, training, monitoring, and so on. But even after that, they still reached a stage that many do and faced one or more of the following issues (these are just a few):

- Still seeing some threats happening
- Managing too many portals to maintain day-to-day security operations
- A few things are out of control
- Not able to quickly react, which is very time-consuming for triage, investigation, and remediation
- Finding resources and providing training for them
- Controlling who has access to what
- Limited visibility or insights into what's going on
- Trying to reduce the risk of data breaches
- Failing to establish a certain level of trust at each access point
- Providing adaptive and continuous protection

> **Tip**
> It is never too late to adopt the Zero Trust security model.

So, in short, with Zero Trust, instead of assuming only things beyond the firewall need to be verified and everything behind the firewall is safe, this model assumes there is a breach and that nothing should be trusted, and it verifies each and every request regardless of where it originates. The core fundamental rule is: never trust, always verify, and continuously assess.

Zero Trust in security operations

Now let's see how Zero Trust is related to **security operations** (**SecOps**). As we know, SecOps is nothing but security and operations. Some of the core responsibilities include security monitoring, alerting, orchestration, defense, and incident response. In general, SecOps teams use a variety of tools and techniques to harden the organization's attack surface. Adopting a Zero Trust strategy helps SecOps to create or establish a more secure environment that can withstand attacks.

It's very important for the SecOps team and management to have end-to-end visibility on security with advanced optimized logging, analytics, and monitoring. Zero Trust architecture can provide visibility, which helps to mitigate threats effectively.

An effective **security operations center** (**SOC**) should be designed to deliver continuous protection, detection, prevention, and mitigation of threats for all attack surfaces.

User Entity Behavior Analytics (UEBA) provides powerful insights and helps to detect advanced threats based on user behavior.

SecOps teams should not spend time on incidents that can be easily addressed before they happen; they should be auto-remediated, semi-remediated, or handled through a playbook's automation. Adopting the Zero Trust security model can significantly improve the response time.

SecOps teams should be able to address security issues quickly.

When we consider Zero Trust, it's very important for any organization to have end-to-end visibility of what is going on and how soon they can react. This is why **extended detection and response (XDR)** and **security information and event management (SIEM)** are much needed for any organization, which we will be discussing in the next chapter. When we implement end-to-end Zero Trust across all the Zero Trust pillars, visibility will increase, which will give us better data and insights to make decisions as well as help us to act quickly on security incidents.

So, adopting a Zero Trust strategy is worth considering. Implementing the right tools to enhance security is crucial. These tools need to be correctly configured with the necessary settings specific to your organization and have the relevant features enabled. This is vital for hardening the attack surface, considering that every case varies. In addition, most security tools aren't plug-and-play. Don't expect instant results. Each one has its own learning curve as it adapts to your enterprise's specific needs and vulnerabilities.

> **Note**
> Zero Trust architecture helps to prevent threats and protect your entire digital estates at scale with end-to-end visibility.

Remember to continually adjust the settings and act responsively when needed. Before you even start choosing the tools and technologies, you need to have a clear understanding of your organization's security landscape, needs, types of threats you deal with in general, data sensitivity, roadmap, vision, resource availability, training, and so on. Finally, do not forget that it's also very important to assess these tools as a continuous process and update as required, as threats are increasing and expanding to every corner we can think of.

Adopting a Zero Trust strategy is very important. The security model helps organizations quickly adopt a security system that embraces the hybrid workplace and protects people, devices, apps, and data wherever they're located (on-premises, cloud, or hybrid).

Zero Trust principles and architecture

When it comes to reaching the goal of implementing a Zero Trust strategy at the maximum capability, the first company that comes to mind is always Microsoft. There are many other vendors trying to promote Zero Trust, but because of the truly powerful native integration benefits that come with Microsoft, it is always the first choice that comes to mind.

Apart from Microsoft, these days we see plenty of Zero Trust security strategies from different vendors, such as BeyondCorp from Google, LISA from Netflix, NIST, CISA, Gartner's CARTA, and Palo Alto. Irrespective of what we choose, the end goal is the same: to improve security, never trust and always verify, and harden the attack surface.

Here, we will discuss a few Zero Trust architectures from different providers, but our focus is mainly on Microsoft's Zero Trust.

Google created BeyondCorp Enterprise, a Zero Trust cybersecurity architecture (see *Figure 1.3*) in response to the Operation Aurora cyberattacks in 2009.

BeyondCorp streamlines security through several key components: single sign-on for a seamless user experience, customizable access control policies for granular control, a dedicated access proxy for secure external connections, and robust user- and device-based authentication and authorization for layered security.

Here are BeyondCorp's core principles:

- Network neutrality: Access to services is independent of the network of origin

- Contextual authorization: User and device attributes determine access privileges

- Multi-layered security: Authentication, authorization, and encryption ensure secure access

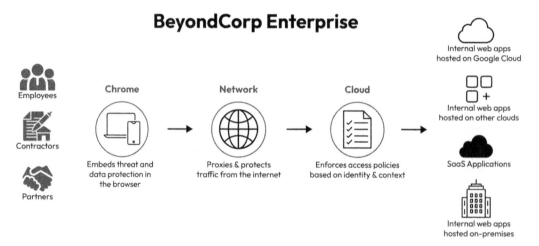

Figure 1.3 – Google's BeyondCorp Zero Trust architecture

Gartner introduced **CARTA** (see *Figure 1.4*) in 2010, which stands for **continuous adaptive risk and trust assessment**; CARTA favors continuous security assessments and contextual decision-making based on evaluations. Zero Trust forms the bedrock of CARTA, serving as a critical pillar within its broader security architecture, as explained here:

- Security should always begin with Zero Trust.

- Make context the key to access. Use relevant information to grant or deny access dynamically and securely.

- Continuous monitoring should be implemented to assess evolving risk levels, informing adaptive access controls that adjust privileges based on the specific context of each access request.

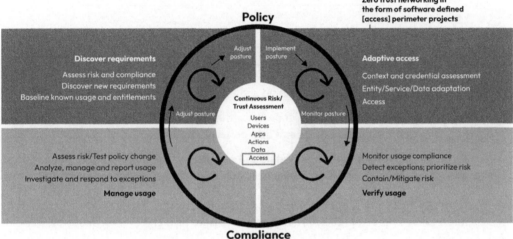

Figure 1.4 – Gartner's CARTA Zero Trust architecture

In **National Institute of Standards and Technology (NIST)**'s **Zero Trust architecture (ZTA)** (see *Figure 1.5*), there are numerous logical components that play a key role in the Zero Trust deployment in an enterprise.

NIST's ZTA components are as follows:

- **Policy engine (PE)**: Responsible for granting access to a resource

- **Policy administrator (PA)**: Responsible for establishing and/or shutting down the communication path between a subject and a resource

- **Policy enforcement point (PEP)**: Responsible for enabling, monitoring, and terminating connections between a subject and a resource

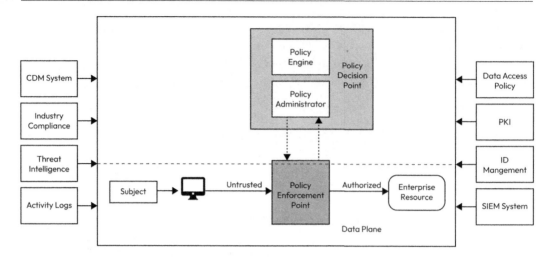

Figure 1.5 – NIST's Zero Trust architecture

Microsoft's Zero Trust has three core principles, which are as follows:

- **Verify explicitly**: Always authenticate and authorize based on all available data points.

- **Use least-privilege access**: Limit user access with **just in time** (**JIT**) and **just enough access** (**JEA**), risk-based adaptive policies, and data protection.

- **Assume breach**: Minimize the blast radius and segment access. Verify end-to-end encryption and use analytics to get visibility, drive threat detection, and improve defenses.

With Zero Trust (*never trust, always verify*), instead of assuming everything is safe behind the enterprise firewall, this model assumes that there is a breach and verifies each and every request regardless of where it originates.

Zero Trust pillars

Implementing Zero Trust controls and technologies across six foundational pillars (see *Figure 1.6*) is required for an end-to-end Zero Trust strategy.

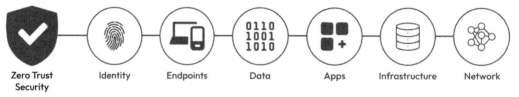

Figure 1.6 – Microsoft's Zero Trust pillars

All these Zero Trust pillars or security layers work together tightly. Let us look at each Zero Trust pillar in short in the following list:

- **Identity**: In the Zero Trust model, this refers to users, services, app credentials, and IoT devices. In the Zero Trust approach, these identities dictate access to vital data and resources, and thus strong authentication, compliance verification, and least-privilege principles are enforced during access attempts.

- **Endpoints**: An endpoint, whether a company-issued device, smartphone, BYOD, IoT device, or a guest device, is anything that connects to your network, whether on-site, remotely, or in the cloud. In Zero Trust, security rules apply uniformly across all endpoints to mitigate risks as data can flow across various endpoints when an identity accesses a resource.

- **Data**: Properly understanding your data and applying appropriate access control are critical to its protection. This extends to limiting access, setting robust data usage rules (all rules will be assigned to the data itself and not the storage location), and employing real-time monitoring to inhibit or prevent the sharing of sensitive data and files.

- **Apps**: Applications, as conduits for data access, require a clear understanding of their functioning and their APIs to manage data flow. In your entire digital ecosystem, all applications should have strictly limited in-app permissions and should be under continuous monitoring for unusual behaviors.

- **Infrastructure**: Your infrastructure encompasses all digital areas, from on-premises servers to cloud-based virtual machines. The primary concern is maintaining configurations and software updates. An effective configuration management strategy guarantees all devices meet essential security and policy standards.

- **Network**: Networks are the gateways to our data. Implementing network access controls and real-time monitoring of user and device activity can enhance threat visibility and prevent cybercriminals from traversing laterally across the network. Measures such as network segmentation, threat detection tools, and traffic encryption can lessen attack probabilities and limit damage from a breach.

A real-life example

Securing our home involves more than just locking the door. We take steps to protect our assets, such as using a safe, keeping confidential documents secure, locking all doors and windows, leaving some lights on, installing cameras inside and out, setting up a security system, and automating tasks such as turning on lights when motion is detected. We don't trust anyone who knocks at the door, but we want to let in the people we trust without disrupting our daily lives. This is what the Zero Trust security model is all about.

Case study analysis

The fictional company High Tech Rapid Solutions Corp presented in the case study faces several security challenges. Implementing a Zero Trust security model represents a strategic response to some of the challenges they are facing, as it demonstrably delivers significant advantages, detailed here:

- Extending the tight security coverage (*never trust, always verify*) across all their digital estates
- Management, including the SOC team, will have end-to-end visibility of the activities by adopting the Zero Trust security model
- Adopting an effective SOC helps them to deliver continuous protection, detection, prevention, and mitigation of threats
- Improved response time
- User behavior-based analytics and monitoring

Future of Zero Trust

According to *2021 Microsoft's Zero Trust Adoption Report*, about 76% of organizations have started implementing or adopting the Zero Trust strategy and about 35% believe that they have fully implemented or adopted it.

Even though, these days, most companies are investing heavily in the security area and aggressively adopting security tools, a few might assume that they have good security coverage and a hardened attack surface. But we strongly feel like this is just the beginning; soon we are going to see lots of IoT devices, expanded digital estates, more automation, and technology growing very fast, so we are expecting increased security challenges ahead. In short, early security adaptors will be rewarded, with no doubt, and we would expect Zero Trust to be the standard approach or concept for any organization.

With all this noise, some organizations are even confused about their security maturity level and are looking for guidance to understand their Zero Trust state. It will be very interesting to see how security will be handled, especially with **artificial intelligence**-based solutions leveraging language models growing at a high speed in both directions.

Summary

The introduction and history in this chapter highlighted the evolution of Zero Trust and how important it is to adopt this security model today and going forward. We have also covered the need to consider Zero Trust in security operations along with a few Zero Trust frameworks in the cybersecurity world.

With the foundation laid here, in the next chapter, we will dive into the compelling reasons why XDR and SIEM should be integral parts of every organization's security architecture. We'll examine their benefits, the clear advantages of modern cloud-based SIEM tools over traditional ones, and essential considerations for making the right XDR and SIEM selection.

Further reading

Refer to the following resources for more information about the topics covered in this chapter:

- Microsoft's Zero Trust: `https://aka.ms/zerotrust`
- Microsoft's *Zero Trust Adoption Report 2021*: `https://packt.link/quaoZ`
- Microsoft's Zero Trust adoption article – *Zero Trust Adoption Report: How does your organization compare?*: `https://packt.link/NyP8N`
- *Planning for a Zero Trust Architecture: A Planning Guide for Federal Administrators* (`nist.gov`): `https://packt.link/zdtT9`

2
Introduction to XDR and SIEM

As we begin this chapter, we'll explore the fundamental concepts of XDR and SIEM, understand their importance for enterprises and CISOs, and examine their core capabilities, use cases, and strategies. We'll also differentiate between modern and legacy approaches and demystify prevalent cybersecurity buzzwords such as EDR, XDR, MDR, NDR, and SIEM. We will also discuss how these solutions help to eliminate siloed architecture and make the lives of **Security Operations Center** (**SOC**) teams easy with better triaging, investigation, and hunting processes.

This chapter will cover the following main topics:

- What are XDR and SIEM?

- What do these *DR acronyms mean?

- The benefits of having XDR and SIEM solutions in the enterprise

- How to choose the right XDR and SIEM tool

- Case study analysis

Understanding XDR and SIEM

First, let's start with the history before we try to understand the importance of XDR and SIEM platforms and why organizations need to switch from the traditional model to modern platforms. According to an article by The Wall Street Journal, many CISOs or security chiefs are no longer looking for individual products to solve single problems but prefer platforms that can solve a range of issues. They are also considering automated technologies to free up their human resources. With all this, XDR and SIEM platforms' adoption rates will keep rising in the future.

What is XDR and how did it start?

XDR stands for **extended detection and response**. According to FireEye, the average global dwell time in 2020 was 56 days, which means an attacker could spend about two months' worth of time on a network before remediation. That dropped to a 21-day median in 2022, based on various reports, and then further dropped to just 16 days according to the cyberthreat landscape M-Trends report from Mandiant. Modern XDR can help reduce this dwell time by detecting and responding to threats quicker.

Let's discuss EDR before we even try to understand what exactly XDR is and why we need it.

EDR stands for **endpoint detection and response** and is an endpoint security solution that continuously monitors endpoints and helps organizations detect, prevent, and remediate threats. It is also often referred to as **Endpoint Detection and Threat Response (EDTR)**. Modern EDR solutions often come with next-generation antivirus.

Most modern EDR solutions are agent based, where agent(s) will be deployed on endpoints and managed via a unified cloud-based portal. Once installed, these agents continuously monitor, analyze, and collect telemetry data and report it to the cloud portal for triage, investigation, and remediation. Depending on the case, these logs will be ingested into a SIEM solution directly, which we will be discussing later.

Some of the core capabilities and features of an EDR solution are as follows:

- Real-time protection and responses for the endpoint
- Threat hunting
- Behavioral-based protection
- Proactive **Indicators of Compromise (IoCs)** search
- Comprehensive enhanced visibility of the endpoint
- Vulnerability data (depending on the EDR solution)
- Data collection for analysis
- Automated workflows

Today, the move to the cloud and remote work has pushed the border of an organization's estate beyond the boundary of the on-premises network, which has created challenges for an organization to manage and protect their assets. On the other side, digital estates are rapidly expanding to meet business needs. Modern networks have IoT, firewalls, multi-cloud assets, containers, Kubernetes, storage, filesystems, cloud and SaaS apps, and many other areas that must be considered for security threats. Deploying an EDR solution is just not enough anymore; focus needs to go beyond that, and this is where XDR comes into play.

The term XDR was coined by Nir Zuk, the CTO and co-founder of Palo Alto Networks, in 2018. Even though Palo Alto Networks came up with the XDR definition in 2018, it started gaining momentum and increased adoption during and after the COVID-19 pandemic, for example, with the zero-trust security model. The *X* in XDR stands for *extended*; however, it is intended to represent *anything* or *any data source* from which data can be collected from siloed security tools across an organization's technology stack for better correlation and faster investigation.

Gartner defines XDR as a *"unified security incident detection and response platform that automatically collects and correlates data from multiple proprietary security components."*

Modern XDR is a **SaaS-based** platform, typically offered from the cloud, that integrates with other security products that a specific vendor can link together. In general, agent(s) are installed on site, and these agents are responsible for gathering telemetry data and reporting it back to the XDR portal.

Some of the characteristics and capabilities of modern XDR are as follows:

- Vendor-specific platform
- Powerful threat intelligence
- Auto-disruption of an attack
- Correlation of multiple security tools and natively stitching together endpoints, identities, mailboxes, networks, apps, and so on into a single story
- SaaS-based platform
- Unified portal experience or unified interface
- Comprehensive behavior analysis or powerful integrated **User Entity Behavior Analytics (UEBA)** engine
- **Artificial Intelligence (AI)**-based threat detection and incident response
- Powerful vulnerability assessment with recommendations
- Automated investigation and auto-remediation (or semi-automation)
- Exploit prevention
- Simplified investigations
- Comprehensive endpoint threat protection with next-generation antivirus and cloud-delivered protection
- Powerful actionable insights
- Smart recommendations for targeted response actions

Typically, a modern XDR solution consists of the following three stages (see *Figure 2.1*):

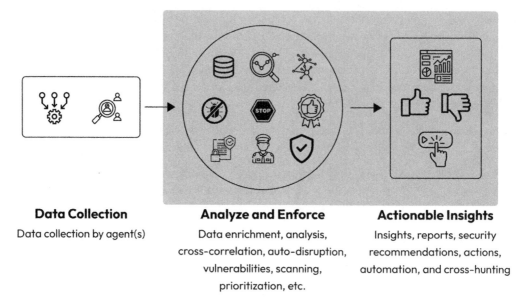

Data Collection

Data collection by agent(s)

Analyze and Enforce

Data enrichment, analysis, cross-correlation, auto-disruption, vulnerabilities, scanning, prioritization, etc.

Actionable Insights

Insights, reports, security recommendations, actions, automation, and cross-hunting

Figure 2.1 – Typical XDR solution stages

Let us look at the three stages:

- **Data collection stage**: This is where we generally deploy agent(s) to collect data from different sources for the XDR platform to analyze

- **Analyze and enforce stage**: Different kinds of activities take place at this stage, such as data analysis, correlation, scanning, vulnerability assessment (depending on the tool), enforcement (rules and policies), auto-disruption of attacks, and full or semi-remediation

- **Actionable insights stage**: Once the telemetry data is pushed to an XDR cloud-based SaaS platform, further features are available, such as deep insights for better triaging, investigation and remediation, security recommendations, and actions to take

What is SIEM and how did it start?

SIEM stands for **security information and event management**. Like most buzzwords in the cybersecurity area, the term SIEM is not new; it was coined by Garter in 2005 and originated out of several security techniques a few decades ago.

SIEM is derived from two main security techniques: **Security Information Management (SIM)** and **Security Event Management (SEM)**. If we look at its history, a couple of decades back, log analysis used to be a challenging activity as there were more logs to analyze, and each activity log used to have its own location and was not centralized. For example, operating-system logs were kept separate for system and boot-related events, and the respective applications were used to maintain their own logs.

Here are some of its major milestones:

- Syslog was invented by Eric Allman in the 1980s to log data in Unix systems as part of the sendmail project.

- From 2000 to 2005, SIM and SEM solutions provided log aggregation across different data sources with basic event correlation techniques. The SOC team relied on these solutions to detect an attack but were unable to deal with zero-day attacks. With the growing threats along with expanding digital estates, this was not enough for the SOC team to deal with the threats.

- SIM tools automate the process of historical log data collection and the storage of event data for analysis, as well as providing reporting. Log data is nothing but a file that collects and stores the system activities. The SIM tool responds to the event as soon as it notices any suspicious activities by alerting the admin and generating graphical reports. SIM solutions are often agent-based, running on the servers being monitored.

- SEM is an improvement on SIM but focuses on real-time network security events. It supports the correlation, aggregation, and notifications of events. The primary purpose of SEM is to identify alerts or events worth investigating.

- The **Common Event Format** (**CEF**) was developed by ArcSight, a SIEM provider (now part of OpenText), in the mid-2000s to standardize the logs generated by different products to simply the process of logging events and integration.

SIEM evolution

Log Management Systems (**LMSs**) -> **Security Information Management** (**SIMs**) and **Security Event Management** (**SEM**) solutions -> legacy SIEM -> next-generation SIEM

How does a SIEM solution work?

SIEM solutions have similar capabilities to XDR. They collect and aggregate log data from various sources, such as endpoints, networks, firewalls, cloud apps, office activity, and user activity (pretty much any data source with either an out-of-the-box connector or API or custom connectors). They then analyze the data with the help of **Threat Intelligence** (**TI**), UEBA, and correlation and generate incidents or alerts. Some modern SIEM solutions come with **Security Orchestration Automation and Response** (**SOAR**) capabilities to automate threat responses. It can take months to build a SIEM solution and even longer to tune it for organizations unfamiliar with threat modeling and rule creation.

Figure 2.2 depicts the architecture of SIEM in general. This can vary depending on the vendor and SIEM features. The automation layer comes into the picture if a specific SIEM has SOAR capabilities. Some of these features (such as UEBA, TI, data retention, and data archive) can be manual integrations depending on the SIEM solution you pick.

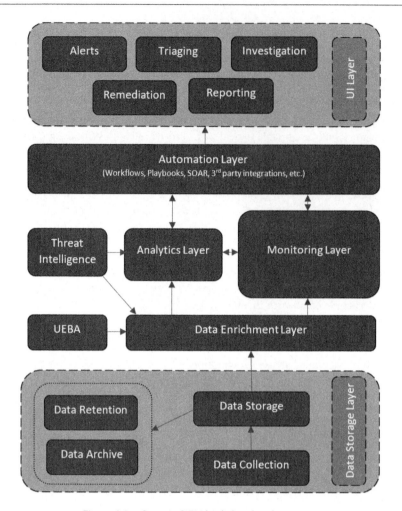

Figure 2.2 – Generic SIEM high-level architecture

> **Recommendation**
>
> Always consider a cloud-based modern SIEM solution with best-of-breed capabilities, such as UEBA, TI, SOAR, AI, and native integration support.

What do these *DR acronyms mean?

It's easy to get confused when coming across all these acronyms: EDR, NDR, XDR, ITDR, MDR, MXDR... But in the cybersecurity world, each acronym has its own core function in threat detection and response. Let's look at each at a high level to understand what exactly these acronyms mean and what they are used for.

EDR stands for **endpoint detection and response**. It is an endpoint security solution that continuously monitors endpoints and helps organizations detect, prevent, and remediate threats. This is also often referred to as EDTR. Modern EDR solutions often come with next-generation antivirus. Typically, the primary role of any modern EDR solution is focused on protecting the endpoint by providing in-depth visibility and threat protection. Modern EDR solutions often come with AI and next-generation antivirus capabilities.

EPP stands for **endpoint protection platform**. Typically, these are tools and technologies such as antivirus, data encryption, and data loss prevention that protect endpoint devices.

NDR stands for **network detection and response**. It collects a wide range of network data, such as firewall logs, NetFlow data from switches, and north/south traffic (internet communications), to detect threats. NDR also supports east/west (LAN/WAN communication) traffic; however, it is recommended to go with an EDR solution for cost benefits. These tools (along with UEBA) have emerged to address some of the challenges faced by SIEM in detecting unknown attacks. However, the tools have certain limitations; for example, they are capable of monitoring network activity but are unable to track or monitor local events or activities on the endpoint side, for which we need to rely on an EDR solution.

XDR stands for **extended detection and response**. It is an evolution of EDR that collects and correlates data across various security layers, such as endpoints, emails, apps, networks, and on-premises, hybrid, and cloud workloads. Adopting XDR will eliminate the siloed architecture tools, reduce complexity, and take a wider view by integrating various security solutions.

ITDR stands for **identity threat detection and response**. It is a security approach (a combination of security tools and processes with best practices) to identify, detect, and respond to targeted threats on identity and identity-based systems.

MDR stands for **managed detection and response**. It is a managed security service offering that monitors your EDR activity. This kind of managed service is ideal for cases where organizations do not have a specific team or expertise to handle security incidents or need 24/7/365 monitoring. We will be discussing this in more detail in *Chapter 9*.

MXDR stands for **managed extended detection and response**. It is also a managed security service offering like MDR but for XDR. With growing threats, these managed services would benefit many organizations by allowing them to react fast and protect their digital assets as deeper triaging, investigation, and remediation require a lot of expertise. We will also be covering this in more detail in *Chapter 9*.

Table 2.1 provides a high-level comparison of these tools by some of the core capabilities and features:

	Investigation	Prevention	Detection	Remediation
EDR	X	X	X	X
EPP		X	X	X
NDR			X	X
XDR	X	X	X	X

	Investigation	Prevention	Detection	Remediation
SIEM & SOAR	X	X	X	X
ITDR	X	X	X	X
MDR	Managed EDR Service			
MXDR	Managed XDR Service			

Table 2.1: High-level comparison of different terms

> **Note**
> XDR is not a replacement for EDR, NDR, or EPP.

The benefits of having XDR and SIEM solutions in an enterprise

By now, you will understand the basics of XDR and SIEM, their history, and the high-level architecture of how they work. Now let's look at the benefits and why we need to consider these tools.

XDR's benefits and reasons to adopt it

As discussed in *Chapter 1*, these days, threats are rapidly expanding and many organizations have extended remote working to their workforce, which has led them to adopt many security tools quickly and resulted in siloed architecture. We don't blame them; in fact, we are very impressed with the way many organizations quickly adopted these security tools.

So, technically when it started, organizations' focus was more on solving the challenges of remote work, and then they started filling in the gaps along with other challenges that arose, such as the following:

- How they could stitch all these tools together.
- Resource challenges.
- Training.
- Integration.
- Automation.
- Reducing alert fatigue.
- Improving response time.
- Eliminating siloed architectures, reducing budgets, and maintenance. (We could list many more here.)

To start with, without XDR, the core challenge is *too many tools in place and too many alerts to deal with*. If an organization encounters this kind of painful situation (see *Figure 2.3*), it's very likely that they are either low on resources, need to train resources, or are spending too much time addressing incidents. Typically, the larger the company, the more security incidents or alerts you will see as each tool might generate hundreds or thousands of incidents or alerts. This can be even more challenging for the SOC team to handle, in terms of monitoring, triaging, investigating, remediating, and correlating the information across the tools, as most of these are disconnected. It will be a very challenging and painful exercise for a SOC team to correlate and group related alerts before taking any action. Not only this, but the SOC team also needs to access multiple portals to capture data for further investigation. Even after that, there could be many unknown things.

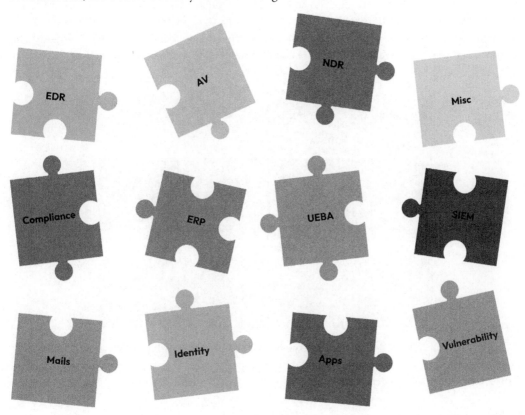

Figure 2.3: Siloed architecture alerts without XDR in place

With the ever-increasing threats these days, we need smart security tools and automation in place, rather than a SOC team spending time identifying the threats, integrating with other tools, automation, and so on. It's also worth knowing the potential user blast radius, attack paths, weak areas, and so on. Modern security tools should be smart enough to collect the required log data, correlate and enrich the data, tightly integrate with UEBA and TI tools, auto-remediate (semi or full), and provide powerful insights.

With XDR in place (see *Figure 2.4*), it allows analysts to quickly detect threats from various sources (whether endpoints, apps, networks, the cloud, containers, or servers), which were previously challenging to discover with limited sensors or agents in place. XDR tools are smart enough to analyze, enrich, and correlate data by collecting log data from various sources. These tools can identify the potential attack paths and user blast radius with recommendations to fix these. Some modern XDR tools are also capable of auto-disrupting attacks at machine speed. These tools can also help reduce alert fatigue by reducing false positives, auto-suppressing alerts, and providing semi or full auto-remediation.

Not only this, but the SOC team will also gain better visibility into a full attack with detailed investigations along with deep insights to react quickly to situations. Most modern XDR tools come with many out-of-the-box features that can be deployed quickly with minimal effort. Considering these kinds of modern XDR tools will increase the productivity of an SOC team and help them to concentrate more on strategic initiatives, rather than struggling to identify the source of threats and fine-tuning the systems. We will continue learning about the capabilities of XDR in the next section.

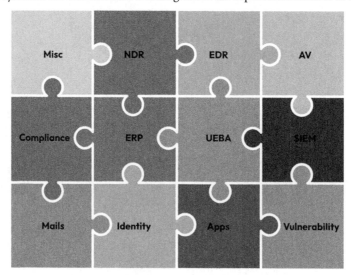

Figure 2.4 – Alerts from various security tools with XDR in place

Now let's look at why we need to consider SIEM when we already have XDR.

Why do we need to consider SIEM?

A SIEM solution collects and analyzes log data from various sources, provides real-time alerts based on rules defined out of the box or configured, and generates dashboards and reports for a SOC team. Some modern SIEM solutions also come with SOAR and UEBA capabilities, which help to automate threat response and detect abnormal behaviors or activities. These SIEM tools can help the SOC team to monitor and guard their environment and reduce the **Mean Time to Respond** (**MTTR**). They also provide a comprehensive and centralized view of security events and incidents, insights into activities, reports, and MITRE mapping, and help in triaging, investigation, and remediation processes.

SIEM goes to the next level (beyond XDR) as it ingests pretty much any data; doesn't need to be vendor specific; allows any third-party log data through either out-of-the-box connectors, API connectors, or custom connectors; and analyzes and detects any potential threats across the collected data and alerts the SOC team.

Another core difference between XDR and SIEM is that XDR focuses on automating (semi or full) the detection and response, meaning XDR will automatically take action on the threats it discovers. On the other hand, with SIEM, you typically ingest the log data from any data source, define the rules, or use the out-of-the-box configuration to detect the threats, and then it's up to the SOC team to decide what steps need to be taken or to automate the process by building the playbooks to respond.

It's very important to define a plan and strategy before adopting and implementing SIEM; otherwise, this can be very expensive and challenging to handle. Here are some tips to avoid your SIEM from turning into a monster that will eventually wipe out your entire budget if you don't plan and design it well:

- The more log data you try to ingest into a SIEM solution, depending on the rules configured, the more likely it will generate noise due to too many incidents or alerts. Hence, it's important to fine-tune the rules.
- Don't just blindly ingest the data you see; separate operations data versus security data. Define and implement data collection and security monitoring strategies.
- Define clear data retention strategies.
- Implement automation for routine tasks rather than relying on a SOC team.

These are just a few things that need to be considered. More will be discussed in *Chapter 8*.

Traditional SIEM versus modern SIEM

We strongly believe that it's time for every organization to move away from the traditional SIEM solutions they have and adopt modern SIEM solutions, for many reasons (see *Table 2.2*):

Traditional SIEM	Modern SIEM
On-premises infrastructure	Cloud based; SaaS-based platform.
Scalability challenges	Scalable and flexible.
Requires complex and resource-intensive implementations and often involves time-consuming maintenance activities	Can be easily onboarded, and there is no need to worry about infrastructure maintenance for SaaS-based modern SIEMs.
Heavily relied on rules-based detection	Uses advanced analytics techniques (such as machine learning and behavior analysis).

Traditional SIEM	Modern SIEM
Integration challenges (not easy to integrate with other tools)	Can easily integrate with any system via out-of-the-box connectors, APIs, and custom connectors. Many modern SIEM solutions integrate with SOAR platforms and few come with SOAR capability as well.
Provides limited context about events and the SOC team needs to collect it manually	The tool generates context-rich insights for better triaging and understanding incidents.
Manual investigation	Powered by automation and orchestration.
Heavy resource requirements (people, hardware, software, process, etc.)	Out-of-the-box automation for many manual processes.
Manual correlation	System built-in correlation
No User Entity Behavior Analytics (UEBA)	Integrated UEBA.
Limited reporting capabilities	Provides powerful context-rich insights.
Too many false positives or missed alerts to deal with due to the rule-based nature of detection	Advanced threat detection leverages machine learning, behavioral analytics, and anomaly detection to identify complex threats. False positives can be reduced easily.
No predictive analytics available	Few modern SIEM solutions use predictive analytics to identify potential future threats based on historical data.

Table 2.2 – Traditional SIEM versus modern SIEM

At this point, you must be thinking, which one should we adopt: XDR or SIEM? Honestly, there is no easy answer to this. Each has its pros and cons, but these days, both are needed by most organizations to deal with threats and enhance their security to protect themselves from bad actors. But adopting these tools and making use of the benefits they provide requires expertise. Not using them might put the organization at risk. Now, the next question would usually be, "Fine, you've convinced me to adopt a modern XDR or SIEM tool, but how do I choose which one to pick out of all the many vendors on the market these days, and which would benefit me?" We will be discussing this in the next section; you will also find more details on why you should consider Microsoft's XDR and SIEM solution in *Chapter 3*.

How to choose the right XDR and SIEM tool

Now, let's look at some of the key capabilities or features you need to consider when choosing a modern XDR or SIEM security tool:

- Look for a modern cloud-based and AI powered XDR or SIEM solution with native integration benefits for better coverage.

- Invest in products that are growing rapidly. It might be frustrating to keep it updated, but updates are much needed these days to provide enhanced security to your attack surface.

- Pick products that can be easily integrated (either out of the box or with simple clicks) with security products for log ingestion, analyzing, triaging, investigation, and remediation.

- Consider products with deep integration with UEBA and SOAR (in the case of SIEM).

- The modern XDR product you pick should provide insights into the potential attack paths with recommendations to address them and should be capable of auto-disrupting attacks when they happen.

- Consider products with simplified deployment, such as agentless scanning or lightweight agents. They should be able to deploy to any (or at least most) operating systems, including mobile devices and private, public, hybrid, and multi-cloud environments.

- Look for an EDR solution that comes with next-generation antivirus.

- It should have supervised and unsupervised machine learning capabilities.

- Entity definitions and intelligence should be sharable across other security tools with native integration or simple click integration.

- It should provide auto-mapping of incident evidence and artifacts with the **MITRE ATT&CK** framework's tactics and techniques for improved investigation.

- The analytics platform must be powered by an automation engine. This enables automated stitching of security alerts and provides a unified view of the attack with the entities involved, such as endpoints, identities, apps, and mailboxes.

- It should auto-disrupt attacks (semi or full) across entities to prevent the attack.

- The solution should provide a unified one-stop portal for end-to-end investigation rather than the SOC team switching between multiple portals.

- It should provide a built-in capability to perform deep forensic analysis, comprehensive insights, and reports for the SOC team and management.

- In the case of SIEM, it should be able to ingest log data from any source with minimal effort. Data retention and restore options should be available from the portal itself for hunting.

- It must be easily scalable and easy to compute considering the persistence of today's threats. You don't want to compromise and ignore telemetry data, which provides forensic evidence of the attack activity.

- XDR and SIEM should stitch the data received from multiple tools, analyze and enrich the data, and correlate it for better triaging and investigation. They should also apply intelligence to show the complete story, from end to end, of an incident in a single view.

- Individual product evaluation is good but always consider and give priority to holistic view benefits. Look for strong API support for extension and integration with other products outside of the vendor's security stack (e.g., an end user ticket system) and migration.

Case study analysis

Now, let's look at some of the challenges High Tech Rapid Solutions Corp is facing as mentioned in the *Case study* section at the beginning of this book. We will be discussing more of these security challenges in the upcoming chapters, but adopting modern XDR and SIEM tools can solve some of the core challenges and improve the company's security posture.

Here are some of the security challenges High Tech Rapid Solutions Corp (the fictional company discussed in the case study) is struggling with:

- **Siloed security architecture**: This challenge can be eliminated by adopting modern XDR and SIEM tools. However, this requires a security monitoring strategy and roadmap, which will be discussed in detail in *Chapter 8*.

- **Incomplete security insights**: XDR and SIEM can provide powerful security insights based on analytical engines.

- **Inefficient threat response**: There are a couple of ways these tools can help with addressing this security challenge. These tools provide very powerful insights into incidents with evidence and artifacts, along with the MITRE ATT&CK framework mapping for improved triage, investigation, and remediation. Also, these tools will either auto-disrupt the attack or initiate an automation to remediate the threat and improve the MTTR.

- **Regulatory compliance**: Security baselines can be configured easily to monitor regulatory compliance using these tools and automation can be implemented. This will significantly reduce the manual SOC effort.

- **Ransomware attacks**: Deploying these tools can significantly reduce the chances of ransomware attacks. Some of the capabilities these tools can bring in this area are as follows:

  - Enforce strong attack surface capabilities

  - Implement next-generation antivirus (signature-based and ML-based) with cloud-delivered protection to identify the malware

  - Review the potential attack paths with the recommendations

  - Provide vulnerability scanning with recommendations

  - Enable powerful insights

  - Help with identifying reconnaissance activities early

A few of these attacks will be discussed in detail in *Chapter 5*.

Summary

This chapter helped you to understand the concepts of XDR and SIEM, also providing the history behind these tools. We have also covered details on the importance of these tools for any organization, their capabilities, and how they work in general. We hope this chapter helped you to understand the reasons why organizations need to switch away from traditional SIEM solutions and the importance of doing so, as well as providing guidance on adopting a better modern XDR and SIEM tool out of the many available in the current cybersecurity market.

This sets the stage for the next few chapters, where we will start discussing an important Microsoft unified XDR and SIEM solution. We hope you are enjoying reading this book so far and have learned something new.

Further reading

Refer to the following links for more information about the topics covered in this chapter:

- Best EDR solutions – Reviews, 2023 | Gartner Peer Insights: `https://packt.link/l0aNq`

- What is XDR? Palo Alto Networks: `https://packt.link/gUEAf`

- *Security Chiefs Trim the Fat as Budgets Bite – Cyber teams are looking to do more with less in an uncertain economy*: `https://packt.link/t5O2f`

- *More Cyber Companies Announce Layoffs – Vendors have cut hundreds of employees in recent weeks* – This article shows how, many CISOs and security chiefs are no longer looking at individual products but rather prefer platforms that can solve a range of issues: `https://packt.link/6o26L`

3
Microsoft's Unified XDR and SIEM Solution

The description "Microsoft's unified XDR and SIEM solution" refers to Microsoft's integrated approach to **extended detection and response (XDR)** and **Security Information and Event Management (SIEM)**. In modern security monitoring architecture, SIEM acts as a primary detection tool, while XDR security solution complements enterprise SIEM solutions. In this chapter, we will explore Microsoft's unified XDR and SIEM solution in more detail, highlighting the value it offers to organizations.

The following topics will be covered in this chapter:

- What is Microsoft's unified XDR and SIEM solution?

- Microsoft Defender XDR overview

- Extending the XDR capabilities to on-premises and hybrid cloud by leveraging Microsoft Defender for Cloud

- Microsoft Sentinel – SIEM and SOAR

- XDR and beyond – exploring commonly used security solutions

- Microsoft's unified XDR and SIEM solution benefits over non-MS solutions

Let's get started!

What is Microsoft's unified XDR and SIEM solution?

Microsoft's unified XDR and SIEM solution was designed to consolidate various Microsoft cloud-based security solutions under one umbrella. Its primary goal was to enhance security operations efficiency, detect and remediate sophisticated threats faster. This was achieved by introducing a unified portal, that brought all defender solutions into one portal. Together these solutions offer a comprehensive solution for cybersecurity threats and complex attacks. In the early stages of Microsoft's cloud-based security solutions architecture, they were designed across multiple portals. This architecture made it challenging for security analysts to get a holistic view when investigating alerts and incidents, or when evaluating the environment's security posture.

The concept of Microsoft's unified XDR and SIEM solution combines multiple security solutions across the Microsoft ecosystem into a single platform to provide improved detection and response capabilities. Over recent years, Microsoft's unified XDR and SIEM solution has undergone significant development to support workloads across multi-cloud and on-premises environments. Large enterprises, often operating in multi-cloud or hybrid environments, are discovering significant holistic benefits from Microsoft's unified XDR and SIEM solution. This unified approach allows organizations to fully benefit from Microsoft's unified XDR and SIEM solution within their own ecosystems.

This comprehensive unified solution accelerates preventing, detecting, and responding to threats across the following domains:

- Identities, endpoints, email, and applications

- Infrastructure (on-premises/hybrid)

- Multi-cloud platforms (Azure, AWS, and GCP)

- IoT environments

To summarize, Microsoft's version of unified XDR and SIEM solution is delivered through the following experiences: **Microsoft Defender XDR** for endpoints, identities, emails, collaboration tools, **Software as a Service (SaaS)** applications, cloud workloads, and data; **Microsoft Defender for Cloud** for Azure, multi-cloud (AWS and GCP), and hybrid workloads, and **Microsoft Sentinel** acting as a SIEM tool.

One of the main advantages of using Microsoft's unified XDR and SIEM solution is native integrations across the products, which means they share signals and events, and sync alerts and incidents. One key benefit of XDR is its ability to automate correlations, enabling the SOC team to focus on complex threats and prioritize investigations effectively.

In the rapidly evolving cybersecurity landscape, there is a need for constant development to address the threats and risks. The latest innovation is **Microsoft Copilot for Security**, a cutting-edge generative AI solution that aims to boost security outcomes using machine speed and scale by increasing the effectiveness and capabilities of Microsoft Defender. It integrates natively with Microsoft security solutions such as Defender XDR, Sentinel, Intune, Defender for Cloud, Defender for **External Attack Surface Management (EASM)**, Defender Threat Intelligence, and third-party solutions, at the time of writing.

By now, we understand what XDR and SIEM are, along with their benefits and why an organization should adopt this combination to enhance their SecOps. Let's take a closer look at the actual solutions behind the Microsoft's unified XDR and SIEM concept starting with Microsoft Defender XDR, Microsoft Defender for Cloud, and Microsoft Sentinel.

Microsoft Defender XDR

Microsoft Defender XDR is a solution that natively integrates multiple security solutions into one unified user experience (`defender.microsoft.com`, formerly `security.microsoft.com`). It provides comprehensive visibility across the environment, advanced threat detection, automated incident response, and proactive hunting for unknown threats, enabling organizations to detect and respond to sophisticated cyberattacks faster than compared to a siloed architecture, where security solutions don't share signals and events, as mentioned in *Chapter 2* under the *Benefits of having XDR and SIEM solutions in the enterprise* section. Microsoft Defender XDR provides visibility for identity, endpoints, applications, email, and documents, as well as cloud workload alerts, signals, and asset information. It uses **Artificial Intelligence (AI)** to reduce the SecOps team's workload by consolidating a high number of alerts in to a low number of high-priority incidents.

Microsoft Defender for Cloud

Microsoft Defender for Cloud (MDC) is a comprehensive cloud-native security solution designed to protect organizations' cloud environments from a wide range of threats. It integrates advanced threat protection, vulnerability management, and cloud security posture management to provide robust security capabilities for cloud workloads and services. Also known as a **cloud-native application protection platform (CNAPP)**, it provides XDR capabilities for both Azure and on-premises infrastructure as well as multi-cloud platforms (AWS and GCP at the time of writing), including servers, virtual machines, databases, containers, key vaults, IoT, Azure Stack HCI, and more. One of the key areas in MDC is developer platforms and application security posture across platforms. At the time of writing this book, MDC supports GitHub, Azure DevOps, and the latest addition GitLab (in public preview).

Microsoft Sentinel

Microsoft's version of SIEM, **Microsoft Sentinel**, is a powerful and scalable cloud-native solution that combines the capabilities of a SIEM tool with **security orchestration and automated response (SOAR)**. It offers intelligent security analytics and threat intelligence, empowering organizations with comprehensive alert detection, threat visibility, proactive hunting, and streamlined threat response capabilities, all in a single unified solution.

Microsoft Sentinel can be deeply integrated with Microsoft XDR solutions (Microsoft Defender XDR and Defender for Cloud) in only a few clicks with out-of-the-box configuration. **User and entity behavior analytics (UEBA)** is another powerful Sentinel feature that analyzes user and entity activities and behaviors across various data sources. UEBA can identify anomalous or risky actions that might indicate malicious activities such as compromised accounts and data exfiltration.

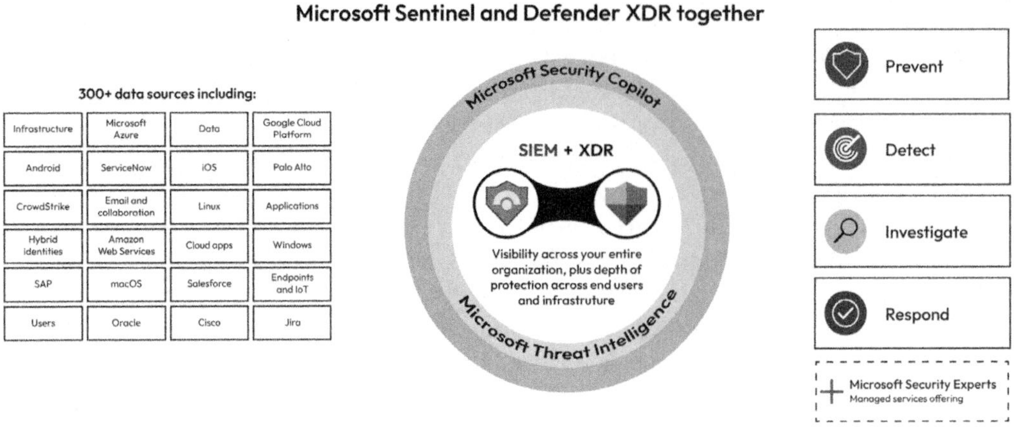

Figure 3.1 - Microsoft's unified XDR and SIEM platform

In the case study analysis sections of this chapter, we will delve deeper into these solutions, as illustrated (see *Figure 3.1*). We'll explore how Microsoft's XDR security solution addresses *High Tech Rapid Solutions Corp*'s security challenges and how Microsoft Sentinel complements this approach.

Other relevant Microsoft Security solutions

In addition to the security solutions mentioned previously, this book will also cover various other Microsoft Security solutions that can significantly enhance an organization's capabilities for threat protection and environment security posture. The seamless integration of XDR solutions with these tools show the strength of the unified security approach, leading to numerous benefits for the organization if these solutions are deployed. The solutions we are referring to are as follows:

- Microsoft Defender for EASM
- Microsoft Defender Threat Intelligence

Both of these solutions are based on RiskIQ's former solutions, which Microsoft has further developed and rebranded after acquiring RiskIQ in 2021. We will discuss more of Defender for EASM and Defender Threat Intelligence capabilities later in the chapter.

Microsoft Defender XDR overview (MDE, MDO, MDA, and MDI)

The Microsoft Defender XDR is the key component in the unified XDR solution. In the early stages of Microsoft's security solutions, every solution in Microsoft's 365 side had its own dedicated admin portal. In the last few years, all Microsoft 365 security solutions have been integrated underneath one unified portal (`defender.microsoft.com`, formerly `security.microsoft.com`) called **Microsoft Defender XDR**. The portal combines the management of the security solutions (protection, detection, investigation, and response) into one single pane of glass in terms of endpoints, email and documents, apps, and identities (see *Figure 3.2*).

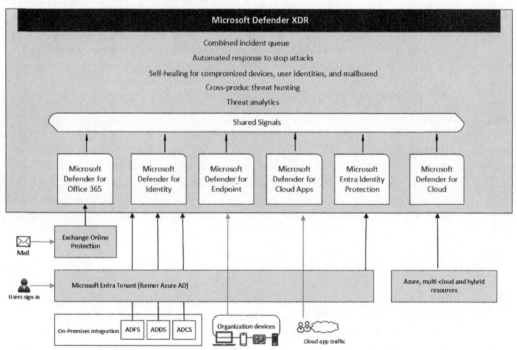

Figure 3.2 - Overview of Microsoft Defender XDR

Microsoft Defender XDR solutions

The Microsoft Defender XDR umbrella has multiple solutions covering different attack surface areas. In the following table (see *Table 3.1*), you can find short descriptions of security solutions that belong to the Microsoft Defender XDR solution. In the sections that follow, we will go through each Microsoft Defender XDR solution and evaluate how the organization presented in the case study can benefit from deploying the solutions, and how these solutions can help the organization address current security challenges.

Security Solution Name	Description
Microsoft Defender for Endpoint (MDE)	MDE is an advanced endpoint security platform. It offers comprehensive tools to defend against, detect, and respond to sophisticated threats, ensuring protection for enterprise endpoints. It also provides vulnerability management and attack surface management, which are some of the key features of MDE, and many more. Provides deep insight into hosts and is the key investigation tool for platform-related detections in SOC.
Microsoft Defender for Office 365 (MDO)	MDO is a comprehensive solution that protects organizations from email-related threats. It integrates various Microsoft security solutions to detect, prevent, investigate, and respond to sophisticated attacks. MDO helps to identify and remediate email-based attacks, such as phishing, malware, and business email compromise. While not directly a tool within MDO, Microsoft offers an attack simulator within the solution. It allows security teams to run realistic phishing attack simulations for user training and awareness.
Microsoft Defender for Cloud Apps (MDA)	MDA is the Microsoft version of a cloud access security broker (CASB). It provides threat protection and visibility for a variety of cloud applications, including Office 365 and many third-party cloud services. Additionally, the platform enhances an organization's security posture through SaaS Security Posture Management (SSPM), offers advanced threat protection and the control of shadow IT, and extends protection to OAuth-enabled apps accessing critical data, especially together with Application Governance (an MDA add-on). With MDA, you can also protect sensitive data in the cloud.
Microsoft Defender for Identity (MDI)	MDI provides detection and investigation for attacks targeting on-premises Active Directory using UEBA (identifies anomalies with adaptive built-in intelligence), and direct threat detection of many attacks such as pass-the-hash, golden ticket, skeleton key, and many more. It also provides mitigation capabilities for on-premises entities as well as security posture management for on-premises that reduces the attack surface.

Microsoft Entra ID Protection	Microsoft Entra ID Protection assesses risk based on billions of login attempts as well as shared signals from other Microsoft security solutions (MDE, MDA, and Threat Intelligence data) and utilizes this information to determine the risk levels. What happens when the risk level is raised depends on how Microsoft Entra Conditional Access policies have been configured.

Table 3.1 - Overview of Microsoft Defender XDR solution

MDE

Endpoint security is a critical aspect of cybersecurity, and there are several common questions and challenges associated with it. Here are some typical questions and challenges around endpoint security:

- How secure are our organization's endpoints?

- What is the scope and impact of security incidents on our endpoints?

- Have any attacks on our endpoints gone unnoticed?

- Are there any indicators of compromise across our network?

- How do we select the right endpoint security solution for our business?

- How can we ensure that our threat and vulnerability management solutions and processes are properly in place?

- Can I rely on traditional endpoint security solutions that are currently used in my environment?

If we look into the history a bit, MDE has been there for a while. Previously, it was known as **Microsoft Defender Advanced Threat Protection** (**MDATP**), and you might still find community content by this name on the web. Over time, MDE has grown from an anti-spyware tool to a comprehensive endpoint security solution, demonstrates Microsoft's commitment to developing its products in line with the constantly changing security landscape and the needs of modern enterprises.

In this chapter, we will introduce some of the key capabilities of MDE (see *Figure 3.3*) and how they can help you protect your organization from sophisticated threats.

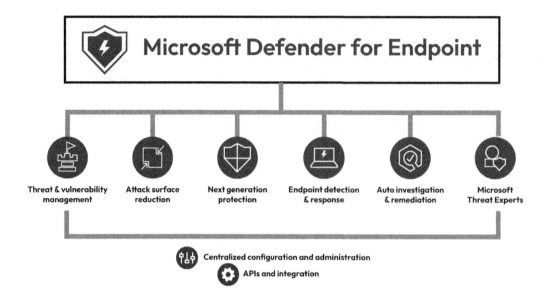

Figure 3.3 - Key features of the MDE solution

MDE key features

MDE is an advanced endpoint security solution that offers vulnerability management, endpoint protection, endpoint detection and response, and mobile threat defense in a single, unified platform. This solution empowers organizations with multi-platform environments to effectively manage and secure their endpoint devices. It facilitates efficient threat mitigation, optimizes security resource allocation, and fosters the development of robust defenses across diverse operating systems and network infrastructure.

Some of the core capabilities of MDE (see *Figure 3.3*) are as follows:

- **Blocks sophisticated threats and malware**: Detect and respond to advanced attacks with deep threat monitoring and analysis (**Endpoint Detection and Response (EDR)**).

- **Eliminates risks with vulnerability management**: Discover vulnerabilities and misconfigurations in real time with Microsoft Defender Vulnerability Management. We will cover Microsoft Defender Vulnerability Management in *Chapter 6*.

- **Next-generation protection**: Microsoft Defender Antivirus is an integrated anti-malware tool designed for desktops, portable computers, and servers. It features cloud-delivered protection with machine learning and the **Intelligent Security Graph (ISG)** for threat detection. The solution offers continuous scanning using advanced behavior monitoring (real-time protection) and provides protection updates through machine learning and comprehensive threat analysis (by humans, automated big-data analysis, and threat research).

- **Attack surface reduction (ASR) rules**: MDE ASR rules are a set of security policies that help protect endpoints from common attack vectors. ASR rules can block or audit malicious behaviors such as credential theft, code injection, script execution, and more. ASR is one of the key features of Microsoft Defender for Endpoint.

- **Automated investigation and response (AIR)**: In addition to being able to quickly respond to attacks, MDE provides automated investigation capabilities that help SOC teams significantly reduce the number of alerts. Customization options depend on the MDE license level (Defender for Business versus Defender P1 versus Defender P2).

- **Eliminates the blind spots in your environment**: Discover unmanaged and unauthorized endpoints and network devices and secure these assets using integrated workflows.

- **Integrated threat protection with SIEM and XDR**: Empower defenders to effectively secure organization digital estate by combining XDR and SIEM.

MDE supports multiple platforms and the supported features between platforms vary. The full list of the supported MDE capabilities by platform is found on the Microsoft website (`https://packt.link/Tr4rl`).

Some of the use cases for MDE

MDE is a powerful solution that helps enterprises prevent, detect, and respond to advanced cyberattacks. But what are some of the use cases and benefits of using this product? Here are some examples:

- One product to cover antivirus, hardening, EDR, and vulnerability needs

- Same product for Windows workstations and servers, macOS, and most popular Linux servers

- Threat intelligence data shared across Microsoft security solutions

- Built-in reports regarding weakness

- Security recommendations for connected devices

- Built-in integration with other Microsoft security tools (synergy advantages with data correlation)

- Automated response to security events (AIR)

- Advanced hunting capabilities (threat hunting)

- Integrated device inventory

Case study analysis

Let's look at how implementing MDE could bring additional value and address security challenges for *High Tech Rapid Solutions Corp* (our fictional company) mentioned in the *Case study* section at the beginning of this book:

- **Incomplete security insights**: Microsoft Defender XDR (including MDE, MDO, MDA, and MDI) provides visibility for incidents across organization as well as deep security insights in one unified portal. Microsoft Defender XDR threat analytics, powered by threat intelligence, detects unusual behaviors and threats from the organization endpoints. MDE's capability to correlate information across endpoints provides contextual threat detection, and its integration with the whole Microsoft Defender XDR security stack and SIEM solutions, such as Sentinel, enhances holistic security event analysis.

- **Attacks targeting Microsoft 365 collaboration workloads**: MDE's integration with Microsoft's threat intelligence helps in identifying phishing and **business email compromise** (**BEC**) patterns, and alerting on suspicious activities. By offering these insights, MDE empowers organizations with proactive defense against BEC and other attacks, ensuring safer collaboration and reducing potential financial and reputational damages.

  In May 2023, the *automatic attack disruption* capability in Microsoft Defender XDR reached **general availability** (**GA**). It helps organizations protect against ransomware, BEC types of attacks by using signals across endpoints, identities, email, and applications. The capability enables the containment of active attacks quickly, halting their progression and limiting their impact on the environment.

- **Ransomware attacks**: By leveraging MDE, an organization can gain protection against advanced threats, such as ransomware attacks. The next-generation protection and ASR capabilities are designed to protect this area and detect advanced threats. Organizations can improve endpoint protection by leveraging MDE's built-in protection. These features need to be configured as a pre-requisite for built-in protection:

  - Enable cloud protection

  - Turn tamper protection on

  - Set standard ASR rules to block mode

  - Enable network protection in block mode

  In addition, by integrating with other defenders part of Microsoft Defender XDR solution, such as MDI, MDO, MDA, Microsoft Entra ID Protection, and **Microsoft Defender for Cloud** (**MDC**), Microsoft Defender XDR can provide a holistic and unified view of the ransomware attack chain.

> **Tip**
>
> MDE can co-exist with non-MS products. Consider running MDE as EDR block mode to have enhanced protection on your endpoints, even if Defender Antivirus is not the primary antivirus product. This way, you can also get vulnerability statuses from your endpoints to the Microsoft Defender XDR portal.

- **SOC team notices too many incidents and is confident that handling certain vulnerabilities would fix these incidents and reduce the number of incidents/alerts but is struggling to gain visibility on the vulnerabilities**: One of the common security challenges many organizations are facing is how to deal with an increasing number of incidents and alerts that overwhelm their SOC teams. Often, these incidents are caused by known vulnerabilities that could have been prevented or mitigated if they were detected and remediated in time. However, many organizations lack the visibility and the tools to manage their vulnerabilities effectively. This is where MDE can help. One of the key features of MDE is its built-in **threat and vulnerability management** (**TVM**) solution, which helps to identify and prioritize the most critical vulnerabilities in your environment and provides guidance on how to remediate them. We cover TVM in more detail in *Chapter 6*.

Refer to the Microsoft Defender for Endpoint documentation at Microsoft Learn (`https://packt.link/uXhhx`) for further learning.

MDO

Even though cybersecurity attacks are becoming more and more sophisticated, traditional phishing still works. Also, if we look at the "illicit consent grant" type of attack, it typically starts with some form of phishing. That said, here are some typical questions and challenges around email security:

- How are we protecting our collaboration workloads?
- How can we protect email accounts from unauthorized access?
- How can we prevent email spoofing and phishing?
- How can we filter out spam and malicious emails?
- How can we educate employees on email security best practices?

In this section, we will go through the next Microsoft Defender XDR security solution, MDO. Many of the Microsoft security solutions have been rebranded lately to match the Defender family by name, including MDO. It was formerly known as Office 365 **Advanced Threat Protection** (**ATP**). MDO is a cloud-based email filtering service that plays an important role for protecting organizations from advanced threats across email and collaboration workloads, such as phishing, BEC, and malware attacks. And like all the defenders part of Microsoft Defender XDR security solution, it helps to detect, investigate, and respond to attacks that target users, collaboration workloads, and data.

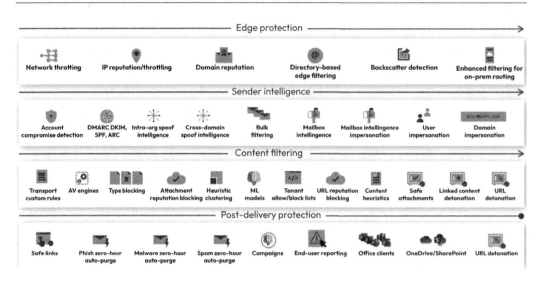

Figure 3.4 - MDO protection stack

MDO key features

MDO offers several key features (see *Figure 3.4*) that enhance its efficacy for collaboration workloads, and in this section, we will introduce the key features:

- **Threat protection**: MDO applies multiple layers of protection to prevent malicious emails and files from reaching your users. It uses advanced techniques such as Safe Links, Safe Attachments, anti-phishing, anti-spoofing, anti-malware, and anti-spam to block known and unknown threats. Safe Links and Safe Attachments are especially useful for protecting end users from malicious URLs and attachments that may contain ransomware or malware. They work by scanning and verifying the links and attachments before opening them and blocking them if they are found to be harmful.

- **Threat detection**: MDO monitors the environment for suspicious activities and anomalies. It uses behavioral analysis, machine learning, and threat intelligence to identify and prioritize potential attacks. It also provides rich alerts and reports to help you understand the nature and severity of the threats.

- **Threat response**: MDO provides AIR capabilities to analyze and mitigate threats (with zero-hour auto purge or quarantine). Additionally, it offers full visibility and control over the environment, allowing manual actions such as quarantine, delete, report, or restore emails and files with Threat Explorer. One significant advantage is its capability to search for similar messages (with AIR and Threat Explorer) across the current Exchange Online environment, which helps analysts prevent potentially malicious content from spreading within the environment.

- **Threat hunting**: MDO empowers analysts to proactively hunt for threats in the cloud environment with Microsoft Defender XDR capabilities. It provides advanced tools such as **Threat Explorer** and **advanced hunting** that let analysts search and query across email and collaboration data. Threat Explorer can be used to initialize an investigation in AIR.

Some of the use cases for MDO

MDO provides protection, detection, and prevention for collaboration workloads and also attack simulation training to educate end users. But what are the use cases and benefits of using this product? Here are some examples:

- Protecting against phishing and impersonation attacks where adversaries try to trick your users into revealing sensitive information or compromise their accounts

- Protecting against ransomware and malware attacks by scanning and filtering all incoming and outgoing emails and files for malicious content

- Protecting against insider threats and data loss. MDO can monitor and control (with the collaboration of Exchange Online) the flow of data within and outside the organization

- MDO has built-in reporting capabilities and provides built-in reports and dashboards in the Microsoft Defender XDR portal that can be leveraged to analyze the security of email and collaboration environments

- Attack simulations that provide real-world **Microsoft 365** (**M365**) attack simulation or training campaigns directly to users

M365 attack simulation lets organizations launch simulated attacks on their own M365 environment. By doing so, the SecOps team can evaluate how users, devices, and policies respond to these attacks, and identify any gaps or weaknesses in the security in the area of simulated attacks.

Tip

Consider implementing MDO as an additional layer of security even if you have a non-MS security solution in place for email security. By doing so, you can leverage additional coverage and protection with Safe Links, Safe Documents for SharePoint, Microsoft Teams, and OneDrive, to name a few benefits.

Case study analysis

Let's look at how implementing MDO could bring additional value and address security challenges for *High Tech Rapid Solutions Corp*:

- **The organization faces security challenges related to their M365 collaboration workloads and they are increasingly concerned about the rising threat of malware and ransomware attacks**: MDO can be leveraged to detect possible adversary activities in this area with the help of other defenders in the XDR security solution. Here is some background information about malware and ransomware attacks:

  - **Malware** is a general term for any malicious software that can harm or compromise data, devices, or networks.

- **Ransomware** is a specific type of malware that encrypts or deletes data and demands a ransom for its recovery. Both malware and ransomware can disrupt business operations and cause financial losses.

Exchange Online Protection (EOP) and MDO can provide protection for the organization's collaboration workloads with the following methods:

- EOP scans email messages and attachments with the help of MDO for malware using anti-malware policy. It also quarantines and blocks any suspicious or malicious content.

- MDO extends EOP with several policies such as Safe Attachments and Safe Links, which protect against unknown malware and viruses by opening attachments in a secure cloud environment before delivering them to users.

- **There is also a possibility to report suspicious emails, files or URLs to Microsoft as a end-user or administrator**:

  - The company can leverage the submissions report that is available in the Microsoft Defender XDR portal for organizations with Exchange Online mailboxes. In addition, they can use Threat Explorer (also known as Explorer) to report email content.

  - The submissions report is a useful tool for improving email security and hygiene. It helps to report false positives and false negatives to Microsoft, get feedback on submissions, and fine-tune policies and overrides. The organization's security teams can also use it to monitor and manage the user-reported messages in their organization.

- **The security team noticed too many users responding to spam messages and clicking on URLs, so management asked the security team to control these activities and train the end users**: One of the features of MDO is the Safe Links policy, which protects end users from clicking on malicious links in email messages. When a user clicks on a link in an email message that has been scanned by MDO, the link is checked against a list of known malicious URLs:

  - If the link is safe, the user is redirected to the original destination

  - If the link is malicious, the user is shown a warning page that informs them of the potential danger and advises them not to proceed

Another feature of MDO is the anti-spam policy, which helps organizations control the flow of spam messages in an environment. There are various settings to customize how spam messages are handled, such as the following:

- The MDO detection engine determines how likely a message is to be spam based on various factors, such as sender reputation, message content, and message headers

- The actions to take on messages that are classified as spam, such as deleting them, moving them to the junk folder, adding a prefix to the subject line, modifying X-headers or giving a quarantine message

- The end user quarantine notifications, which allow you to send periodic reports to your end users that show them the messages that have been quarantined and give them the option to release or report them

In addition, quarantine policies control how end users and admins view, release, or delete messages. Quarantine policies also control which users or admins receive notifications of quarantine messages.

However, these MDO features alone are not enough to fight against phishing. *High Tech Rapid Solutions Corp* also needs to educate their end users on how to recognize and avoid possible phishing messages. This is where the attack simulator can help. It provides different attack simulations and training campaigns that can be targeted for all users or a selected number of users. Also, it's important to educate users so that they can use the reporting feature because it improves spam and phishing detection capabilities.

- **High Tech Rapid Solutions Corp is using various collaboration tools, such as Microsoft Teams and SharePoint Online, and they need to address potential data leaks, phishing attempts, and other security risks associated with cloud-based collaboration (phishing and BEC attacks):**

Scenario 1 – Possible data leaks

Data leaks are a serious threat to any organization, as they can expose sensitive information, damage reputation, and incur legal liabilities. MDO, as well as MDA, can help you detect and respond to data leaks in the following ways:

- Monitoring collaboration workloads for any unusual or unauthorized activities, such as forwarding, downloading, or sharing files

- Alerting of any suspicious or anomalous behaviors, such as accessing data from unusual locations or devices, or using uncommon applications or protocols

- Enabling the application of policies and controls to prevent further data exfiltration, such as blocking or quarantining emails, revoking access to files, or deleting data

Scenario 2 – BEC attacks

BEC attacks are a form of phishing attacks that target specific individuals or organizations (often impersonating trusted contacts or executives) and attempt to trick them into transferring money or revealing confidential information. MDO can help to defend (with MDA and Entra ID Protection) against BEC attacks in the following ways:

- Analyzing emails for any signs of spoofing, impersonation, or deception, such as mismatched sender names, domains, addresses, or unusual language or requests

- Alerting to any potential BEC attempts, such as asking for urgent payments, wire transfers, gift cards, or personal information

- Providing detailed information on the sender's identity, reputation, and history, as well as the links and attachments in the email

- Enabling actions to be taken to stop the BEC attack, such as reporting it as phishing, blocking the sender, or notifying the intended recipient

The organization should also verify that they are following best practices to prevent and minimize potential BEC attacks in their organization.

Further reading about BEC attacks can be found here: `https://packt.link/oWuGP` and `https://packt.link/Ln7lj`.

- **Conduct regular security awareness training for employees**: Even though third-party solutions are available for this area, the organization is considering the full M365 license stack where attack simulation is included. It enables you to pinpoint and identify vulnerable users before an actual attack occurs.

At the time of writing, the available simulations are as follows:

- **Credential Harvest**

- **Malware Attachment**

- **Link in Attachment**

- **Link to Malware**

- **Drive-by-URL and OAuth Consent Grant**

These allow admins to launch realistic phishing, malware, and ransomware campaigns against their own users and devices, and monitor the results.

Refer to the MDO documentation (`https://packt.link/vLrQX`) for further learning.

MDA

Here are some of the common questions and challenges around cloud applications:

- What measures are taken to protect against cloud application vulnerabilities?

- How can access management for applications be strengthened by Microsoft security solutions?

- Difficulty in identifying which applications are secure and which are potentially risky.

- Having to manually analyze app by app and make sure secure configurations are in place.

- How can we detect when data is being exfiltrated from apps and how can we prevent it?

- How can we gain visibility into data stored in the cloud?

- How can we discover the apps being used in the organization with their usage?

When looking into the history of MDA, we see that it goes back to 2015 when Microsoft acquired a company called Adallom. Microsoft's version of a CASB was introduced in 2016 and was called **Microsoft Cloud App Security (MCAS)**. In 2022, MCAS was rebranded as *Microsoft Defender for Cloud Apps* to align with other Defender solutions.

MDA has a wide range of features, which we will go through at a high level in this chapter.

MDA key features

MDA provides rich visibility to connected applications, controls data over travel, and has a sophisticated analytics and threat protection layer for detecting possible adversary activities in the ecosystem.

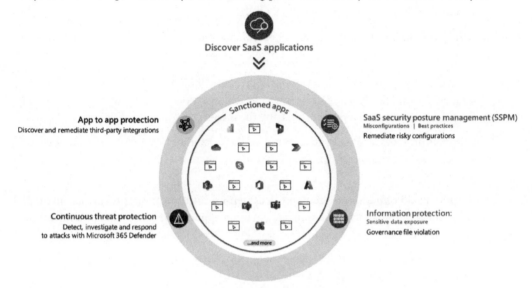

Figure 3.5 - MDA key capabilities

MDA offers a wide range of key capabilities, features, and possibilities (see *Figure 3.5*), such as the following:

- **Discover and control the use of shadow IT**: With MDA, the organization can identify the cloud apps used by the organization and assess whether those apps meet the relevant compliance requirements, including regulatory compliance and industry standards. Collected data is shown in the Cloud Discovery dashboard, and the cloud app catalog contains more than 31,000 cloud apps and 90+ risk indicators.

  Logs data can be ingested from MDE clients (endpoints) or from supported firewalls or proxies to get the full picture of applications being used in the environment.

  In addition, access to the discovered applications can be controlled through MDA (sanctioned, unsanctioned, monitored, or by using custom tags).

- **Threat protection**: With threat protection capabilities, you can have visibility of anomalous activity as well as malware detection.

  Malware detection includes governance action possibilities that help organizations perform mitigation actions immediately when malware is found in the applications (depending on the actions supported by the application).

  MDA enables the detection of unusual behavior across cloud apps to identify ransomware, compromised users, or rogue applications and analyzes high-risk usage to limit the risk to the environment.

  In addition, MDA provides SSPM data in Microsoft Secure Score for any supported and connected apps (`https://packt.link/xd11t`).

- **Secure access to applications**: Session control and monitoring for application access and activities allow for limiting access to apps or even blocking activities during the active session:

  - **Session control** – By leveraging the CASB core functionality, organizations can have more insights into the application sessions and, if needed, can block certain activities (downloading, copying, printing, etc.) in real time during the session.

  - **Controlling access** – MDA provides natively a possibility to control access to integrated applications (the recommended approach is to use Microsoft Entra Conditional Access with MDA session controls).

  - In addition, **adaptive access** (also known as step-up authentication) provides an additional layer to strengthen authentication for sensitive applications. Step-up authentication is established through Microsoft Entra Conditional Access policies.

  One thing to keep in mind is that MDA is built mainly for protecting browser-based applications in terms of access and session policies.

  For example, session policies don't support mobile and desktop apps. Mobile apps and desktop apps can also be blocked or allowed by creating an access policy.

- **Information protection for sensitive information anywhere in the cloud**: MDA has out-of-the-box policies that can be used to detect and see data in the cloud, as well as automated processes to apply controls in real time across cloud apps.

  At the time of writing this book, MDA supports the automatic application of sensitivity labels on Box, GSuite, SharePoint, and OneDrive for Business.

  The information protection layer contains the following key features:

  - **Files** – The ability to scan files from the connected applications and apply file-based policies

  - **Content inspection** – MDA has deep integration with Microsoft Purview (unified data governance solution), which provides **data loss prevention** (**DLP**) and data classification capabilities

> **Tip**
>
> Consider integrating MDA and MDE and *enforce app access* to block applications that are marked as *unsanctioned* or warn about usage of applications that are marked as *monitored*. The access is controlled by MDE's indicators (URLs/domains).

Some of the use cases for MDA

Based on our experience with MDA, we have often seen that organizations don't always utilize it to its fullest potential. While MDA is often set up to conduct active security monitoring, there are often missed opportunities. These include application integrations that don't exist (except M365 and Azure), uncontrolled application access (shadow IT), custom use cases that haven't been created (policies), governance actions that are missing from policies, and a lack of session controls for accessing sensitive applications. Let's look at some of the typical use cases for MDA:

- Cloud Discovery – detection of shadow IT applications

- Security monitoring and threat protection capabilities for connected applications

- Access and session controls (CASB features) when accessing applications that contain sensitive data

- Detecting threats from users inside your organization together with UEBA

- Detecting threats for supported SaaS applications

- Gaining visibility into corporate data stored in the cloud

Application governance – part of MDA

Application governance, introduced in 2020, was conceived to provide enhanced security for Microsoft Entra ID-integrated OAuth applications. The need for such a development emerged from the rise of *illicit consent grant* attacks, also recognized in the **MITRE ATT&CK framework Tactics, Techniques, and Procedures (TTPs)** as *Steal Application Access Token* (T1528).

Starting typically with some form of a phishing attempt, this kind of attack stands out for its sophistication compared to the usual credential theft methods. It has proven to be an effective strategy for implanting backdoors and circumventing **multi-factor authentication (MFA)** within the victim's systems.

In cooperation with MDA and Microsoft Entra ID, application governance can offer further security advantages (see *Figure 3.6*) when protecting and detecting possible threats from the applications. Application Governance provides insights into Entra ID registered non-Microsoft OAuth-enabled applications, supporting also Google and Salesforce. For Entra ID apps, Microsoft 'first-party apps' are excluded. more information about 'first-party apps' at `https://packt.link/4X7ms`.

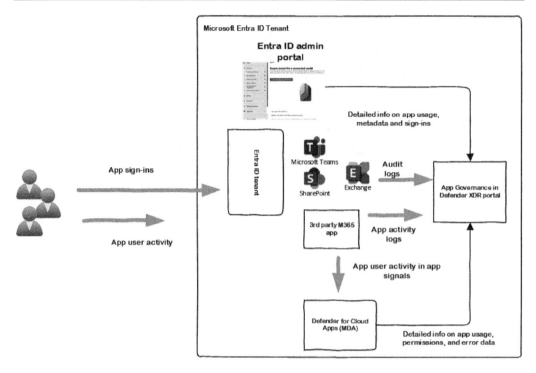

Figure 3.6- Application governance integration with MDA

Case study analysis

Let's look at how implementing MDA leveraging Microsoft Defender XDR, MDC, and Microsoft Entra ID Protection could bring additional value to addressing security challenges for *High Tech Rapid Solutions Corp*:

- **The finance department noticed some suspicious activities in their mailboxes, suspicious mail rules created, and a few confidential emails leaking outside their department**: If suspicious activity is detected in the user's mailbox, Entra ID Protection has detection rules in place for the scenarios. MDA has deep integration with Entra ID Protection, which creates an alert by using information gathered by MDA.

To detect suspicious activity in the mailbox, Entra ID Protection has built-in detection available. These detection rules are *offline* detections:

- **Suspicious inbox forwarding** – This triggers an alert when suspicious rules that delete or move messages or folders are set on a user's inbox. This detection may indicate that a user's account is compromised, messages are being intentionally hidden, or the mailbox is being used to distribute spam or malware in your organization.

- **Suspicious inbox manipulation rules** – This detection is discovered using information provided by MDA. This detection profile triggers alerts when suspicious rules that delete or move messages or folders are set on a user's inbox. This may indicate that the user's account is compromised, messages are being intentionally hidden, or that the mailbox is being used to distribute spam or malware in your organization.

- **Management asked the security team to keep an extra eye on certain assets, terminated employees, and contractors/vendors**: MDA is very useful for monitoring user activities both in the cloud and on-premises. With MDI integration natively in place (if MDI is deployed), you can see identity-related activities in one place (in MDA Activity Log). This helps when an analyst is doing an active incident investigation and provides the possibility for creating custom alert rules based on the activities.

- **The security team noticed too many false positives and spent more time addressing these**: The false/positive ratio can be reduced with the following actions:

  - Define known organization IP ranges in MDA – This helps in the identification of an IP address during the investigation.

  - Behavior detections – Microsoft introduced a new data layer in Microsoft Defender XDR called *Behaviors*. It's a representation of an abstraction above the raw data level to offer a deeper understanding of events.

  Like alerts, *Behaviors* are attached to the MITRE ATT&CK categories and techniques. Security teams can consume them by creating queries or custom detections using the `Behaviors` data tables (`BehaviorInfo` and `BehaviorEntities`) in advanced hunting.

  Some MDA detection rules were deactivated due to the *Behaviors* layer announcement. The full list of deactivated rules can be found in the Microsoft Learn documentation (`https://packt.link/LuX4t`).

- **Security teams are struggling to track the apps in the organization and control them**: MDA's **Cloud Discovery** (also known as **shadow IT management**) provides visibility for applications used by organization end users. To perform discovery and get the full picture of the applications being used, it's recommended to ingest network-based data for analysis from MDE as well as using firewalls and proxies.

  The discovered applications can be managed (sanctioned, unsanctioned, monitored, or using a custom tag) from MDA. With MDA and MDE deep integration, access to applications can even be blocked from endpoints.

Application governance provides additional protection in this area by providing advanced insights into OAuth-enabled application integration to Microsoft Entra tenants and also, to some extent, to Google and Salesforce. The main advantages of using this solution would be detailed information about each application, such as its usage, traffic, and data exposure through the Graph API.

Refer to the MDA documentation (`https://packt.link/w9ZAs`) for further learning.

MDI

Here are a few common questions and challenges about identities, especially around MDI:

- Why do we need to consider MDI and configure domain controllers?
- Does MDI protect any other workloads than the domain controllers?
- How can I capture some of the reconnaissance activities early?
- How can I quickly notice lateral moment activities and take remediation actions?
- How can I detect compromised identities and is it possible to automatically mitigate compromised identities?
- How can I get UEBA insights from an on-premises Active Directory?
- Does MDI also protect cloud-based identities?

MDI has been in the market for a while. Its predecessors were **Azure Advanced Threat Protection (Azure ATP)** and **Advanced Threat Analytics (ATA)**. Nowadays, it is a cloud-based security solution even though it provides protection for on-premises environment entities.

MDI key features

MDI fulfills visibility in the ecosystem by monitoring on-premises Active Directory signals to identify and detect advanced threats, users, and devices to discover suspicious activities (*see Figure 3.7*). MDI natively integrates with other security solutions underneath the Microsoft Defender XDR umbrella. MDI can also be integrated with Microsoft Sentinel UEBA, which is one of the key advantages.

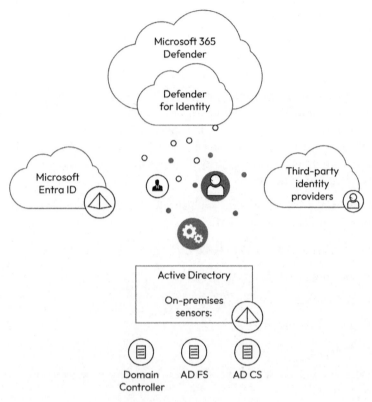

Figure 3.7 - MDI solution architecture

Here are a few more advantages:

- **Monitoring and analyzing entities**: MDI monitors the authentication traffic of domain controllers through packet inspection technology, offering visibility into the authentication and authorization processes within an organization. This is established by installing sensors to domain controllers that send audit data to the MDI cloud service. To synchronize user entities from on-premises Active Directory, ensure the following:

    - The Entra ID tenant is integrated with MDI (either as a standalone solution or as part of Microsoft Defender XDR)

    - The MDI sensor is successfully installed on Active Directory domain controllers

- **Protection for AD FS and AD CS**: Besides on-premises Active Directory, MDI provides additional protection for **Active Directory Federation Services** (**AD FS**) and **Active Directory Certificate Services** (**AD CS**, aka **PKI**) workloads. The MDI sensor needs to be installed on these workloads for coverage. By installing the MDI sensor, organizations can detect on-premises attacks on AD FS and provide visibility into authentication events generated by AD FS.

> **Tip**
> To get the best possible visibility for AD FS and AD CS workloads, consider installing both the MDI sensor and MDE agent on the servers running the workloads.

- **Secure Score and attack surface**: In addition, MDI also collects relevant Windows events from all **domain controllers** where the sensor is installed and creates entity profiles based on information from **Active Directory Domain Services (AD DS)**. One of the benefits of having MDI deployed is better threat protection for the workloads and enhanced visibility for possible weak configurations in terms of security posture reports. The organization's security posture can be found in **Secure Score**.

- **Detections**: MDI provides multiple sophisticated out-of-the-box detections for scenarios, which are categorized as follows in MDI:

  - **Reconnaissance and discovery alerts**

  - **Persistence and privilege escalation alerts**

  - **Credential access alerts**

  - **Lateral movement alerts**

  - **Other alerts**

  The full alert list with details can be found on the Microsoft website: `https://packt.link/Npwla`.

  If the organization needs to create custom detection based on MDI raw data, this can be achieved in several ways:

  - **MDA** – The activity log includes MDI events and custom alerts can be created based on the MDI events

  - **Defender XDR advanced hunting** – By utilizing MDI raw data through the advanced hunting feature, there is a possibility to create custom detection based on custom queries

  - **Microsoft Sentinel** – If MDI raw data is ingested through the Microsoft Defender XDR data connector to Sentinel and the Log Analytics workspace, **Kusto Query Language (KQL)** can be used to create custom detections based on the data

- **Mitigation actions**: If there is a suspicion of identity compromise, MDI allows taking mitigation actions against the compromised account, and an on-premises account can be disabled or enabled (see *Figure 3.8*).

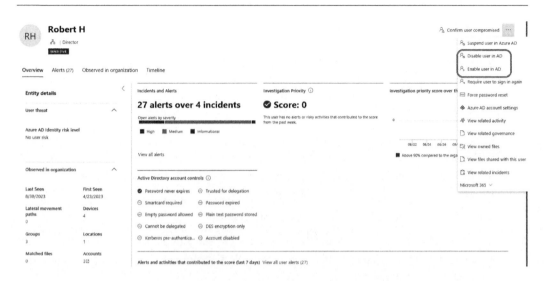

Figure 3.8 - Microsoft Defender XDR portal (sample incident)

- **Integrations**: Furthermore, MDI seamlessly integrates with other Microsoft security solutions, which enriches the security capabilities of the organization by leveraging the collective intelligence and insights across the Microsoft security stack.

  Another important feature is Microsoft Sentinel's UEBA, which can leverage MDI as a data source for the Sentinel UEBA engine. The user entity information that Microsoft Sentinel uses to build its user profiles comes from two sources (at the time of writing): Microsoft Entra ID and on-premises Active Directory (if enabled).

  When UEBA is enabled, it synchronizes Microsoft Entra ID with Microsoft Sentinel, storing the details in an internal database that can be viewed via the `IdentityInfo` table in Log Analytics. There is also a possibility to sync on-premises Active Directory user entity information, using MDI.

MDI comes with multiple out-of-the-box alert definitions and provides protection for several on-premises environment attack scenarios, which are categorized underneath the following categories:

- **Reconnaissance and discovery alerts**
- **Persistence and privilege escalation alerts**
- **Credential access alerts**
- **Lateral movement alerts**
- **Other alerts**

The full list of these built-in alert rules can be found on the Microsoft Learn website (`https://packt.link/tOR6D`).

Some of the use cases for MDI

MDI gives valuable insights from the on-premises Active Directory environment, which is sometimes overlooked when the focus is purely on cloud-based technologies. By utilizing MDI, organizations will get much better visibility of potential malicious activities in on-premises environments. Here are some use cases for MDI:

- MDI is excellent at detecting potentially compromised user identities by monitoring and analyzing user behavior and activities. It can identify suspicious activities such as unusual resource access, multiple failed login attempts, and logins from suspicious locations.

- MDI can monitor and identify instances of privilege escalation or abuse of elevated privileges, which is a common tactic used in advanced attacks.

- MDI provides detailed information on the source of the attack, the devices and identities affected, and the techniques used, which can be very useful when trying to investigate and remediate a security incident.

- MDI provides invaluable insights on identity configurations and suggested security best practices related to on-premises Active Directory configurations. These recommendations can be seen in the Secure Score reports.

- MDI raw data is synced to Microsoft Defender XDR and is available in advanced hunting data tables (`IdentityInfo`, `IdentityLogonEvents`, `IdentityQueryEvents`, and `IdentityDirectoryEvents`). Threat hunting capabilities are one of the key features in the whole Defender XDR stack and provide an effective way to do threat hunting across XDR solutions and workloads.

Case study analysis

Now, let's look at some of the challenges that *High Tech Rapid Solutions Corp* is facing, as mentioned in the *Case study* section at the beginning of this book. Let's see how Microsoft Defender XDR and MDI can address some of the challenges:

- **Management asked the security team to keep an extra eye on certain assets, terminated employees, and contractors/vendors**: MDI, together with MDA, provides insights from certain assets, such as identities. This information can be leveraged when investigating activities of critical assets (VIP users, etc.). *Figure 3.9* shows the **Identities** blade in Defender XDR portal, filtered to show external users:

Identities

Filters:

| × | Affiliation ∨ | Is | 🔍 Internal | 🔍 External |

+ Add a filter

⤓ Export   ▼ 1 - 20 of 236

	User name ↑ ∨	Investigation priority ∨	Affiliation ∨	Type ∨	Email ∨	Apps ∨	Groups ∨
●	045350f58c024871b59e60a4	—	🔍 External	Account	—	🗂	2 groups
●	2431894d10504ba494975c0	—	🔍 External	Account	—	🗂	2 groups
●	4ff8512ce1014b0b8ca13b43	—	🔍 External	Account	—	🗂	2 groups
●	5c04be93d37643109e171e9	—	🔍 External	Account	—	🗂	2 groups
●	7cac59d66a754ba9a9219248	—	🔍 External	Account	—	🗂	2 groups
Ⓐ	aad-extensions-app. Do not	—	🔍 External	Account	—	🗂	2 groups
Ⓐ	AADC01	—	🔍 External	Account	—	🗂	2 groups
Ⓐ	AADConfigIngestion	—	🔍 External	Account	—	🗂	Application (Defender for Clou...
Ⓐ	AADPB1	—	🔍 External	Account	—	🗂	Application (Defender for Clou...
Ⓐ	Add-IP-Entity-To-Named-Lo	—	🔍 External	Account	—	🗂	2 groups
Ⓐ	Add-UserToWatchlist-Incide	—	🔍 External	Account	—	🗂	2 groups
Ⓐ	ae539e4ec1094e3fa1a48970	—	🔍 External	Account	—	🗂	2 groups

Figure 3.9- Picture from Microsoft Defender XDR portal with external users filtered (Identities blade)

- **The security team noticed too many false positives and spent more time addressing them**: The alert learning period in the context of MDI starts after the solution has been deployed. During the learning period, MDI collects data and learns what is normal behavior in the environment. By default, the learning period for MDI workspaces is 30 days but it can be turned off if needed (for example, testing the solution capabilities).

  The recommendation is to keep the learning period enabled. The setting for it can be found in the **Microsoft Defender XDR** portal | **Settings** | **Identities** | **Advanced settings**. At the time of writing this book, the learning period varies from 8 to 30 days, depending on the alert rule.

  MDI configuration needs to be addressed to reduce the number of false/positive alerts during the learning period.

  A good example is scanning machines (vulnerability scanners) or a Microsoft Entra Connect instance that might need to be excluded from some of the detection rules in MDI configuration.

- **The SOC team doesn't have active security monitoring for on-premises identities**: This is exactly what MDI does. It provides protection for on-premises Active Directory identities:

  - Monitors users, entity behavior, and activities with learning-based analytics

  - Protects user identities and credentials stored in on-premises Active Directory

  - Determines and investigates unusual user actions and advanced attacks throughout the entire kill chain

- **There is no active security posture management solution for on-premises Active Directory in the SecOps team**: MDI provides identity posture management for on-premises Active Directory identities. This feature is sometimes neglected but provides very useful information from the on-premises **Active Directory (AD)**.

  Nowadays, it's integrated natively into Microsoft Defender XDR Secure Score, which provides more granularity for managing posture findings. At the time of writing this book, these are the assessments available in the portal:

  - Domain controllers with the print spooler service available

  - Dormant entities in sensitive groups

  - Entities exposing credentials in clear text

  - Microsoft LAPS usage

  - Legacy protocols usage

  - Riskiest lateral movement paths (LMP)

  - Unmonitored domain controllers

  - Unsecure account attributes

  - Unsecure domain configurations

  - Unsecure Kerberos delegation

  - Unsecure SID History attributes

  - Weak cipher usage

Refer to the MDI documentation at Microsoft Learn (`https://packt.link/alxZU`) for further learning.

Microsoft Entra ID Protection (formerly Azure AD Identity Protection)

Initially, Microsoft Entra ID Protection (formerly Azure AD Identity Protection) was purely an Entra ID (formerly Azure AD) security solution. It protects identities in two different ways: either in real time during the authentication process or offline after the authentication process (by own detections or receiving signals from other solutions). The following diagram (*Figure 3.10*) shows the high-level architecture of the solution.

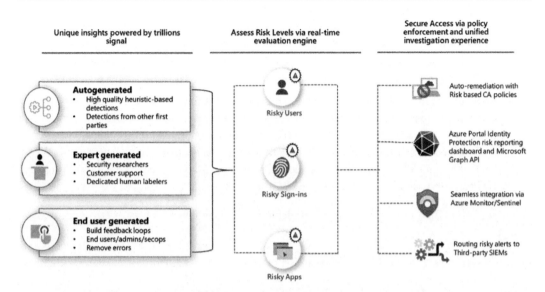

Figure 3.10- High-level overview of Microsoft Entra ID Protection risk engine

Real-time detection (online)

Real-time detections are based on the detection rules that are evaluated during the authentication pipeline. The initial purpose is to detect possible malicious activity during the authentication process. The latency with real-time detections before they show up in reports is 5–10 minutes.

A few example detections are as follows:

- **Unfamiliar sign-in properties**: This real-time risk detection type takes into account previous sign-in history to identify for possible anomalous sign-ins. The risk engine stores information about earlier user sign-ins and triggers risk detection when a sign-in occurs with properties that are unfamiliar to the user sign-in history.

- **Anonymous IP address**: Sign-ins from an anonymous IP address (such as the Tor Browser or an anonymous VPN) are triggered by this risk detection. Adversaries who wish to hide their sign-in details (IP address, location, device, and so on) for perhaps malicious reasons usually utilize these IP addresses.

- **Offline detections**: Offline detections are malicious activities detected after the user has signed in.

A few example detections are as follows:

- **Anomalous token**: This detection identifies unusual characteristics in the token, such as an unusual token lifetime or token replay from an unfamiliar location based on user sign-in history. Session tokens and refresh tokens are covered by the detection.

- **Password spray**: In a password spray attack, several usernames are targeted with the same password in a coordinated brute-force manner to obtain unauthorized access. High severity risk is triggered when a password spray attack has been successfully performed and medium severity ri is triggered sk when there is an unsuccessfull password spray attack attempt.

- **Possible attempt to access primary refresh token (PRT)**: PRT access detection is a great example of cross-product benefits and signal sharing in Microsoft security solutions. PRT detection is initiated in MDE, which shares the signal with Entra ID Protection. The PRT is a key artifact of Microsoft Entra authentication on several platforms and is used for enabling SSO. If the PRT is extracted on the device, MDE detects the attempt and sends a signal to Entra ID Protection, which raises the user risk to high.

Full list of Entra ID Protection detections is available at Microsoft Learn `https://packt.link/btJgo`.

Use cases for Entra ID Protection

Entra ID Protection detects possible malicious activity against identities, and we have seen, in many cases, the benefits of having it deployed and configured properly. It needs a learning period and sign-in history to be present to be able to correlate activities properly (take this into account when deploying the solution). The most common use cases with Entra ID Protection are as follows:

- Protects risky sign-ins (real-time) – end users and admins

- Protects from risky users (offline) – end users and admins

- Detects suspicious activities from applications (workload Identities)

- Detects leaked credentials

Case study analysis

Now, let's look at some of the challenges that *High Tech Rapid Solutions Corp* is facing, as mentioned in the *Case study* section at the beginning of this book. The following section provides insights into how Entra ID Protection, together with the unified XDR stack, can address security challenges:

- **The finance department noticed some suspicious activities in their mailboxes, suspicious mail rules created, and a few confidential emails leaking outside their department**: Entra ID Protection has detections in place for suspicious activity in user mailboxes. We already covered the scenario in the *MDA* section as the actual detection is happening on the MDA side, which sends the signal to Entra ID Protection. The detection rules (which are used to identify suspicious activity) are offline detections, as follows:

  - **Suspicious inbox forwarding** – This triggers an alert when suspicious rules that delete or move messages or folders are set on a user's inbox. This detection may indicate that a user's account is compromised, messages are being intentionally hidden, or the mailbox is being used to distribute spam or malware in your organization.

- **Suspicious inbox manipulation rules** – This detection is discovered using information provided by MDA. The detection looks for suspicious email forwarding rules – for example, if a user created an inbox rule that forwards a copy of all emails to an external address.

- **The company operations run in three different continents and some of the employees are traveling between office locations, factories, and so on. For the SOC team, it's complicated to identify false/positive and true/positive logins with the current security monitoring solutions**: Entra ID Protection has deep integration with the Entra ID **Conditional Access (CA)** engine. With this integration, an organization can configure auto-remediation in place when suspicious activity is detected. In a nutshell, this means that when suspicious activity is detected by the solution risk engine, the user risk is raised and CA requires conditions, such as MFA or a password change (depending on real-time/offline detection) on the next authentication attempt.

  The latest enhancement was especially targeted at hybrid users. The ability to remediate risk has been there for years already, but in a hybrid scenario, it has had some challenges. For example, earlier, when the on-premises synced user (hybrid) risk level was raised and CA (or Entra ID Protection policies) required a password change for auto-remediation, the password change notification didn't reach Microsoft Entra ID, even though the password was changed at the on-premises user. This led to a situation in some organizations where user risk was not remediated on Entra ID Protection and, in the worst-case scenario, the user was not able to access cloud services.

  The feature can be enabled from the **Entra ID Protection** blade (by enabling the **Allow on-premises password change to reset user risk** settings) and is in public preview at the time of writing this book. The company should configure Entra ID Protection auto-remediation capabilities with CA policies and enable **Allow on-premises password change to reset user risk** to strengthen the identity security posture and mitigate identity-based threats detected by Entra ID Protection whenever possible.

> **Important**
>
> To ensure appropriate mitigation actions are initiated, it's recommended to configure Entra ID Protection policies in Conditional Access. Legacy policies will be retired October 2026.

- **The security team noticed too many false positives and spent much time addressing them**: The Entra ID Protection learning period varies between detections from 5 to 14 days after deployment. The learning period refers to the duration during which the system familiarizes itself with the user's sign-in behavior, establishing a baseline for what is considered normal activity. During this period, the system will not block or challenge any sign-ins.

  After the learning period, Entra ID Protection can reduce false/positive alerts, and reduce noise from the SOC if configured correctly. Plus, you have Entra ID CA policies in place for possible remediations.

If you would like to learn more about Entra ID Protection, we encourage you to read the following blog post by Sami Lamppu (co-author of this book): *Azure AD Identity Protection Integrations with Microsoft Security Solutions* (`https://packt.link/YCYmr`).

More information about Microsoft Entra ID Protection can be found here: `https://packt.link/aBzFf`.

Extending XDR capabilities to on-premises and hybrid cloud by leveraging MDC

The following are some common questions and challenges around Azure resources, hybrid cloud, and multi-cloud environments:

- How can I get a holistic view of my environment security status when using hybrid and multi-cloud infrastructure?
- Is it mandatory to use a third-party **Cloud Security Posture Management** (**CSPM**) solution to efficiently manage security posture in a multi-cloud environment?
- What are the benefits of leveraging Microsoft's unified XDR and SIEM solution with MDC and what benefit am I getting for my multi-cloud and on-premises workloads from it?
- How can I ensure that I have visibility and protection in my DevOps environment and CI/CD pipelines?
- How can I control most of the security controls (if not all) from a single portal?

Azure Security Center (launched in 2016) and **Azure Defender** were the predecessors of MDC. These products were rebranded in 2021 under the name **Microsoft Defender for Cloud**. MDC is a comprehensive solution that provides end-to-end protection for cloud resources across Azure, multi-cloud, and hybrid environments. MDC is also categorized as a CNAPP solution that consolidates security and compliance capabilities, providing a cohesive defense against modern cloud security threats from development to runtime.

MDC key features

In this section, we will explore the MDC key features that protect cloud environments no matter where resources are located (Azure, AWS, GCP, or on-premises). The MDC core features can be divided at a high level into three different categories (as shown in *Figure 3.11*):

- Unified DevOps security management
- **Cloud Security Posture Management** (**CSPM**)
- **Cloud Workload Protection Platform** (**CWPP**)
- **Cloud Infrastructure Entitlement Management** (**CIEM**)

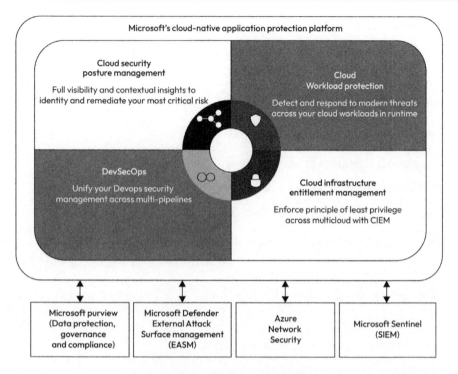

Figure 3.11 - MDC core capabilities

Unified DevOps security management

Let's start with DevOps platform security management. By utilizing DevOps integration with MDC, organizations can include security controls early in the software development life cycle, preventing the need for expensive changes later. MDC provides protection for both code management environments and development pipelines. At the time of writing, MDC supports Azure DevOps, GitHub (Free, Pro, Team, and Enterprise Cloud), and GitLab environments.

> **Note**
>
> GitHub Enterprise with GitHub Advanced Security is required to gain all the benefits of this DevOps platform security management solution.

MDC features for DevOps could add enhanced protection for the DevOps environment, continuous monitoring, and the improvement of security practices with key features such as the following:

- Visibility into DevOps environments
- Strengthening cloud resource configurations by enabling IaC templates and container images
- Prioritization of critical issues in code

Cloud Security Posture Management

MDC CSPM plays an important role in preventing breaches by continuously proactively scanning weak configurations from the environment. It provides actionable recommendations, ensuring a secure and compliant cloud infrastructure and reducing the risk of security incidents. CSPM is available in two versions at the time of writing this book:

- Foundational CSPM (free) contains the following:

  - Continuous assessment of security configurations

  - Recommendations for assessment findings

  - Secure Score to summarize security status

- Defender CSPM (paid version) contains all the free features plus the following:

  - Identity and role assignments discovery

  - Network exposure detection

  - Attack path analysis

  - Cloud security explorer for risk hunting

  - Agentless vulnerability scanning

  - Governance rules to drive timely remediation and accountability

  - Regulatory compliance and industry best practices

  - Data-aware security posture

  - Agentless discovery for Kubernetes

  - Agentless vulnerability assessments for container images, including registry scanning

Let's take a closer look into Defender CSPM capabilities and how they can strengthen environment security posture and defenses.

Defender CSPM (DCSPM) is one of the newest additions to the MDC toolbox that organizations can leverage to enhance their cloud security posture. Features such as attack path analysis, Cloud Security Explorer, and agentless scanning are solutions that many organizations have been asking for to get better visibility for high-risk security vulnerabilities. Next, let's look at a high-level introduction of the DCSPM features.

Attack path analysis uncovers hidden vulnerabilities and prioritizes risks in your cloud infrastructure by highlighting potential adversary targets. Utilizing graph-based analytics and machine learning, it maps potential attack paths (as shown in *Figure 3.12*) that could be exploited by adversaries, offering actionable steps for remediation.

The latest innovation for MDC attack path analysis and recommendations are as follows:

- Attack paths are given a risk prioritization based on the possible impact on the company as well as their exploitability

- This evaluation considers variables including potential for lateral movement, data sensitivity, and internet exposure

> **Note**
>
> If EASM is configured, it complements the attack surface view and might provide additional information when investigating attack paths.

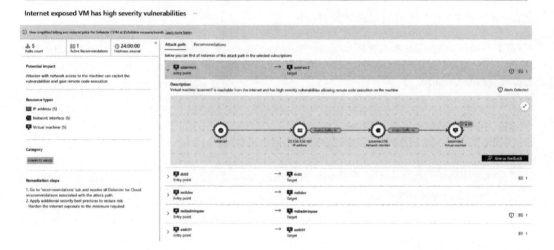

Figure 3.12 - Attack path blade in the Azure portal (demo environment)

Cloud Security Explorer utilizes graph-based queries run on MDC's context engine, known as the **cloud security graph**. This feature allows your security team to focus on high-priority issues, and helps to reduce the risk of breaches in Azure environment.

Using either pre-designed query templates from Cloud Security Explorer or crafting custom queries, you can uncover insights into improperly configured data resources that may be publicly accessible and contain sensitive information, even in multi-cloud settings.

> **Info**
>
> A reference list for available cloud security graph components can be found at https:// packt.link/6Aznc.

With the MDC **agentless scanning** approach, there isn't a need for any additional software or agent installations on cloud resources. It leverages the native APIs provided by cloud service providers to evaluate cloud environments, identifying potential misconfigurations, security exposures, or malware intrusions. In today's fast-paced cloud security landscape, where resources can be quickly deployed, agentless scanning offers an alternate strategy.

> Tip
> We recommend leveraging DCSPM to safeguard cloud, hybrid, and multi-cloud resources. The solution provides proactive protection and helps to enhance the environment's overall security posture.

Cloud Workload Protection Platform

CWPP (also referred to as **CWP**) is a combination of workload-specific recommendations and threat protection for workloads (in terms of security alerts). You can imagine it as a reactive part of **Defender for Cloud**.

CWPP threat protection (Defender) plans are available for the following workloads listed at the time of writing. These plans provide additional protection and features to workloads and give more visibility and control in the environment as well as reducing the attack surface:

- Defender for Servers (Plan 1 / Plan 2)
- Defender for App Service
- Defender for Databases (Azure SQL, SQL on Servers, open source relational DB, Cosmos DB)
- Defender for Storage
- Defender for Containers
- Defender for Key Vault
- Defender for Resource Manager
- Defender for APIs

With the threat protection layer, organizations get workload-specific signals and threat alerts with deterministic, AI, and anomaly-based detection mechanisms.

Cloud infrastructure entitlement management

CIEM, a vital component of the CNAPP capability by MDC, ensures that everyone, from users to applications, only has the bare minimum access needed to do their work, following the principle of least privilege. Think of it like a "security gate keeper" or a "traffic controller" for your cloud, which ensures access rights follow the **principle of least privilege** (**PoLP**), meaning users and services only have the minimum permissions needed to do their jobs. This keeps unauthorized users out and keeps your valuable cloud resources safe.

By integrating with Permissions Management, Defender for Cloud empowers security teams with a single, comprehensive cloud security dashboard. This dashboard offers unified visibility into user access controls and delivers actionable recommendations to optimize security posture.

At the time of writing it supports only Azure, AWS, and GCP clouds. Also, Microsoft Defender for Cloud integration currently excludes AWS or GCP accountts initially onboarded to Entra Permissions Management.

Benefits of using unified XDR for on-premises, multi-cloud, or hybrid cloud scenarios

The following question has been frequently asked: *What are the benefits of leveraging Microsoft's unified XDR and SIEM solution with MDC and what benefit will I get for my multi-cloud and on-premises workloads from it?*

In the following sections, we will elaborate on the benefits of using the unified XDR stack outside Azure.

Background information

Before going deeper into how MDC can protect workloads located anywhere outside Azure, let's clarify the definitions of multi-cloud and hybrid cloud given by Microsoft.

The **hybrid cloud** combines private cloud infrastructure located at on-premises with public cloud services. These services are provided over the public Internet by third-pary providers.

Multi-cloud computing refers to the use of several cloud computing services in a heterogeneous environment from different cloud providers (including private and public clouds)Most of the organizations we have worked with or observed have hybrid cloud and multi-cloud architecture in place. This means that part of the workload is located on-premises and part of it is located in the cloud (the balance varies between organizations). More details are in the sections that follow.

Hybrid cloud workloads

Defender for Cloud provides the same protection for server workloads (Defender for Servers) no matter where the server is located (Azure, multi-cloud, or on-premises). This is established in collaboration with MDC, MDE, the Azure Arc framework, and Azure Monitor agents (**Azure Monitor Agent –AMA** or **Microsoft Monitoring Agent - MMA**).

Defender for Servers (which automatically deploys the MDE extension if the prerequisites are configured) provides two options for deployment:

- Through the Azure Arc management framework
- Direct onboarding to MDE

The Azure Arc framework enables us to manage hybrid cloud resources from a single control plane. From the server's point of view, it provides the possibility to deploy MDE, and Arc gives tools to implement antivirus and security policies through MDE-Intune integration.

Basically, if you want to control exclusions, for example from Azure, Arc is required, otherwise, settings must be distributed via scripts or Group Policies (GPO) for hybrid servers.

Direct onboarding is a tenant-level setting that provides you with the option to deploy MDE automatically without any agent deployments. Sounds almost too good to be true, right? Direct onboarding is established with integration between MDC and MDE.

At the time of writing this book, direct onboarding still has some limitations, for example the P2 license plan is not supported, the multi-cloud scenario has some limitations, and simultaneous onboarding has limited support. Take these into account when planning MDE deployment to server workloads.

More information can be found at `https://packt.link/jnLxA`.

The next topic we look at is CSPM and how it brings additional benefits in multi-cloud and hybrid-cloud scenarios.

CSPM is fully supported for servers and SQL servers on machines (SQL servers on-premises and Azure Arc-enabled SQL servers) no matter where resources are located. With CSPM, you can proactively mitigate weak configurations based on regulatory standards (using Azure Policy as an engine) and reduce the risk of breaches. In the following figure (*Figure 3.13*), you can see the Azure Arc-connected machine in the **Inventory** blade.

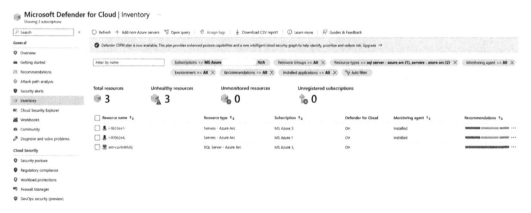

Figure 3.13 - Inventory blade in the Microsoft Defender for Cloud portal

CWP provides threat protection for supported workloads. Some examples are as follows:

- Servers connected through Azure Arc
- Servers connected through direct onboarding

If servers are onboarded through direct onboarding, some of the MDC features are not available (in some cases, event log data is needed from the servers). Event log data can be sent to Azure through **AMA** or **MMA** – the latter will be deprecated in September 2024. It's important to understand that visibility into the security of workloads depends on the data that the monitoring components collect. The components ensure security coverage for all supported resources.

Let's look at which of the Defender plans (as of this writing) use monitoring components (AMA/MMA) to collect data in hybrid and multi-cloud scenarios:

- Defender for Servers:

    - Azure Arc agent (for multi-cloud and on-premises servers)

    - MDE vulnerability assessment

    - AMA or Log Analytics agent

- Defender for SQL servers on machines:

    - Azure Arc agent (for multi-cloud and on-premises servers)

    - AMA or Log Analytics agent

    - Automatic SQL server discovery and registration

- Defender for Containers:

    - Azure Arc agent (for multi-cloud and on-premises servers)

    - Defender profile, Azure Policy Extension, Kubernetes audit log data

Multi-cloud – AWS and GCP

If an organization has multi-cloud architecture in place, as many enterprise organizations do, MDC can provide additional benefits to gain holistic visibility to the whole environment as well as additional protection for threat detection, centralized dashboards (based on Azure Resource Graph data), and for managing the security posture in the environment.

There are many third-party tools available in this area, especially for multi-cloud security posture management, but the challenges have been (based on our experience) integrations capabilities and pricing.

MDC supports Microsoft Azure, AWS, and GCP in multi-cloud scenarios (as of this writing).

> **Note**
> Supported workloads vary between AWS and GCP cloud environments. It is essential to consider this factor when planning deployment.

In the following screenshot (*Figure 3.14*), you can see that AWS Defender CSPM is available and CWP servers, databases, and containers are supported:

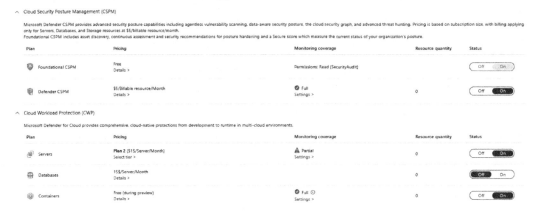

Figure 3.14 - CSPM plans for AWS resources

Let's take a closer look at the benefits of having both CSPM and CWP covering workloads in multi-cloud scenarios. In the next figure (*Figure 3.15*), you can see an EC2 instance (virtual machine) that is running in AWS and connected to Azure and Defender for Cloud through Azure Arc.

From the inventory (resource health), you can evaluate posture management information and mitigate possible weak configurations that could prevent potential breaches. Also, if malicious activity is seen on the machine, there are a few solutions that protect against possible adversary actions and create alerts on the activities. This can be achieved by utilizing solutions such as Defender for Servers, Defender for Endpoint, agentless vulnerability scanning, and AMA/MMA.

Recommendations   Alerts   Installed applications   Secrets

Severity ↑↓	Description	Status ↑↓
Low	OS and data disks should be encrypted with a customer-managed key	• Unhealthy
High	Adaptive network hardening recommendations should be applied on internet facing virtual machines	• Unhealthy
Low	Audit Windows machines that do not have the minimum password age set to specified number of days	• Unhealthy
Medium	Windows Defender Exploit Guard should be enabled on machines Preview	• Unhealthy
Low	Audit Windows machines that do not have the password complexity setting enabled	• Unhealthy
High	Windows virtual machines should enable Azure Disk Encryption or EncryptionAtHost. Preview	• Unhealthy
Low	Audit Windows machines that allow re-use of the passwords after the specified number of unique passwords	• Unhealthy
High	File integrity monitoring should be enabled on machines Preview	• Unhealthy
Low	Azure Backup should be enabled for virtual machines Preview	• Unhealthy
High	Install endpoint protection solution on virtual machines	• Unhealthy

Figure 3.15 - MDC inventory recommendations for VMs

One question that is very often asked (in every Defender for Servers-related project) is *How can I monitor agents that are deployed to servers (Azure and non-Azure)?* Luckily, community members and Microsoft have published Azure workbooks to address this challenge. Here are a few workbooks that might be useful in this area:

- *Defender CSPM Dashboard*: `https://packt.link/EX1tt`
- *Defender for Servers Deployment Status*: `https://packt.link/0mn9G`
- *Defender for Servers Monitoring*: `https://packt.link/oGhgr`

Some of the use cases for Defender for Cloud

MDC can be compared to a Swiss Army knife; it has multiple features that solve most of your security challenges on the infrastructure level. At a high level, here are some of the use cases for MDC:

- Security posture monitoring: CSPM (covering hybrid and multi-cloud scenarios)
- Workload protection: CWPP
- Defender CSPM:
  - Agentless scanning and agentless discovery
  - Sensitive data discovery
  - Attack path analysis and Cloud Security Explorer
  - Data-aware security posture
- DevOps posture visibility
- Cloud infrastructure entitlement management
- Regulatory compliance
- Vulnerability scanning for servers and SQL

Case study analysis

Now, let's look at some of the challenges that *High Tech Rapid Solutions Corp* is facing, as mentioned in the *Case study* section at the beginning of this book. They have several security challenges around infrastructure and resources that span Azure, AWS, and on-premises environments:

- **Regulatory compliance**: MDC fully supports multi-cloud environments, offering a valuable solution for the organization's regulatory compliance challenges. As the organization utilizes Azure and AWS for hosting resources in the cloud, MDC's support for various known regulatory standards and frameworks (and custom standards) aligns with the organization's specific requirements. This adaptability ensures a simplified approach to compliance across different platforms. For a comprehensive overview of the regulatory standards that MDC provides, the full list is available on the Microsoft site (`https://packt.link/hP9Fa`).

- **Siloed security architecture**: *High Tech Rapid Solutions Corp's* current security challenge, marked by isolated products and limited visibility within a multi-cloud architecture, can be efficiently addressed by Microsoft Defender for Cloud. This solution offers a unified security dashboard that centralizes monitoring across all cloud platforms (CSPM and CWP).

  Leveraging MDC's adaptability, they can have better control over their multi-cloud environment security and transform a siloed architecture into a holistic, and resilient defense system.

- **Incomplete security insights**: MDC manages the security posture for a multi-cloud environment. It offers a centralized, single pane of glass view for security posture management across the various cloud platforms (Azure, AWS, and GCP) as well as DevOps and on-premises server workloads.

  Bidirectional sync capabilities between MDC and Sentinel makes incident handling more efficient, but also leverages AI in detection on the MDC side. This collaboration enhances the correlation of security events and allows for sophisticated alerting by taking on analytical tasks on behalf of security analysts.

  The newest addition to the family of integrations is the MDC and Microsoft Defender XDR bidirectional integration. The latest integrations to Defender XDR (Entra ID Protection and MDC) helps SOC analysts to investigate and manage incidents and alerts more efficiently from a single portal, as well as allowing them to investigate and manage asset information in multi-cloud scenarios.

- Compared to isolated, siloed solutions, the combined approach of MDC and Sentinel streamlines incident management and provides a holistic security posture status across the multi-cloud environment.

- **The HR department raised concerns to the security team about unauthorized users accessing their apps or servers**: MDC has a threat protection layer (Defender plans) that can be used to protect both workloads natively. Defender for App Services provides protection for organization applications running over Azure App Service. When enabled, the environment will get protection for the following:

  - VM instances in which Azure App Service is running (and its management interface)

  - Requests and responses sent to and from App Service apps will be monitored

  - Protection for underlying sandboxes and VMs

  - Visibility for App Service internal logs

  Server workloads can be protected with Defender for Servers plan 1 or plan 2. Which one to use depends on the organization's security requirements on server workloads.

  The organization has server workloads in **Azure**, **AWS**, and on-premises environments. By leveraging **MDC**, **MDE**, and **Azure Arc**, they would have a consistent threat protection framework across all platforms.

Depending on application architecture and used Azure resources, there are additional MDC enhanced plans they could leverage, such as the following:

- Defender CSPM – Provides additional protection (posture management) for workloads such as attack path analysis, Cloud Security Explorer, and agentless vulnerability scanning, to name a few

- Defender for APIs – Provides visibility into business-critical APIs that are published through Azure API Management

- Defender for Containers – Protects container nodes and clusters (such as Kubernetes), vulnerability assessments, and so on

- Defender for Databases – Provides protection for a variety of database resource types, both SQL servers and managed cloud database services

- Defender for Storage – Detects threats on storage workloads and data, including malicious access, data exfiltration of sensitive data, and malware uploads

- Defender for Key Vault – Detects possible malicious attempts to access or exploit Azure Key Vault accounts

- **In a multi-cloud environment, High Tech Rapid Solutions Corp has been struggling to deploy agents on all servers**: Leveraging an agentless approach, Defender for Cloud utilizes existing infrastructure and resources, effectively minimizing any impact on system performance and resource availability, while also reducing management complexity. This would help the organization to address security and operational challenges in a multi-cloud environment.

  MDC is a flexible platform, supporting both agent-based and agentless methods, allowing it to adapt to various operational models within an organization. They could prefer agent-based (because of MDE) and agentless for the workloads when an agent-based strategy is not practicable.

  By offering a hybrid cloud security strategy that combines both agent and agentless security solutions, Defender for Cloud enables them to leverage the advantages of both approaches, providing a tailored and efficient security framework.

- **High Tech Rapid Solutions Corp's SecOps teams have been lacking in identifying possible attack paths to cloud resources**: By leveraging DCSPM, the company would get insightful information about possible attack paths to the organization's exposable resources. Attack path analysis supports (at the time of writing) the following:

  - Attack scenarios on VMs in Azure, AWS, and GCP

  - Attack scenarios on data in Azure, AWS, and GCP

  - Azure containers and GitHub repositories

  The company has server workloads running in both Azure and AWS environments, so it is very useful for the SecOps team to get information on VM-related attack paths from both cloud environments.

In addition, they are leveraging SQL on VMs in Azure as well as managed databases and Azure Blob Storage, which all have attack paths available.

Microsoft Sentinel – SIEM and SOAR

In the cybersecurity world, all roads lead to the SIEM tool, right?

Common questions and challenges we hear around Microsoft Sentinel are as follows:

- Can I use Sentinel if I'm not using Microsoft Defender XDR security solution?
- If I'm using Microsoft Defender XDR, do I need Sentinel?
- How can I avoid alert/incident fatigue in ever-evolving multi-cloud and hybrid environments?
- I am happy with my non-MS SIEM solution; what is a strong case to switch to Sentinel?

Initially introduced in 2019 under the name **Azure Sentinel**, this service was designed to offer security analytics on a cloud-based scale. Azure Sentinel was built on top of **Azure Log Analytics**, a service that collects and analyzes data from various sources such as Azure resources, applications, devices, and other cloud platforms. Azure Sentinel leveraged the power of AI and **machine learning** (**ML**) to correlate and analyze large volumes of data and provide actionable insights for security teams. Later, the solution was renamed **Microsoft Sentinel**.

Its feature set (see *Figure 3.16*) includes data connectors, analytics rules, a content hub for installing solutions, hunting capabilities, notebooks, an automation layer, a workspace manager (for **Managed Security Service Providers** - **MSSPs**), and many more. Additionally, Microsoft Sentinel seamlessly integrates with other security offerings from Microsoft's whole XDR stack, Azure solutions, and so on. It also accommodates third-party data sources and solutions via its rich partner ecosystem.

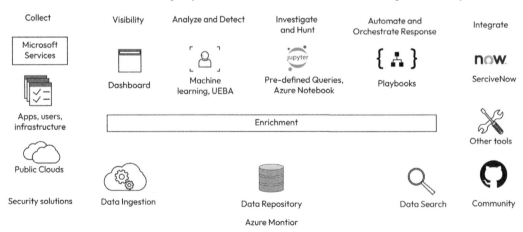

Figure 3.16 - Microsoft Sentinel architecture

Sentinel key features

Here, we have listed a few Sentinel key features that make it a powerful SIEM solution:

- **Cloud-native, which also means the ability to collect data at the cloud scale**: Microsoft Sentinel can ingest data from various sources, both Microsoft and non-Microsoft, on-premises and from multi-cloud environments. You can use built-in or custom data connectors, common event format, Syslog, or REST APIs to connect your data sources with Microsoft Sentinel.

- **SIEM capabilities**: Sentinel provides core SIEM functionalities, helping organizations aggregate and analyze security data from various sources. With rich set of collected data, organizations can detect possible attacks faster, detect anomalies efficiently, do correlations more easily, and perform threat hunting against various data sources.

- **AI**: The platform uses built-in AI to analyze large volumes of data, making threat detection and response more efficient.

- **SOAR**: By adopting SOAR in Sentinel, organizations can manage incidents effectively, thanks to its automation features (SOAR capabilities).

  Sentinel SOAR is organized into two distinct layers – automation and playbooks:

  - The automation layer enables analysts to centrally manage incident handling through automation rules

  - A Sentinel playbook (built on top of Azure Logic Apps) is a collection of response and remediation actions and logic that can be executed within Microsoft Sentinel as a routine

- **Integrated XDR solutions**: One of the major advantages of using Microsoft security solutions is the seamless integration with Microsoft Defender XDR.

  This integration not only simplifies the setup and deployment process but also enhances operational efficiency. Through bidirectional synchronization with Microsoft Defender XDR, there is improved control over the management and handling of incidents and alerts.

- **Content Hub solutions**: The Content Hub is a centralized platform for discovering, installing, enabling, and managing pre-packaged content and solutions specifically designed for Microsoft Sentinel. It simplifies content management and deployment in Sentinel. You can expect to find analytic rules, data connectors, hunting queries, parsers, playbooks, watchlists, and workbooks in the Content Hub.

- **Workspace manager**: The workspace manager is a new feature in Sentinel, but it was a game changer for **MSSPs**. By leveraging the workspace manager, MSSPs can manage the content they are publishing to their clients in a central place.

  At the time of writing this book, the supported content types are analytics rules, automation rules (excluding playbooks), parsers, saved searches and functions, hunting and live stream queries, and workbooks.

> **Tip**
>
> Consider having Sentinel deployed even if you have a non-MS SIEM tool as a primary solution. It will be beneficial to ingest incidents from Microsoft cloud workloads to Sentinel and then to non-MS SIEM. Also, UEBA can be turned on with just simple clicks.

Microsoft Sentinel versus Microsoft Defender XDR

Often, we hear people asking, *What is the difference between Sentinel and Microsoft Defender XDR and are there overlapping features? Do I need both, or can I move forward with only one in place?*

In *Chapter 2* we covered the importance of XDR vs SIEM in general. Even though some capabilities overlap with Microsoft Defender XDR, Sentinel offers many capabilities that organizations are not able to achieve with Microsoft Defender XDR. Here are a few:

- **Data ingestion**: In Sentinel, you can configure data collection based on your needs and ingest data from Azure, multi-cloud environments, on-premises, and so on. In Microsoft Defender XDR, you receive data mainly from Defender solutions: MDE, MDO, MDA, MDI, and MDC, as well as Entra ID Protection.

- **Threat detection and investigation**: Both solutions provide advanced capabilities for threat detection. The major difference is Sentinel's wider support for Azure and third-party data sources including the Fusion detection engine (advanced multistage attack detection). This leads to better correlations with multiple data sources.

- **Data retention**: The maximum data retention in Microsoft Defender XDR is 180 days, and in Sentinel, it can be up to 12 years. Sentinel, or the underlying Azure Log Analytics, is not the ideal place for long-term storage of logs. For this purpose, the Azure Monitor data retention and archive or Azure Data Explorer can be used.

- **Automation**: As Microsoft Defender XDR has AIR capabilities for MDE, MDO, and MDI (and for MDA with custom policies), Sentinel provides a wide range of automation capabilities. This is established in two layers: the automation layer and custom playbooks that are built on top of Azure Logic Apps.

- **Advanced UEBA capabilities**: Even though Microsoft Defender XDR has UEBA capabilities (in MDA and MDI), Sentinel UEBA has some advanced capabilities. UEBA raw data is also available for threat hunting or investigation.

- **Threat hunting**: Both solutions provide threat hunting features. Microsoft Defender XDR has advanced hunting that can be used in two different ways: building KQL queries from scratch or with the query builder, which is helpful if the user is not an expert in creating KQL queries. The main difference is that, in Sentinel, you can ingest data from third-party data sources and in Microsoft Defender XDR you have data from (at the time of writing of this book) MDE, MDO, MDI, MDA and Entra ID. In addition, Sentinel has **Jupyter Notebook** integration for advanced scenarios.

- **Threat intelligence (TI)**: In Microsoft Defender XDR, TI capabilities are out-of-the-box features and it provides information on the **Threat Analytics** dashboard and uses it when analyzing threats. In Sentinel, you can ingest data from various TI platforms. In addition, Microsoft Defender TI can be ingested for free, even if your organization didn't purchase the Microsoft Defender TI solution.

Case study analysis

Now, let's look at some of the challenges that *High Tech Rapid Solutions Corp* is facing, as mentioned in the *Case study* section at the beginning of this book:

- **High Tech Rapid Solutions Corp has siloed architecture that operates in isolation, resulting in limited visibility, fragmented threat intelligence, and inefficient incident response capabilities**: Microsoft Sentinel connects the dots with a unified view and workbooks, and the use of the whole XDR stack would benefit the SOC organization significantly. A combination of Microsoft Defender XDR and SIEM (unified XDR) would bring security events from the environment in a single management view. The bidirectional sync feature between the solutions addresses inefficient incident response capabilities.

- **Incomplete security insight – the lack of centralized security monitoring and analytics hinders the ability to correlate and analyze security events, making it difficult to identify emerging threats**: One of the greatest benefits of using the unified XDR stack is that the solutions are sharing signals, events, alerts, and incidents and leverages Microsoft TI data behind the scenes. The solution makes a correlation on behalf of the analyst and hastens the incident management process.

- **Alert fatigue is real; analysts don't have time to investigate all the incoming incidents**: Understanding your digital environment is foundational. Ask yourself this: What are the crown jewels of your organization? What are you safeguarding, and from whom?

  When the security monitoring strategy (as discussed in *Chapter 8*) is crystal clear, an organization can focus on collecting the data they need to build effective security monitoring that the automation layer and TI data support, to be as effective as possible. At the end of the day, the incident queue should show only actionable incidents.

  One option is to leverage the Sentinel watchlist feature. With this, the company can generate allowlists to mute alerts originating from a specific set of users, including those operating from approved IP addresses, who carry out activities that would typically activate alerts. This prevents benign events from rising up into the incident queue.

- **Due to the overwhelming amount of data ingested, SIEM costs have gotten out of hand**: The **Chief Information Security Officer (CISO)** has realized that the security monitoring strategy is an important topic that needs to be addressed in the early stages of SIEM deployment.

Collect the data you need for security monitoring, define the use cases, evaluate and define data retention requirements and strategies, and verify possible compliance requirements for data, to name a few ways to address increasing data ingestion costs.

Sentinel has multiple ways to reduce data retention costs such as basic logs, the possibility to reduce long-term data retention costs with Azure Data Explorer or archived logs, separating non-security data to a separate workspace, or even using dedicated Log Analytics clusters if daily ingestion is a minimum of 500 GB per day.

In the cloud, monitoring of costs is easily established and one of the key elements of operational mode.

- **High Tech Rapid Solutions Corp is using a legacy SIEM (on-premises) solution and is keen to modernize security operations and SIEM with a cloud-based solution**: Nowadays, there are several cloud-based SIEM solutions on the market such as Microsoft Sentinel, Google's Chronicle, and Rapid7's own solution, to name a few.

The company is planning to implement the whole Microsoft security stack into use, so it makes sense to also invest in Microsoft Sentinel as a SIEM solution.

Companies will gain more benefits when using Sentinel when they heavily use the Microsoft ecosystem because of true native integration between solutions, less latency, built-in AI, TI, and so on.

Even though they would continue using non-Microsoft SIEM as their primary SIEM solution, it would be beneficial to implement Microsoft Sentinel workloads (M365, Azure, etc.), and forward incidents to third-party SIEM tools.

XDR and beyond – exploring commonly used security solutions

Let's discuss Microsoft Security solutions that can complement an organization's security monitoring strategy and provide valuable benefits when configured and deployed. The solutions we are referring to include the following:

- Microsoft Defender for IoT
- EASM
- Microsoft Defender TI
- Microsoft Copilot for Security

By deploying and integrating these solutions with the Microsoft XDR platform, organizations can achieve an even more comprehensive view of the environment and digital estate.

In this section, we will explain what these commonly used security solutions are and how *High Tech Rapid Solutions Corp* can benefit from using them together with the unified XDR security stack.

Microsoft Defender for IoT

Let's start with Microsoft Defender for IoT. The solution protects IoT devices (see *Figure 3.17*). The foundation of Defender for IoT is based on CyberX expertise and technology, which Microsoft acquired in 2020. After the acquisition, Defender for IoT was integrated into the Azure platform and added one missing piece to the XDR platform (visibility in **Internet of Things/IoT/Operational Technology/ OT** environments). *Figure 3.17* describes Defender for IoT components at a high level.

Some of the main features of Microsoft Defender for IoT are as follows:

- **Agentless monitoring**: It does not require any software installation or configuration on IoT devices, which reduces the risk of performance or compatibility issues

- **Behavioral analytics**: It uses ML and AI to analyze the normal behavior of IoT devices and networks and detect any anomalies or deviations that indicate a potential attack

- **Automated response**: It can automatically block or isolate malicious devices, or trigger alerts and actions in other security tools, such as firewalls, SIEMs, or ticketing systems

- **Cloud scalability**: It can scale up or down according to the size and complexity of the IoT environment

- **Integrations**: It has native integrations with Microsoft Security solutions such as Microsoft Defender XDR and Microsoft Sentinel

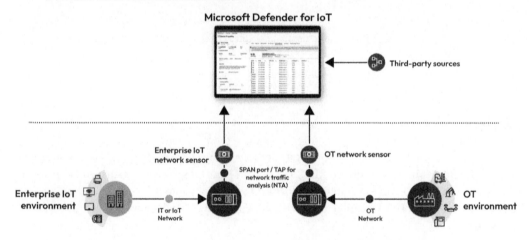

Figure 3.17 - Microsoft Defender for IoT solution architecture

Added value in Microsoft Defender XDR comes with an Enterprise IoT plan, which needs to be configured in the Microsoft Defender XDR portal (**Settings | Device discovery | Enterprise IoTs**). After configuring, an organization can see IoT-specific alerts, recommendations, and vulnerability data in the Microsoft Defender XDR portal (an MDE P2 license is needed).

Even though we are not focusing on licenses in this book, it is worth mentioning that the M365 E5 license plan was updated in October 2023 to contain up to five IoT devices per user license, as shown in *Figure 3.18*. This service plan provides E5 and E5 Security customers with real-time device discovery, continuous monitoring, and vulnerability management capabilities.

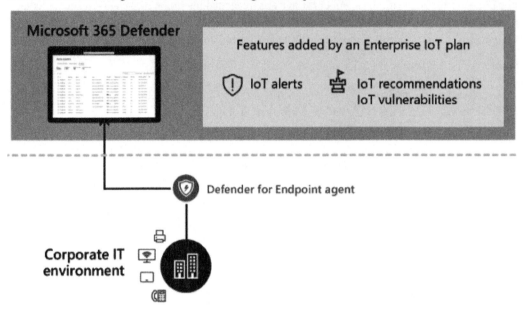

Figure 3.18: Microsoft Defender XDR new IoT plan

Refer to the Microsoft Defender for IoT documentation for organizations for more information (`https://packt.link/1K2Um`).

EASM

Microsoft Defender EASM is one of the newest additions to the Defender family. It was announced in August 2022, after Microsoft acquired RiskIQ, a global TI and attack surface management platform. After acquiring RiskIQ, Microsoft integrated RiskIQ technology into its own platform and created both EASM and **Microsoft Defender Threat Intelligence (MDTI)**, which we will go through in the next section.

EASM is a service that helps discover and monitor the external attack surface and prioritize the remediation of vulnerabilities. EASM scans the internet for assets that belong to or are associated with an organization, such as domains, IP addresses, certificates, web servers, and cloud services. EASM then analyzes these assets for vulnerabilities, misconfigurations, and other risks that could be exploited by attackers.

It provides native integration with Azure Log Analytics and Azure Data Explorer, which allows organizations to leverage EASM data in Sentinel. When establishing the integration, you have the flexibility to choose between migrating asset data, attack surface insights, or both data types. Asset data offers comprehensive details about your entire inventory, while attack surface insights deliver actionable information through Defender EASM dashboards (see *Figure 3.19*).

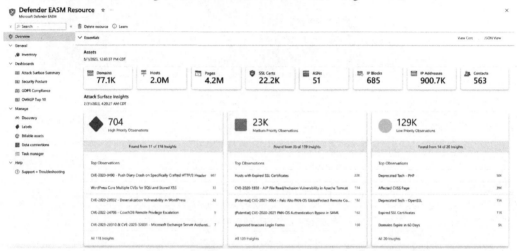

Figure 3.19 - Microsoft Defender EASM portal diagram from microsoft.com

MDTI

MDTI (see *Figure 3.20*) aims to provide the ultimate analyst experience driven by feedback from the community. MDTI provides real-time insights into the latest threats, vulnerabilities, and malicious activities, as well as guidance on how to respond and remediate them. MDTI leverages the power of the cloud, AI, and ML to deliver comprehensive and actionable intelligence that can help reduce the risk and impact of cyberattacks.

Some of the features and benefits of MDTI are as follows:

- It collects and analyzes data from millions of sources, including Microsoft's own products and services, third-party vendors, open source platforms, and partner networks

- It uses advanced algorithms and models to identify patterns, trends, and anomalies in the threat landscape, and to prioritize the most relevant and urgent threats for each organization

- It provides customized and contextualized intelligence reports, alerts, and recommendations that are tailored to the specific needs and preferences of each organization.

- It enables organizations to automate and orchestrate their threat response and remediation processes, using built-in tools and integrations with other Microsoft security solutions

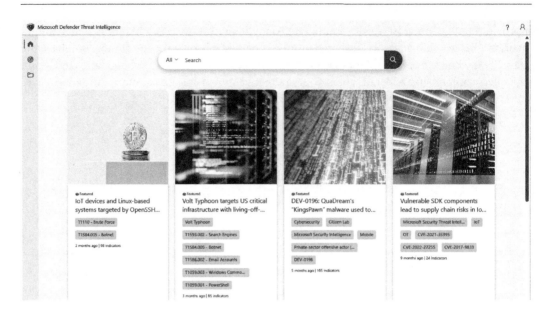

Figure 3.20 - The MDTI portal

At Microsoft Ignite 2023 in November, a free version of MDTI was announced and is now available for all Microsoft Defender XDR tenants. This means that certain MDTI features are available in the Microsoft Defender XDR portal, such as threat research information from Microsoft security experts and open source (**Open-Source Intelligence - OSINT**) feeds, IoCs, and threat profiles.

Microsoft Copilot for Security

Microsoft Copilot for Security is a generative AI-powered security solution, and its goal is to improve security outcomes at machine speed and scale by increasing defenders' effectiveness and capabilities. At the time of writing this book, Copilot for Security is an **Early Access Program** (**EAP**), and the focus of this stage of development is on three different scenarios from the SOC perspective:

- Incident response

- Security posture management

- Security reporting

If the solution is used by an organization, Copilot can be accessed as one of two models:

- As a standalone experience when the solution is available in a dedicated portal `https://packt.link/VbY3f` (at the time of writing this book).

- As an embedded experience when Copilot for Security is experienced through other security solutions such as Microsoft Defender XDR

Copilot for Security integrates seamlessly with Microsoft Defender XDR, Microsoft Sentinel, Microsoft Intune, MDTI, EASM, and Microsoft Entra ID. The solutions also integrate with third-party solutions (plug-ins need to be created, few available) such as ServiceNow to bring more context to incidents.

By integrating with MDTI (which is free), Copilot for Security has access to TI data and authoritative content through plugins. These plugins make it easier to search through publications on vulnerability disclosure, Microsoft Defender XDR threat analytics reports, Intel profiles, articles, and more related to threat intelligence. In addition, this integration provides MDTI access via API, MDTI workbench, and MDTI analyst seats (the same number as Copilot for Security seats).

Figure 3.21 highlights Microsoft Copilot for Security's current architecture:

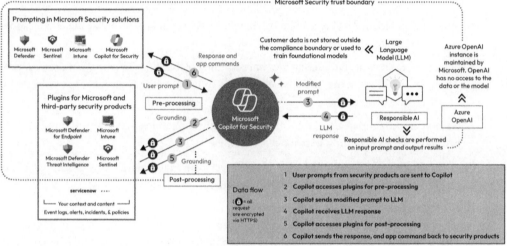

Figure 3.21: Microsoft Copilot for Security Architecture

Case study analysis

Now, let's look at some of the challenges that *High Tech Rapid Solutions Corp* is facing, as mentioned in the *Case study* section at the beginning of this book:

- **Lack of visibility and control in IoT/OT environment**: Microsoft Defender for IoT provides enhanced visibility into the IoT/OT environment. With a combination of passive and active agentless network monitoring, it discovers and profiles devices, identifies their communication patterns, and assesses their risk levels. This improved visibility allows security teams to monitor and control devices effectively. Defender for IoT can also be integrated with XDR and SIEM. This is an important piece in their holistic security monitoring approach.

- **Lack of visibility into internet-exposed digital assets**: To address security challenges on digital assets, *High Tech Rapid Solutions Corp* needs to discover and inventory all the digital assets that belong to them and are exposed to the internet across different domains, subdomains, IP ranges, cloud providers, and technologies.

  The organization can monitor and assess the security posture of these digital assets by identifying vulnerabilities, misconfigurations, outdated software, exposed credentials, sensitive data leaks, and other risks.

  They can prioritize and remediate the most critical security issues, by providing actionable insights, recommendations, and workflows for fixing the vulnerabilities and hardening the digital assets.

  By implementing an effective EASM solution, the organization can address the challenges mentioned and achieve several benefits, such as the following:

  - Reducing the risk of data breaches and cyberattacks that could compromise the organization's reputation, customer trust, revenue, and market share

  - Enhancing the security culture and awareness within organizations by empowering developers, engineers, product managers, and executives to take ownership and responsibility for securing their digital assets

  - Gaining a competitive edge over other technology companies that may not have a robust EASM strategy or solution in place

  They can also leverage DCSPM, which provides attack path analysis and Cloud Security Explorer features to identify possible exposable resources in Azure.

  By deploying MDE to endpoints and servers, they can leverage the Device Discovery feature, which helps identify unmanaged devices from the corporate network. The functionality utilizes onboarded endpoints for gathering, probing, or scanning networks to identify unmanaged devices.

- **TI data (feed) does not exist**: There are a bunch of service providers that provide TI feeds for organizations. *High Tech Rapid Solutions Corp* is planning on putting a cloud-based SIEM solution into use (Sentinel) and it supports connecting **threat intelligence platforms** (**TIPs**), TAXII servers (STIX-compatible TI source), custom solutions that communicate directly with the Microsoft Graph security `tiIndicators` API, and MDTI feeds. Even though *High Tech Rapid Solutions Corp* won't have a license for MDTI, they can ingest TI data through a data connector for free and leverage data in analytics rules and threat hunting (see *Figure 3.22*). Besides that, the MDTI solution offers a range of benefits:

  - **Enhanced visibility**: It provides a detailed view into both the broader threat landscape and environment-specific vulnerabilities.

  - **Real-time alerts**: The organization will receive timely and relevant notifications about threats and vulnerabilities that could impact its operations.

- **Contextual intelligence**: The solution enriches existing security protocols with contextual threat intelligence data, enabling more effective decision-making.

- **Seamless integration**: It automates threat detection and response activities by integrating with Microsoft Defender XDR and Sentinel, thereby streamlining security operations. A Microsoft Sentinel data connector provides all publicly available IOCs from MDTI finished intelligence to the Microsoft Sentinel TI blade (added by Microsoft researchers). Microsoft Sentinel users can access these valuable IOCs for free to drive analytics, hunting, and investigations.

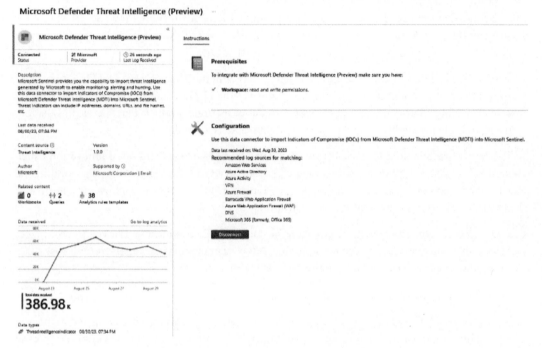

Figure 3.22 - MDTI data connector in Sentinel

By adopting Microsoft Defender for Threat Intelligence, *High Tech Rapid Solutions Corp* can improve its security posture, reduce its vulnerable attack surface, and lessen the impact of potential cyberattacks. In addition, by using Microsoft Copilot for Security, the company can leverage MDTI capabilities (without extra cost) because all threat intelligence data from MDTI is available through Copilot for Security.

Microsoft's unified XDR and SIEM solution's benefits over non-MS solutions

Security is a top priority for every organization, especially in the era of digital transformation and cloud adoption. However, many organizations still rely on multiple, disparate security solutions that are not integrated and do not provide a holistic view of the threat landscape. This leads to inefficiencies, gaps, and blind spots that can compromise the security posture and increase the risk of breaches.

That is why organizations should consider using a unified XDR security solution and SIEM tool for security monitoring. Even if an organization uses non-Microsoft SIEM instead of Sentinel, using the unified XDR stack can provide great benefits for security teams.

As we discussed while addressing security challenges earlier in this chapter, *High Tech Rapid Solutions Corp* would greatly benefit from utilizing Microsoft's unified XDR stack and cloud-based Sentinel instead of existing security infrastructure, which contains disparate products that operate in isolation, resulting in limited visibility and inefficient incident response capabilities.

By leveraging the unified XDR stack, organizations can take advantage of the latest innovations, such as automatic attack disruption, which is designed to contain attacks in progress while also limiting the attack's impact on the organization. It's worth mentioning that the wider the deployment, the greater the protection is with the automatic attack disruption.

One of the key advantages of using the unified XDR stack and Microsoft Sentinel is synergy advantages and true native integrations between the solutions. A few examples of these (apart from the use cases we covered in the respective sections in this chapter) are as follows:

- Deep correlation between related signals in security, which leads to better incidents.
- Defender for Cloud Apps and Defender for Endpoint integration for detecting and managing shadow IT in the environment, as we highlighted in the Defender for Cloud Apps case study analysis.
- MDO and MDE integration, which helps in threat investigation between Office 365 and Windows devices. By enabling the integration, analysts can see device details and MDE alerts in Threat Explorer.
- The integration of XDR and SIEM can help reduce alert fatigue by prioritizing and contextualizing security alerts.
- Also, Microsoft Sentinel UEBA provides a powerful investigation tool combining data (logs and alerts) from Azure, Microsoft Entra ID, on-premises AD, and servers (Windows events).

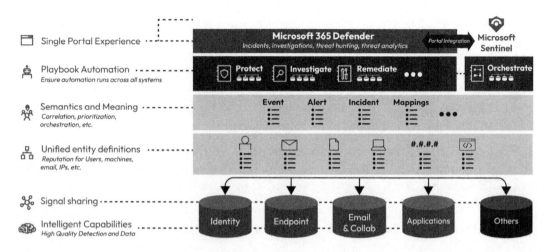

Figure 3.23 - Microsoft Unified Defender XDR solution architecture

- Microsoft Defender XDR provides cross-domain protection and automatically protects, detects, and remediates threats across M365 environments. The diagram in *Figure 3.23* shows that intelligence and signals are shared across all products, which helps to fight against threats. Entity definitions are also the same across all products, which makes integration easier. This makes this XDR solution even more powerful with seamless integration, correlation, and automation. Additionally, Microsoft Sentinel's native integration (you can utilize built-in tools and connectors for simple integration and ingestion) helps to visualize signal and incident data from Microsoft Defender XDR and third-party clouds.

The Microsoft ecosystem has a unified Security Graph API that provides a uniform interface and schema to make integrations of Microsoft Security and partner solutions more straightforward. The Security Graph API can be used for the following operations:

- Centralize and correlate security alerts

- Retrieve and examine all incidents and alerts originating from services integrated with or forming part of Microsoft Defender XDR

- Extract contextual data to enhance investigative insights

- Automate different security-related tasks, business processes, workflows, and incident reporting

- Transmit threat indicators to Microsoft products for tailored detections

As we have described throughout this chapter, Microsoft Defender XDR provides unified visibility, investigation, and response across endpoints, hybrid identities, emails, collaboration tools, cloud apps, cloud workloads, and data. All of that is complemented by Microsoft Sentinel, which provides visibility in to every layer of the digital environment. Both security solutions are natively integrated (bidirectional sync), providing synergy advantages for SecOps teams.

At the time of writing this book, the next phase of evolution is in preview and Microsoft is now bringing Microsoft Sentinel, Microsoft Defender XDR, and Copilot for Security into one unified platform. SecOps teams will ultimately have a single user interface, a single data model, and unified features that are driven by automation, AI, attack disruption, and security posture management recommendations. With the latest innovation, Microsoft Defender XDR extends its support to multitenant scenarios and provides a consolidated view of incidents, devices, vulnerability management, and threat hunting across environments.

In conclusion, a unified XDR security stack (see *Figure 3.23*) is a powerful and effective way to improve the security posture and resilience of every organization. By adopting this approach, organizations can gain more visibility, reduce complexity, and improve performance in their security operations.

The future – Microsoft's influence in cybersecurity

Microsoft's impact on technology is unquestionable, and its influence can be observed in various domains, including the cybersecurity domain. If we look back through history and different technology key areas, we can see the impact left by the corporation.

The graphical Windows OS revolution

When Microsoft introduced its graphical Windows OS, it essentially set the standard for personal computing interfaces. The Windows OS not only made computing accessible to the everyday person but also shaped the way software was designed and distributed. Essentially, in the world of graphical OSs, the majority of roads led (and still lead) to Microsoft.

Reshaping server technology with Windows NT

Microsoft didn't stop at personal computing. With the introduction of Windows **NT** (which stands for **New Technology**), Microsoft reshaped the landscape of server technologies. Windows NT offered ease-of-use, scalability, and compatibility features that were game-changing at the time, pulling corporations into Microsoft's ecosystem.

Outlook and the transformation of email communication

When it comes to email, Microsoft's Outlook was a game-changer. Integrated into the company's Office suite, Outlook changed how businesses and individuals manage and communicate through email. Its seamless integration with other Microsoft products made it a preferred option for corporations, thereby dominating the email solutions market.

MS Office – standard in productivity software

Microsoft Office (Word, PowerPoint, Excel, and other productivity tools) has been widely used in business, education, and home computing. Its features, ease of use, and comprehensive solutions made it the leader in productivity software, further strengthening Microsoft's position in the market.

Internet Explorer – a chapter in web browsing

When Internet Explorer was at its peak, there was no denying that it was the most widely used web browser. Microsoft successfully leveraged its OS monopoly to make Internet Explorer the default browser for millions, shaping the way people accessed and experienced the internet. Things have now changed, and Google Chrome is a leading internet browser, but Microsoft came back with the Edge browser which has started gaining momentum. In addition, with Bing chat and Copilot features, the Edge browser might increase in popularity in the near future.

The future – Microsoft's rising influence in cybersecurity

Given Microsoft's track record in shaping and dominating various sectors in the tech industry, we believe the company is ready to similarly influence the cybersecurity landscape. With Microsoft's growing suite of security solutions, including the unified XDR stack and Microsoft Sentinel, it's realistic to predict that Microsoft will dominate cybersecurity with its expanding portfolio. If history is any indicator, all signs suggest that, in the realm of the cybersecurity domain, the majority (if not all) of roads will eventually lead to Microsoft.

Summary

In this chapter, we have gone through the security solutions behind Microsoft's unified XDR concept and explored how Microsoft Sentinel fits into the picture. Additionally, we discussed the specific security challenges facing *High Tech Rapid Solutions Corp*, as outlined in the case study chapter. This discussion is designed to clearly explain the benefits that organizations can gain from using Microsoft's XDR and SIEM solution. Also, we discussed some of the security solutions that would complement the unified XDR. These solutions, which include Defender for IoT, EASM, and Defender for Threat Intelligence, could be useful in preventing potential breaches seamlessly with the XDR stack.

The following chapter delves into the fundamental principles of Security Operations Centers (SOCs), and explains why organizations of all sizes should consider modernizing their SOC. We'll then explore how Microsoft's unified XDR and SIEM platform simplifies life for SOC teams by offering powerful tools and streamlined operations.

Further reading

Refer to the following links for more information about the topics covered in this chapter:

- MDO plan features: https://packt.link/pNxFx

- More information on stopping BEC attacks with Microsoft XDR: https://packt.link/uFXpR

- Malware and ransomware protection in Microsoft Defender XDR: https://packt.link/n0ryM

- Enabling data connector for Microsoft Defender TI: https://packt.link/ziRb1

- Automatic disruption of ransomware attacks with Microsoft Defender XDR: https://packt.link/rrFJI

- Understanding Microsoft Sentinel's pricing and billing: https://packt.link/4XvIA

- Microsoft 365 licensing maps: https://packt.link/6KFO7

- *Field notes on security strategy* by Truls Dahlsveen: https://packt.link/2vCLR

- *Microsoft Defender XDR Automatic Attack Disruption*: https://packt.link/TQWYe

- The list of available attack paths: https://packt.link/7jqPj

- Microsoft Defender XDR capabilities evaluation: https://packt.link/yVmv6

- More information about Microsoft Copilot for Security: https://packt.link/KVEWJ

- Microsoft Sentinel Zero Trust (TIC 3.0) Solution - https://packt.link/f0VRv

- Get Started with Microsoft Copilot for Security - https://packt.link/MFhwr

Part 2 – Microsoft's Unified Approach to Threat Detection and Response

This part dives deep into the game-changing power of Microsoft's unified XDR and SIEM solution. We'll explore how it transforms the SOC's journey, streamlines its work, and shields organizations against real-world threats. We'll dissect prevention strategies, tackle misconfigurations and vulnerabilities, and unveil the vital role of Secure Score and monitoring in this unified security shield. Brace yourself for a comprehensive exploration of how this solution simplifies and strengthens your cyber defenses.

This part has the following chapters:

- *Chapter 4, Power of Investigation with Microsoft's Unified XDR and SIEM Solution*
- *Chapter 5, Defend Attacks with Microsoft XDR and SIEM*
- *Chapter 6, Security Misconfigurations and Vulnerability Management*
- *Chapter 7, Understanding Microsoft Secure Score*

4

Power of Investigation with Microsoft Unified XDR and SIEM Solution

This chapter serves as your comprehensive guide to the world of SOCs. We begin by covering the essentials – the basics of the **Security Operations Center** (**SOC**) and its fascinating evolution. We then delve into the crucial question: why should every organization make the shift to a modern SOC? Finally, we showcase the seamless SOC experience enabled by Microsoft Unified XDR and SIEM Solution, highlighting its power to simplify and optimize your security operations.

In a nutshell, we will cover the following main topics in this chapter:

- Understanding the basics of SOC
- SOC evolution and the difference between traditional and modern SOC
- SOC experience with the Microsoft Unified XDR and SIEM Solution
- Integration with other solutions

Understanding the basics of SOC

A SOC is the nerve center of an organization's cybersecurity defense. This team of vigilant security professionals, whether in-house or outsourced, monitors every corner of your digital infrastructure, from user accounts to network servers, to identify and neutralize potential attacks in real time. For large, global organizations, a **Global Security Operations Center (GSOC)** may serve as an overarching hub, coordinating security efforts across local SOCs and ensuring worldwide protection.

Typically, a SOC leverages a combination of **Security Information and Event Management (SIEM)** systems, **Extended Detection and Response (XDR)**, **Endpoint Detection and Response (EDR)** tools, **User Entity Behavior Analytics (UEBA)** insights, and **Threat Intelligence (TI)** feeds to provide comprehensive security visibility and incident response capabilities. They actively hunt for vulnerabilities, stay informed about the latest threats, and work tirelessly 24/7 to ensure your data and systems remain secure (see *Figure 4.1*).

Figure 4.1 - Security Operation Center (SOC)

The SOC has undergone a revolution, driven by breakthroughs in technology, shifting threats, and evolving organizational demands, *Figure 4.2* highlights some key aspects of this revolution. Inadequate SOC tools cripple security operations. Expect a deluge of false positives, relentless alert fatigue, repetitive manual tasks, shoddy documentation, siloed data, unreliable metrics, weak correlation, fragmented insights, limited visibility, alert prioritization, and so on. The sudden shift to remote work during and after the pandemic intensified security risks, demanding a rapid transition to remote SecOps for incident management and response.

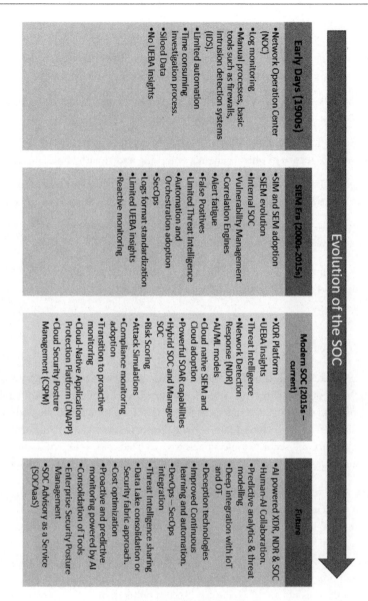

Figure 4.2 - Evolution of SOC

Typical SOC roles

The SOC uses a tiered system to assign responsibilities. Each tier represents a specific level of expertise and involvement in security tasks, creating a clear hierarchy for managing and responding to potential threats.

The common roles and responsibilities of a SOC team are:

- SOC Analyst (T1) – Leverages security monitoring tools to identify vulnerabilities, assesses potential incidents, and escalates critical threats for further investigation.

- SOC Analyst (T2) – Proactively investigates and resolves security incidents, ensuring swift and effective recovery to minimize disruptions.

- Threat Hunters (T3) – Leverages cutting-edge threat intelligence to assess and improve the effectiveness of IT security controls against emerging and stealthy hacking techniques.

- SOC Manager (T4) – Drives the team's response to security incidents and vulnerabilities, keeping the CISO informed of progress and potential risks through clear and concise communication.

- SOC Architect – Designs and implements secure network architectures and endpoint protection in collaboration with SOC analysts and engineers.

These roles vary by organization; there could be more depending on the organization's size and specific requirements, such as Forensics Specialist, Malware Engineer, Security Researcher, Global SOC Lead, SOC Chief, and so on.

Avengers of cybersecurity

A cybersecurity team is like a highly skilled orchestra, with each member playing a crucial role in protecting the organization from potential threats. These roles can be broadly categorized into management or collaboration, offense, and defense. Offensive security specialists are often called the **Red Team**, defensive security specialists are often called the **Blue Team**, and the **Purple Team** for the management or collaboration that occurs between them. Cybersecurity professionals have adopted color-coded nicknames for these roles, reflecting their distinct but complementary functions within the overall security orchestra:

- **Red Team** - Red teams act as controlled adversaries, utilizing **simulated attacks** to identify and exploit vulnerabilities within a system or organization's security posture. Red teams are essentially ethical hackers who help organizations improve their security posture by finding and fixing weaknesses before real attackers can exploit them. Their goal is to find weaknesses in systems and procedures to help the organization strengthen its security posture. They use different methods such as hacking techniques and social engineering to exploit weaknesses. In simple words, they act as the "bad guys" trying to break in.

- **Blue Team** - A blue team is a team of security professionals who are responsible for defending a system or organization from attack. Blue teams work to detect, prevent, and respond to security threats. Their goal is to maintain a strong security posture and effectively mitigate threats by taking actions such as implementing security controls, monitoring systems for suspicious activity, incident response, and so on. They often use a variety of tools and techniques, such as intrusion detection systems, **Endpoint Detection Response (EDR)**, **Extended Detection and Response (XDR)**, **Security Information and Event Management (SIEM)** systems, and so on. In other words, this is a team of security guards monitoring and protecting the organization's digital assets.

- **Purple Team** - A purple team is usually a combination of a red team and a blue team, a collaborative effort to improve an organization's overall security posture. Purple teams combine the offensive skills of red teams with the defensive skills of blue teams to plan and execute security assessments, analyze the results, and make recommendations for improvement. Their goal is to improve collaboration and communication between the offensive and defensive teams to create a more resilient and secure environment. In other words, they bridge the gap between red and blue teams and act as a security leader coordinating between both teams to improve the security posture.

Traditional versus modern SOC operations

The old-school way of running a SOC is no longer cutting it. It's expensive, inefficient, and simply can't keep pace with the evolving threat landscape. Several factors have contributed to this downfall including outdated technology, non-scalability, slow to adapt, maintenance madness, technology-driven inflexibility, and so on. *Chapter 2* and *Chapter 3* laid the foundation for our discussion on XDR and SOC platforms, highlighting their significance in fortifying an organization's security defenses.

The table below (*Table 4.1*) outlines the key distinctions between traditional and modern SOC operations, demonstrating the compelling reasons for organizations to embrace the modern approach.

Traditional SOC	Modern SOC
No automation in place	SOAR automation
Poor insights	Powerful enriched insights
No UEBA insights	UEBA insights
Manual triaging, investigation, enrichment and containment	AI powered investigation
Manual correlation	Enhanced correlation
Alert fatigue	Reduced alert fatigue
Limited alert tuning capabilities	Alert tuning capabilities
Too many false positives and complex processes to reduce them	Reduce false positives
Limited or no Threat Intelligence	Powerful Threat Intelligence
Painful threat hunting process	Easy threat hunting
Overloaded information	Enriched data and information
Siloed architecture	Unified architecture
Triaging and investigation at multiple portals	Unified platform

Time consuming team co-ordination activities	Easy collaboration between teams
Lack of network visibility	Improved network visibility
Challenging third party tools integration	Flexible integration with third party tools
Limited or no workflows	Workflows

Table 4.1 - Traditional versus modern SOC

With some of the SOC fundamentals under our belt, it's time to explore Microsoft's unified platform and discover how it streamlines and empowers SOC operations.

SOC journey with Microsoft's unified security operations platform

In this section, we focus on the investigation experience by highlighting a few key features in a scenario where an organization is utilizing both Microsoft Sentinel and Microsoft Defender XDR in its SOC operations.

Typically, when an incident is created in the Sentinel incident queue, the SOC team receives a notification about the incident. Notifications can be sent to third-party solutions such as ServiceNow or Jira depending on what ticketing system the SOC team uses.

If a third-party SOAR solution is in use (for example, Cortex XSOAR, formerly Demisto), this can be the place where the investigation process starts. In some cases, typically in smaller organizations, there may not necessarily be a ticketing system in use for handling case management in SOC; rather, a Teams channel or email notifications may be the preferred way to get notified about new incidents.

Investigation in Microsoft Sentinel

Let's start an investigation walkthrough with an example incident in Sentinel, 'Multi-stage incident involving Initial access and Defense evasion involving one user reported by multiple sources'. When you navigate to Sentinel and open the **Incidents** blade you can see all the incidents in the incident queue as shown in *Figure 4.3*.

Figure 4.3 - Sentinel incident queue

By opening an incident through 'view full details' link, the analyst can see its basic details (alert product name, evidence, impacted entities, MITRE ATT&CK mapping, owner, and status) as highlighted in *Figure 4.4.*

- **Overview** section contains the timeline and information on impacted entities

- **Similar incidents** contain incidents that match by entity, rule, or alert details

- **Top insights** widget shows a collection of insights to help the analyst better understand the scope of the threat on the affected entities. In our example, you can see threat indicators related to the user and UEBA insights for impacted entities

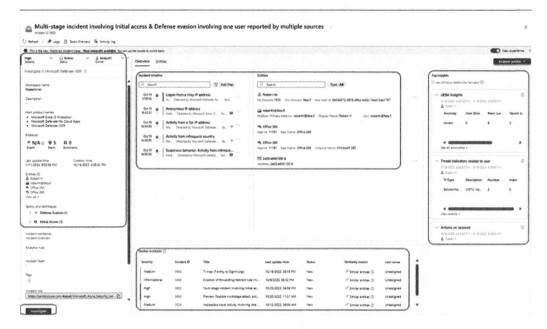

Figure 4.4 - Incident investigation blade in Sentinel

By selecting **Investigate** at the bottom left corner you can open the investigation graph (see *Figure 4.5*) to perform a visual evaluation of the incident details. The investigation graph contains incident details and related activities (alerts, entities, host related, IP-related information, etc.) which might help during the investigation to get the full picture of what happened during the incident and whether there was any other suspicious activity that should be taken into consideration.

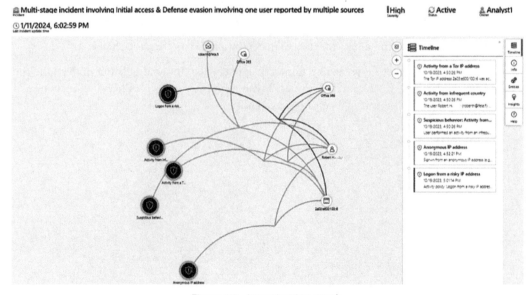

Figure 4.5 - Investigation graph

> **Tip**
>
> To take the investigation deeper in Sentinel you can select the deep link (Events) in the investigation experience that will open an underlying query in the **Logs** panel, in the context of the investigation.

In *Chapters 2* and *3*, we emphasized the importance of SOAR in modern cybersecurity operations. During the investigation, analysts can run playbooks (Azure Logic Apps) on demand from the main **Incidents** blade or, when performing an investigation from the incident 'full details' experience as shown in *Figure 4.6*.

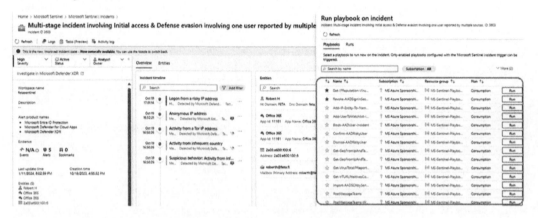

Figure 4.6 - Incident playbook view in Sentinel

During an investigation, the need may arise to create either automation rules or playbooks to automate threat response and incident handling. To address this need, navigate to the **Automation** blade in Sentinel. As you can see in *Figure 4.7*, there are options to create automation rules and playbooks (the top left) and there are several playbook templates available for common scenarios to make deployment and development easier.

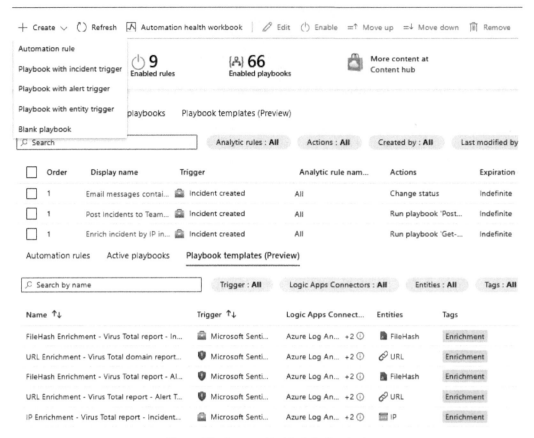

Figure 4.7 - Automation blade in Sentinel

Another key element of investigation in Sentinel is **User Entity Behavior Analytics** (**UEBA**), which is very useful when investigating entities (such as users, hosts, IP-addresses, IoT devices and Azure resources). The feature is found underneath the **Entity Behavior** blade in Sentinel and provides several insights into entities (the specific insights depend on the entity type). With UEBA, you can identify advanced threats and connect the dots by evaluating the entity's behavioral profile as shown in *Figure 4.8*.

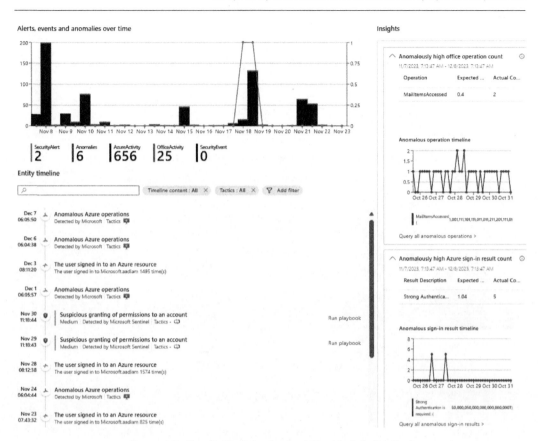

Figure 4.8 - User Entity Behavior Analytics blade in Sentinel

For deeper and more advanced investigation, Azure Log Analytics can be used. The UEBA related data is stored in the `BehaviorAnalytics` table in **Azure Log Analytics**. To get started, here is an example KQL query to get data on failed logon activities from the past 7 days with a connection-based filter included:

```
BehaviorAnalytics
| where TimeGenerated >= ago(7d)
| where ActivityType == "FailedLogOn"
| where ActivityInsights.FirstTimeUserConnectedFromCountry == True
| where ActivityInsights.CountryUncommonlyConnectedFromAmongPeers ==
True
```

In general, **Cyber Threat Intelligence** (**CTI**) plays an important role in security solutions. CTIs are typically threat indicators (indicators of compromise or indicators of attack) that are associated with observed artifacts (domain, email, file hash, IP address, URL, and so on). If your organization is ingesting **Threat Intelligence (TI)** data through data connectors, IOCs can be leveraged in Sentinel analytic rules as well as in threat hunting and custom KQL queries. An example TI-related analytic rule is seen in *Figure 4.9* where you can see IP match in the **TI MAP IP Entity to SigninLogs** analytics rule.

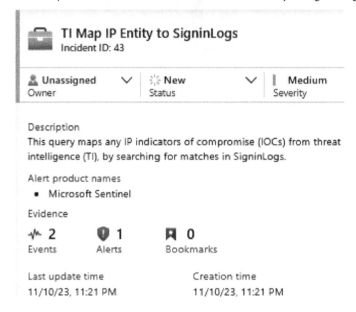

Figure 4.9 - TI-related incident in Sentinel

For proactive investigation, Sentinel provides many threat hunting queries out of the box (see *Figure 4.10*) that can be leveraged. For advanced scenarios, there are also Jupyter notebooks available that run on top of Azure Machine Learning services.

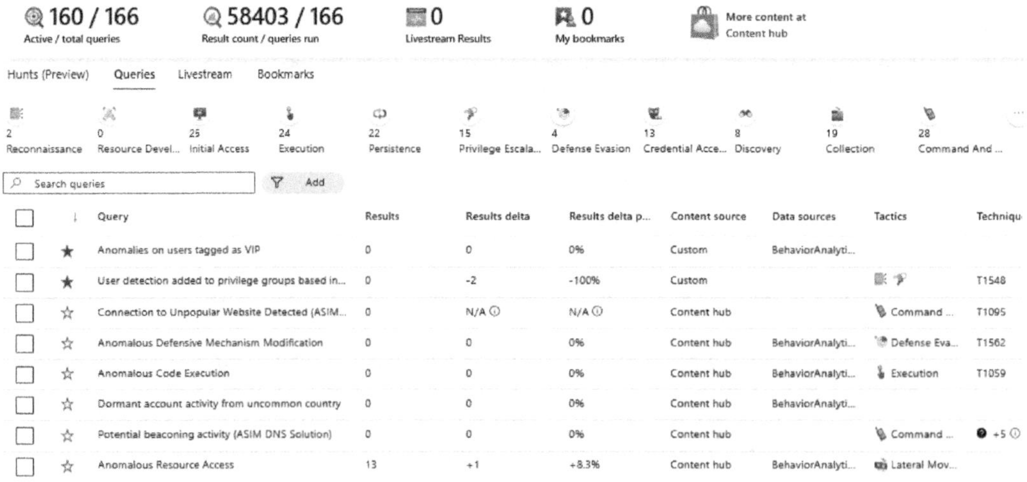

Figure 4.10 - Sentinel threat hunting built-in queries

The **MITRE ATT&CK** framework is widely used by security professionals and many organizations are using it to map detection capabilities to attack scenarios. It is also found in **Sentinel**, where it can be leveraged to evaluate and analyze current and simulated detection coverage in the environment. As we can see in *Figure 4.11*, there are filters at the top that can be used to select the correct **MITRE** matrix and do comparisons.

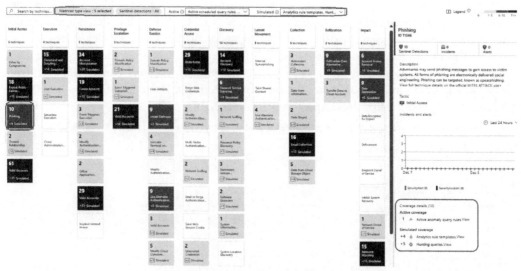

Figure 4.11 - MITRE ATT&CK matrix in Sentinel

Additional features that may prove essential for the investigative process include the following:

- Watchlist:

  With this capability, SOC team can create allowlists, for example, to suppress alerts originating from a specific group of users, including those operating from approved IP addresses, that engage in activities that would typically trigger alerts. This helps prevent benign events appearing in the incident queue. There are a few other use cases where watchlists can be used, such as investigating threats, importing business data, reducing alert fatigue, enriching event data, and so on. Refer to `https://packt.link/ciLZW` to understand these use cases.

- Archive, Search, and Restore operations:

  In some cases, a SOC team might need to go back in time to a specific time frame during an investigation. If a dataset is extremely large, a search job can be built for these kinds of search activities. For deeper analysis, archived log data can be restored to a data table to run high performing queries. Microsoft Sentinel grants SOC teams direct control over data restoration operations through the portal, bypassing the cumbersome multi-team coordination and delays traditionally associated with data retrieval.

Investigation in Microsoft Defender XDR

Now, let's look at the same incident but from the perspective of **Microsoft Defender XDR**. As you can see, there is a deep link (called 'Investigate in Microsoft Defender XDR') on the incident page in the top left corner re-directing the analyst to the unified security portal (`defender.microsoft.com`, formerly `security.microsoft.com`). The incident is created by **Microsoft Defender XDR** and synced to **Sentinel** with bi-directional sync capability. By enabling this integration and sync capability, you can get any incident created by **Defender XDR** to appear in the Sentinel incident queue. In the following example (shown in *Figure 4.12*), there is a multi-stage incident that contains practically the same information as any other incident. The main difference compared to incidents created in Microsoft Sentinel, is that the alert sources are Microsoft Defender XDR solutions (**Entra ID Protection**, **Defender for Cloud Apps,** and **Defender XDR**).

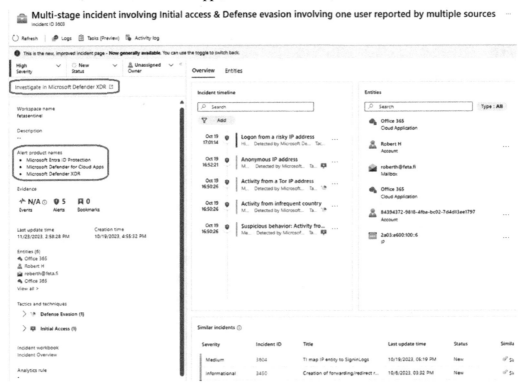

Figure 4.12 - Multi-stage incident created by Defender XDR in Sentinel

With bi-directional synchronization between **Sentinel** and **Microsoft Defender XDR**, all alerts, incidents, and relevant data are synced between the solutions, and the data is populated in Sentinel in the `SecurityAlert` and `SecurityIncident` tables. Bi-directional sync covers the incident's status, owner, and closing reason.

> **Note**
>
> The relevant data connectors in Sentinel are enabled automatically when Microsoft Defender XDR bi-directional sync is enabled. It's also important for getting product alerts (such as Entra ID Protection, MDE, MDO, MDI, and MDA) into Sentinel even though incidents are covered with Sentinel and Defender XDR integration. The ingested data (alerts) is used by the Sentinel Fusion engine for data correlation in Fusion detections

In *Figure 4.13*, you can see the same incident on the **Microsoft Defender XDR** portal and can continue your investigation on that side if required.

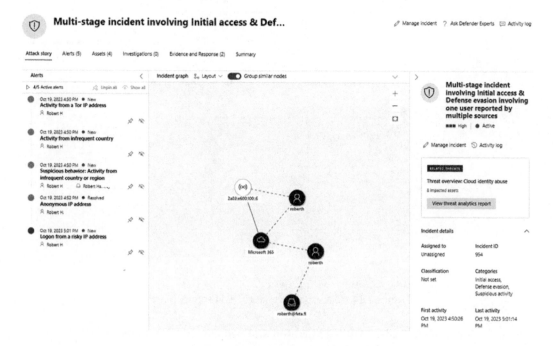

Figure 4.13 - Multi-stage incident in Microsoft Defender XDR

Microsoft Defender XDR brings additional benefits during investigations in terms of integrated solutions. It has all the raw data from devices, email and collaboration tools identities, and applications (out of the box) usable inside of the products, as well as being able to run correlations between the products, producing sophisticated alerts and incidents.

Microsoft Defender XDR also has built-in **Threat Intelligence** and **Threat Analytics** features that provide extensive information on emerging threats. Threat Analytics can be used effectively during investigations to evaluate possible impacts, related incidents, impacted assets, endpoints exposure, and recommended actions. We elaborate on Threat Analytics in more detail in *Chapter 5*.

The Microsoft Defender XDR investigation experience also provides in-depth information about entities such as files, URLs, domains, identities, and more as shown in *Figure 4.14* (file entity page). These pieces of information help security teams to identify the possible impact of the breach during the investigation. The entity pages are accessible from several places in the incident (for example, in the **Evidence** tab, or from the alert story or assets pages), depending on which entities are involved in the incident.

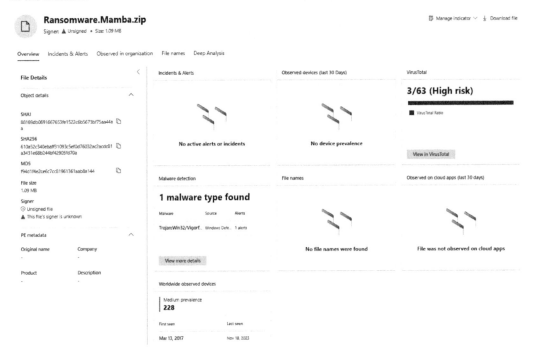

Figure 4.14 - Microsoft Defender XDR file entity page

We covered **Microsoft Defender XDR** and **Microsoft Sentinel** automation layer differences in *Chapter 3*, but to summarize, Microsoft Defender XDR has an automation layer but it's not customizable to the same extent as in Sentinel. **Microsoft Defender XDR** provides automated investigation and response (AIR and Attack Disruption) for certain scenarios and workloads (MDO, MDE, and MDI).

Further investigation with Defender solutions (MDE, MDO, MDI, MDA, and MDC)

For deep investigations, **Microsoft Defender XDR** provides visibility for workloads such as endpoints, collaboration workloads, identities, applications, and cloud resources. We go over some of the most important aspects of each of these categories that will enhance the SOC team's experience in this section.

Endpoints

MDE has many features that can support investigations and security team operations, let's take a look some of them. In Microsoft Defender XDR, you can see raw data from devices divided into 10 different tables in **Advanced Hunting,** which can be used during threat hunting or investigations to do more deeper investigation with KQL queries.

The **Device Inventory** blade (see *Figure 4.15*) provides an overview of the status of devices in your environment as well as other important aspects related to devices, such as name, domain, risk and exposure level, operating system, onboarding status, and more.

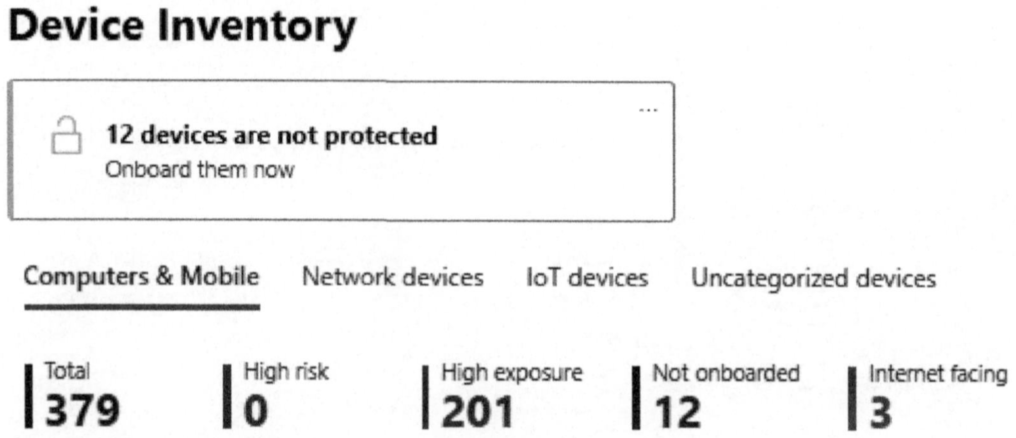

Device Inventory

🔓 **12 devices are not protected**
Onboard them now

...

Computers & Mobile   Network devices   IoT devices   Uncategorized devices

Total	High risk	High exposure	Not onboarded	Internet facing
379	0	201	12	3

Figure 4.15 - MDE device inventory summary

During an investigation, it's common that the security team needs to investigate the device state in more detail, and this can be achieved from the device page. The device overview page contains general information about the device as well as a summary of the risk and exposure level and the device health status. The device page also contains many more informative blades useful for investigations, such as Incidents and alerts, Security recommendations, Inventories, Discovered vulnerabilities, Missing KBs, Security policies, and Timeline, as shown in *Figure 4.16*.

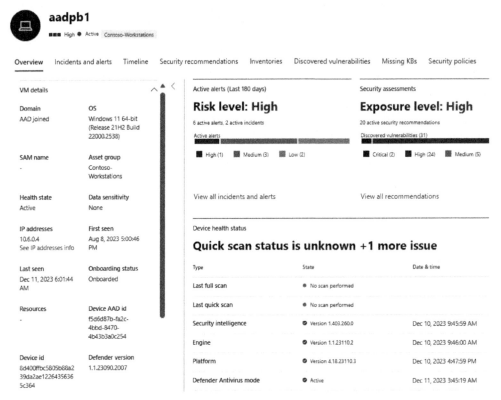

Figure 4.16 - MDE device details in Microsoft Defender XDR

To investigate in detail what has happened during a certain time window, the **Timeline** blade is very useful. It shows events and related alerts on a particular device in chronological order, as shown in *Figure 4.17*.

Figure 4.17 - Device timeline in MDE

> **Important note**
>
> Microsoft Defender XDR **Automated Investigation and Response** (**AIR**) covers MDE but requires Microsoft Defender Antivirus for running in passive or active mode.

If there is a need to investigate some event even further from the device timeline, there is the **Hunt for relevant events** option that redirects to Advanced Hunting and generates a query to search for other relevant events to get you started (see *Figure 4.18*). To hunt for relevant events, the event you are using needs to be in a specific time range (maximum of 30 days) to be usable in advanced hunting in Microsoft Defender XDR.

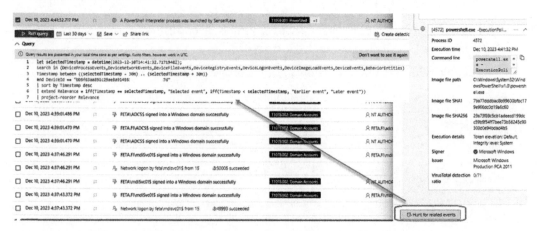

Figure 4.18 - Microsoft Defender XDR Advanced Hunting

> **Note**
>
> There are differences between Defender for Endpoint and Defender for Business for example, not all device tables are available in Defender for Business and advanced hunting is not included.

MDE provides several response actions that can be applied to a device if the analyst needs to respond quickly to a detected attack or collect more information from a device. Some examples are as follows:

- Initiate Automated Investigation

- Initiate Live Response Session

- Collect investigation package

- Run antivirus scan

- Isolate or contain device

The full list of response actions can be found at `https://packt.link/ONVEk`.

We strongly recommend going through the Security Operations Fundamentals, Intermediate, and Expert modules for Microsoft Defender XDR Ninja Training at `https://packt.link/KHJTc`.

Collaboration Workloads

AIR in Microsoft Defender XDR MDO is your friend and investigates alerts and incidents on your behalf (see *Figure 4.19*). This procedure can help you a lot and save your security team's time by providing the necessary details about the incident for a decision to be made. In general, AIR is a very powerful tool for detecting and removing emails that are categorized as phishing or malware.

AIR can be initiated in the following ways:

- An alert can be triggered by any suspicious element in an email: the message content itself, an attachment, a URL, or a compromised user account

- Following incident creation, an automatic investigative process is started

- The security analyst utilizes Explorer's automation features to kick off an in-depth investigation

Investigations

Automated investigation and response (AIR) capabilities enable you to run automated investigation processes in response to well known threats. Learn more

Figure 4.19 - MDO AIR in action

> **Note**
> MDO doesn't trigger automatic remediations. Instead, your security team reviews and approves actions, ensuring informed decisions every step of the way. AIR automates threat identification and gathers crucial details, empowering your security team to make informed decisions about how to address vulnerabilities.

Explorer in MDO is another powerful feature for investigation. If you are not familiar with KQL, Explorer provides a UI-based method for fast search and effective investigations into all email, malware, phishing, campaigns, content malware, or URL click-based content search and mitigations (see *Figure 4.20*). Even though Microsoft Defender XDR Advanced Hunting is the preferred tool for threat hunting, Explorer enables UI-based threat hunting on collaboration workloads if that's a more comfortable way to move forward.

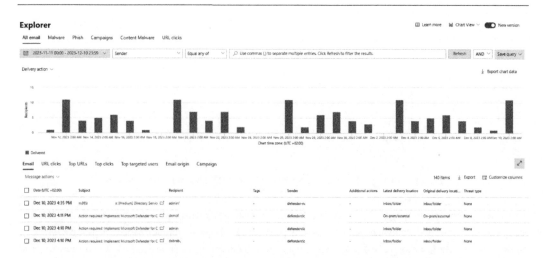

Figure 4.20 - MDO Explorer in the Microsoft Defender XDR portal

We strongly recommend working through the Security Operations Advanced modules for Microsoft Defender for Office 365 Ninja Training (`https://packt.link/3Q9Z0`).

Identities

Identity related attacks have increased a lot in the past year. In the **Microsoft Digital Defense Report 2023 (MDDR)**, it was stated that according to Microsoft Entra data an average of 4,000 password spray attacks per second were identified as targeting Microsoft Entra cloud identities in 2023. This means there is a high likelihood that the SOC team will need to investigate identity related attacks.

In Microsoft Defender XDR, identities are mapped as entities in incidents, no matter the detection source. MDI covers on-premises identities, MDA covers cloud identities, and Entra ID Protection adds additional protection for identities together with Entra Conditional Access.

That being said, there might be multiple solutions involved in any investigation. Let's look at some examples now.

As described in the **Microsoft Defender XDR** incident overview page, there are a lot of details covered on the incident page itself. If there is a user entity involved in the incident, and there is a need to further investigate the user activities, select **Users** under **Assets** and then the user entity, as shown in *Figure 4.21*.

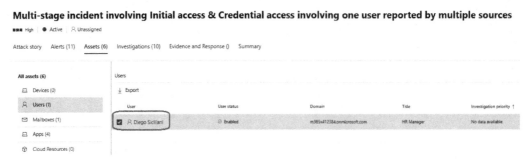

Figure 4.21 - Assets page in a sample Microsoft Defender XDR incident

This opens a user entity page (see *Figure 4.22*), known also as UEBA in Microsoft Defender XDR. The feature was formerly only available in the MDA portal but is now available in the Microsoft Defender XDR portal as well. Within the user entity page, you'll find details such as investigation priority, and risk score, providing a contextual understanding of each individual. One of the MDI core features is **Lateral Movement Paths** (**LMPs**), which can be seen under the **Observed in organization** tab together with devices, groups, and locations.

Figure 4.22 - MDA user entity (UEBA) page

> **Information**
>
> The investigation score is calculated based on activities and alerts from the past 7 days. In addition, user entities have the **Timeline** feature for deeper activity investigation.

The outcome of an investigation could be that mitigations are needed, and the identity entity page provides a way to do so. The available actions are as follows:

- Confirm user compromised:

  - The user is marked as high risk in Entra ID Protection and what happens during their next authentication attempt depends on Entra Conditional Access Policies as, elaborated in *Chapter 3*.

- Suspend user in Azure AD:

  - Disables user account in Entra ID

- Require user to sign in again:

  - Revokes all refresh tokens and session cookies issued to applications in Entra ID by the user entity

- Disable user in AD:

  - Disables user account in an on-premises AD environment

- Enable user in AD:

  - Enables user account in an on-premises AD environment

- Force password reset:

  - Prompts the user to change their password on the next logon

Additional features that may prove essential for the investigative process include the following:

- Entra ID Protection:

  - Entra ID Protection alerts and incidents are synced to Microsoft Defender XDR, and investigation along with mitigations can be done directly from the security portal

- When the security team needs to use raw data, for example, correlation with the identity-related raw data (MDI and MDA) is found at two locations in Microsoft Defender XDR:

  - In MDA Activity Log

  - In Advanced Hunting from several tables:

    - `CloudAppEvents` – basically the same data that the activity log contains but in a different format

    - `IdentityDirectoryEvents, IdentityInfo, IdentityLogonEvents, IdentityQueryEvents` – MDI data from on-premises AD

    - `AADSignInEventsBeta, AADSpnSignInEventsBeta` – part of Microsoft Entra ID sign-in events

Cloud applications

As we covered in *Chapter 3*, **Microsoft Defender for Cloud Apps (MDA)** is a solution used for protecting identities, applications, and data. Let's start by looking at the **Cloud Discovery** feature (also known as **Shadow IT**). If **Cloud Discovery** is configured (data can be ingested from MDE, and supported firewalls, or proxies) the SecOps team can see relevant traffic to known applications on the dashboard (see *Figure 4.23*). This information can be leveraged during investigations, and MDA policies are available to automatically detect possible malicious activities and carry out governance actions for unwanted applications, for example, based on a given application risk score or the amount of traffic.

Cloud Discovery

Updated on Dec 11, 2023, 6:12 AM

| Dashboard | Discovered apps | Discovered resources | IP addresses | Users | Devices |

Apps	IP addresses	Users	Devices	Traffic
1089	7460	573	265	5.6 TB ↑ 909.1 GB ↓ 4.7 TB

App categories — 1-5 of 42 — Traffic

☑ ▎Sanctioned   ☑ ▎Unsanctioned   ☑ ▎Other

Security	1.3 TB
Customer support	938.6 GB
Cloud computing platf...	848.0 GB
Collaboration	676.6 GB
IT services	438.8 GB

Figure 4.23 - MDA Cloud Discovery dashboard

This information can be ingested into Sentinel as well, where it can be leveraged through Log Analytics or Azure Workbooks (data visualization) for investigation. MDA provides the capability to block applications by tagging them (unsanctioned, sanctioned, monitored, or a custom tag). The blocking capability is provided by MDE (custom indicators feature) and applications can be managed from **Cloud Discovery** (when controlling discovered apps) or from **Cloud App Catalog** when controlling apps proactively (see *Figure 4.24*).

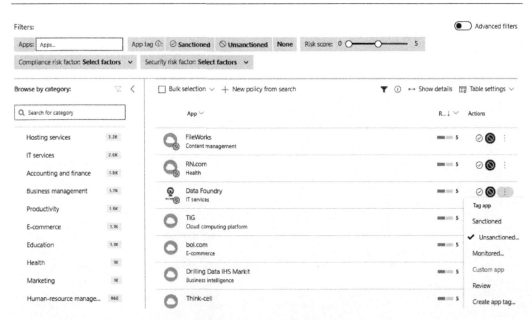

Figure 4.24 - MDA Cloud App Catalog

MDA's threat protection layer provides detection and coverage of possible malicious activities. MDA has deep integration with other Microsoft security solutions such as MDI, Entra ID Protection, and MDE. This leads to better detections and quite often, you will see identity-related multi-stage incidents in the incident queue where MDA is one of the detection sources.

In the *Identities* section, we already covered how to address investigation into identity-related incidents. In addition, there are a few features that we would like to highlight. To find the users with a high investigation priority in your organization (this portal blade leverages Microsoft Defender XDR UEBA as we mentioned earlier), the SecOps team can use the **Identities** blade on the Defender XDR portal, as shown in *Figure 4.25*.

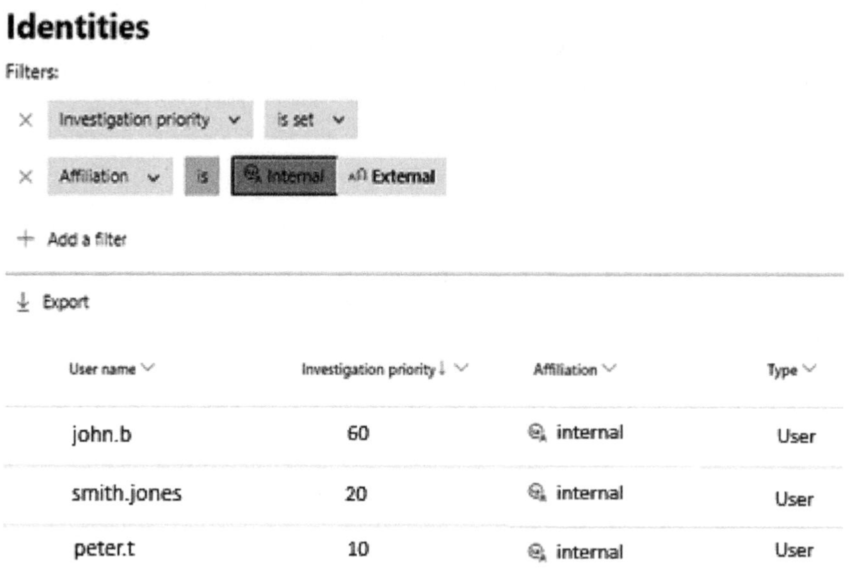

Identities

Filters:

×   Investigation priority ⌄   is set ⌄

×   Affiliation ⌄   is   🔍 Internal   ⌐Ω External

+ Add a filter

⤓ Export

User name ⌄	Investigation priority ↓ ⌄	Affiliation ⌄	Type ⌄
john.b	60	🔍 internal	User
smith.jones	20	🔍 internal	User
peter.t	10	🔍 internal	User

Figure 4.25 - Identities summarized by investigation priority in Microsoft Defender XDR

MDA also provides **App governance** solution and security posture management for SaaS applications (**SSPM**) for evaluating and investigating applications.

The main purpose of **App governance** is to evaluate Entra ID consent framework-related items, such as insight into the integrated OAuth applications. It tracks non-Microsoft apps that use OAuth to authenticate to Microsoft Entra ID, as well as Google and Salesforce at the time of writing this book.

When investigating the *Illicit Consent Grant* type of attack, for example, when applications are leveraged, using **App governance** is beneficial to evaluate applications' usage, permissions, and find any overprivileged apps (as highlighted in *Figure 4.26*) or incidents related to applications.

As also shown in *Figure 4.26*, some features have been moved to require the Microsoft Entra Workload Identities premium license, such as monitoring unused apps and unused and expiring credentials.

App governance

Get in-depth visibility and control over OAuth apps integrated with Azure Active Directory, Google, and Salesforce.

Figure 4.26 - App governance dashboard

On the other hand, SSPM provides a proactive approach to identifying possible risky configurations in integrated SaaS applications. These findings are listed in the **Microsoft Secure Score**, which we cover in more detail in *Chapter 7*.

For the list of app visibility and controls in MDA refer to `https://packt.link/ZFhVn`.

The last item we will touch on in this section is data protection in MDA, which is one of MDA's core features. MDA has deep integration with **Microsoft Purview Information Protection,** which can help to address the following scenarios:

- The ability to apply sensitivity labels as a governance action to files that match specific policies

- The ability to view all classified files in a central location

- The ability to investigate files according to classification level and quantify exposure of sensitive data in your cloud applications

- The ability to create policies to make sure classified files are being handled properly

In addition, MDA provides visibility for files from all apps that have been integrated (through the app connector). This feature provides insights into how files are used and shared in the environment which is useful if you are investigating possible data leaks. We strongly recommend going through the modules for Microsoft Defender for Cloud Apps Ninja Training at `https://packt.link/rWrKL`.

Advanced Hunting

Advanced Hunting is a powerful tool that allows security teams to query data up to 30 days from Microsoft Defender XDR supported data sources (MDE, MDO, MDI, MDA and Entra ID sign-in data), as highlighted earlier in this chapter. Querying such raw data is typically required during investigations when there is a need to investigate deeper or when doing threat hunting on the environment.

> **Note**
>
> Data in Advanced Hunting is divided into two distinct types: **Event or activity data** (alerts, security events, system events, and routine assessments) and **Entity data** (information about users and devices).

Here is an example KQL query where MDA and MDO event data sources are correlated together. This kind of query can be used during an investigation of a possible account breach when the security team wants to have a better understanding of the locations from emails have been accessed:

```
//Review accessed emails
let accountId = '<insert account object id here>';
let locations = pack_array(<insert selected location here, example
'RU'>);
let timeToSearch = startofday(datetime('2023-12-01'));
CloudAppEvents
    | where ActionType == 'MailItemsAccessed' and CountryCode in
(locations) and AccountObjectId == accountId and Timestamp >=
timeToSearch
    | mv-expand todynamic(RawEventData.Folders)
    | extend Path = todynamic(RawEventData_Folders.Path), SessionId =
tostring(RawEventData.SessionId)
    | mv-expand todynamic(RawEventData_Folders.FolderItems)
    | project SessionId, Timestamp, AccountObjectId, DeviceType,
CountryCode, City, IPAddress, UserAgent, Path, Message =
tostring(RawEventData_Folders_FolderItems.InternetMessageId)
    | join kind=leftouter (
        EmailEvents
        | where RecipientObjectId == accountId
        | project Subject, RecipientEmailAddress ,
SenderMailFromAddress , DeliveryLocation , ThreatTypes,
AttachmentCount , UrlCount , InternetMessageId
        ) on $left.Message == $right.InternetMessageId
    | sort by Timestamp desc
```

The preceding query shows the power of Advanced Hunting where you can correlate events and search activities from multiple tables.

Cloud resources (MDC)

The latest addition to the **Microsoft Defender XDR** family is **MDC**. With this new integration, MDC alerts and incidents are synced to **Defender XDR**. This has the following benefits for the investigation experience:

- Incidents are synced to the XDR portal and SOC teams can search and list cloud assets, see cloud resources in the attack story, and view all VMs on their own device pages

- See multi-cloud resources in the assets list

- Get automated event correlation and quickly identify the attack kill chain in the environment

- If the SOC team leverages the Microsoft Defender XDR API, the team will be able to see the MDC alerts and incidents in the Defender XDR API as well

We strongly recommend going through the modules for Microsoft Defender for Cloud Apps Ninja Training at `https://packt.link/0zBS9`.

Managed Security Service Providers (MSSPs)

For MSSPs, there are several solutions that can be used for investigating and managing content in the customer environments. In general, access is needed for Microsoft Entra ID and Azure environments, and these can be established with Entra ID Access Packages, GDAP, and Azure Lighthouse integrations.

The specific permissions required depends on the SOC team's continuous services scope and detailed planning is needed to ensure that the least privilege principle is followed. Many MSSPs around the world leverage Sentinel content management with **Workspace Manager**, which is designed to manage and deploy content to customer environments. In addition, in **Microsoft Defender XDR**, **Multi-tenant Management** provides a single unified view of all tenants the SOC team is managing.

For more information on this, please refer to *Chapter 9*. We also recommend reading *Technical Playbook for MSSPs* at `https://packt.link/4EBTI`.

For more information about Microsoft Defender XDR MTO, refer to `https://packt.link/GqJQ1`.

Now we have covered the investigation experience in Microsoft Defender XDR with an example incident, let's look at how Microsoft Copilot for Security can be leveraged in investigations as of the time of writing.

Microsoft Copilot for Security

When SecOps team are investigating an incident, it can be hard and time consuming to figure out what has happened during an attack. One of the **Microsoft Copilot for Security** scenarios in the embedded experience is the incident summary, which aims to help analysts identify how an attack happened (see *Figure 4.27*). At the time of writing this book, an incident summary can contain 100 alerts with the following items covered:

- The time and date when an attack started

- The specific entity or asset from which the attack originated

- A concise overview of the chronological sequence detailing how the attack progressed

- Identification of the assets implicated in the attack

- **Indicators of compromise (IOCs)**

- Names of threat actors involved

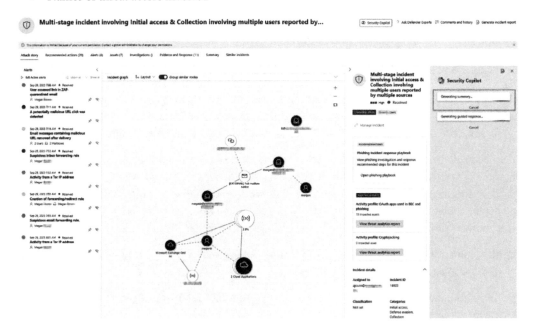

Figure 4.27 - Microsoft Copilot for Security incident investigation

An example outcome of the incident summary is shown in *Figure 4.28*.

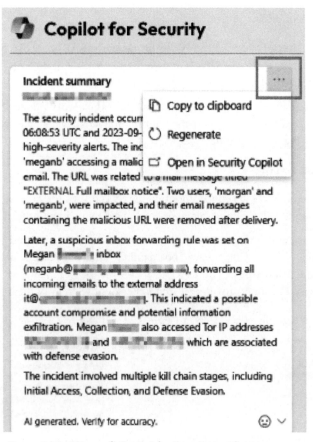

Figure 4.28 - Microsoft Copilot for Security incident summary

Other scenarios of the embedded experience of **Copilot for Security** through **Microsoft Defender XDR** are as follows:

- **Analyze scripts and codes:**

  - Many sophisticated attacks (such as ransomware) contain scripts or code that can be very difficult to evaluate. Copilot for Security provides script analysis capability to support analysis.

- **Use guided responses:**

  - The guided response during investigation provides recommended actions for analysts during investigation. This process is powered by AI and helps analysts decide how to proceed with incident triaging, investigation, remediation, and containment.

- **Generate KQL queries:**

  - **Advanced Hunting** is one of the **Microsoft Defender XDR** core features and provides two options to create queries, either manually in the editor (for advanced users) or using the query builder to get more guidance on the creation process.

  - Copilot for Security helps with this area as well. The security analyst can ask Copilot for Security to create a KQL query using their natural language, which reduces the barrier for people who are not so familiar with KQL.

- **Create incident reports:**

  - In SOC teams, creating reports about incidents is one of the core tasks undertaken on a regular basis. Copilot for Security assists with writing incident reports more efficiently.

  - While an incident summary describes how the incident occurred and provides an overview of it, an incident report aggregates information from diverse data sources within **Microsoft Sentinel** and **Microsoft Defender XDR**. It encompasses both analyst-initiated procedures and automated actions, providing a comprehensive overview of the incident.

The outcome of each scenario can be seen in *Figure 4.29* and *Figure 4.30*:

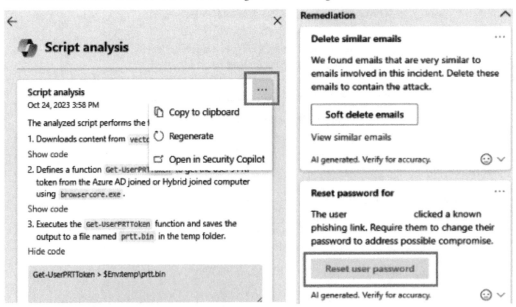

Figure 4.29 - Copilot for Security script analysis (left) and guided responses (right)

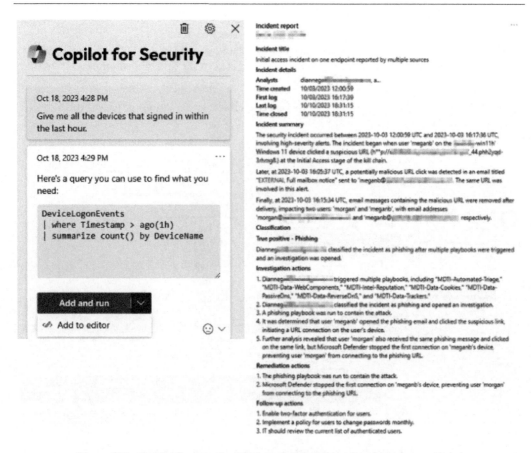

Figure 4.30 - Copilot for Security KQL generation (left) and incident report (right)

Now, we have gone through the highlights of the Sentinel and Defender XDR investigation experience. It's important to mention that these solutions are evolving, and Microsoft is constantly announcing new features that enhance the investigation experience even further.

Integrations with other Microsoft security solutions and third-party tools

As we already noted in *Chapter 3*, there are many security solutions in the Microsoft ecosystem. These solutions are integrated with each other and share signals, events, and alerts. For organizations to truly get the most out of their Microsoft security stack, leveraging inter-connections (integrations between MS solutions) is essential. Most of the available integrations are enabled out of the box, but some you need to enable yourself.

> **Important note**
>
> The best synergy advantages come from using the full stack, which leverages the inter-connections (the sharing of signals, events, alerts and incidents) between the different solutions.

Figure 4.31 elaborates the high-level integrations between security solutions as part of the Microsoft security operations architecture.

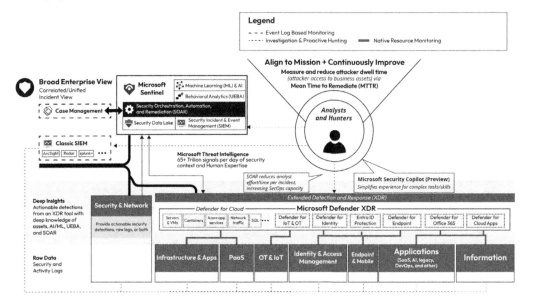

Figure 4.31 - Microsoft security operations architecture

As we can see in *Figure 4.31*, in the modern security operations architecture, the evolution of XDR had a huge impact on SecOps transformation. XDR solutions have an important role to play by providing improved detection mechanisms for common attack patterns compared to static SIEM detections.

In Microsoft's security operations architecture, **Defender XDR** provides high-quality alerts and incidents, supported by deep integrations between the solutions and leveraging behavior analytics, machine learning, and AI, along with automatic attack disruption to stop attacks in their early stages.

Microsoft Defender XDR platform – Single pane of glass

Let's look at the **Microsoft Defender XDR** platform (formerly Microsoft Defender 365) integrations and where they sit in the ecosystem. Microsoft Defender XDR integrates natively with all the Microsoft 'MDx' security solutions (**MDE, MDO, MDI** and **MDA**), **Defender for IoT, Entra ID Protection,** and **Defender for Cloud** (**MDC**).

Microsoft Defender XDR is tightly integrated with Microsoft Sentinel with the option of enabling bi-directional sync of alerts, incidents, and relevant data, as well as the option to bring in raw data from Defender XDR solutions to Sentinel. This integration is one of those you need to enable manually in Sentinel (via the Microsoft Defender XDR data connector).

With this wide set of integrations, its goal is to run most of the security operations from one dedicated portal depending on the security solutions used.

The latest addition to the family of integrations is **MDC**. With MDC integration, SecOps teams can get multi-cloud alerts, signals, and asset information for **Azure**, **AWS**, and **GCP** from MDC into Microsoft Defender XDR, which speeds up the investigation and helps with correlation in the IR process.

Future of XDR

At the Ignite event (November 2023), Microsoft announced a **Unified XDR Platform**. What this means is that there will be a fully integrated toolset that can be used to protect the whole organization's entire digital landscape. In a nutshell, **Microsoft Sentinel**, **Microsoft Defender for Cloud** and **Microsoft Copilot for Security** will be integrated into **Microsoft Defender XDR**. When all these solutions are merged into one portal, and powered by **AI** and **TI**, organizations can investigate and respond to incidents better and faster. When most of the solutions needed for the security operations are contained in one portal, it is obvious that portal switching will not be needed, as it is at the time of writing this book.

Also, Microsoft Defender XDR capabilities (**Automatic Attack Disruption**) will be extended beyond non-Microsoft data brought in through **SIEM** (Sentinel), and in the first phase, capabilities will be extended with SAP.

Microsoft Sentinel

In the legacy security operations architecture, all log sources are integrated in a SIEM tool, but in most cases, this approach doesn't provide enough actionable incidents and can lead to alert fatigue in the SIEM solution.

In the modern **SecOps** architecture that Sentinel represents, both XDR and SIEM tools complement each other. The SIEM tool can basically collect data from any data source that can be further leveraged for event correlation between various sources such as identities, applications, data, devices, hybrid and multi-cloud resources, and so on. Third party security solutions can be integrated in Sentinel through APIs, which is not possible in Defender XDR. On the other hand, Defender XDR provides sophisticated alert rules, **Automatic Attack Disruption** and **EDR** with *deception tactics* to catch adversaries on the fly, whereas Sentinel has more static rules that work in combination with an automation layer. You can find more information about *Automatic Attack Disruption* in *Chapter 3* and *Chapter 5*.

Let's consider an example. Even though the XDR platform provides a great toolset, it doesn't provide the possibility to collect logs from network devices (firewalls) or other custom log sources. For these kinds of data sources, organizations might want to create custom detections.

Another layer that is more enhanced in Sentinel than in XDR is automation (SOAR). In Defender XDR, automation is established through **Automated Investigation and Response – AIR**. In general, SOAR has an important role in modern SecOps architecture where incidents can for example be trimmed, enriched, and managed to reduce the manual work required from the analyst. In Sentinel, automation is provided by two separate features; Sentinel Automation and Azure Logic Apps, which are tightly integrated into Sentinel.

There are also other differences between the solutions, which can be found in *Chapter 3.*

Future of Sentinel

Sentinel as a SIEM tool isn't going anywhere; it has its place in the Microsoft cybersecurity architecture. In the near future, organizations will have the option to use the Unified Security Operations Platform to manage both solutions (Sentinel and Defender XDR) with a fully integrated toolset and single data model, advanced hunting, and incident management for integrated solutions. As we covered in the *Microsoft DefenderXDR platform* section, this integration into one platform will speed up investigations and the overall management of SecOps-related content because solutions will be available through one portal. From an architecture standpoint, Sentinel will be utilized as of right now, as an individual solution with integration to Microsoft Defender XDR as an optional step in the future.

Microsoft Copilot for Security is in the **Early Access Program** (**EAP**) phase at the time of writing this book and is integrated with Microsoft security products including Sentinel. If an organization leverages Copilot for Security, it can be used in the Sentinel context as well.

Third Party integrations

Let's focus on third-party solutions and integration possibilities when using the Microsoft Defender XDR and SIEM solution. As was covered earlier, native integrations are one of the key advantages of using Microsoft security solutions. There are different architectures in place along with variety of other vendors leveraged by many organizations. What are the possibilities for integrations in such an ecosystem? Let's elaborate on a few items that are beneficial when you need to consider and plan integrations.

Microsoft Sentinel

In a nutshell, Sentinel content based on SIEM components help organizations to ingest data, monitor, alert, hunt, investigate, respond, and connect with different products, platforms, and services. This content include data connectors, analytic rules, hunting queries, and workbooks among others. The content can be deployed to Sentinel either standalone or as solutions.

More information about different content types can be found at `https://packt.link/yRLiP`.

These solutions are deployed to the Sentinel workspace through Content Hub and are packaged integrations with easy deployment. From the Content Hub you can find the following:

- **Packaged content**: Collections of Sentinel content such as data connectors, analytic rules, workbooks and more

- **Integrations**: These solutions are services or tools built using Sentinel or Azure Log Analytics APIs that support integrations of applications and data (among others) into Microsoft Sentinel.

You can learn more about partner integrations at `https://packt.link/iWBdA`.

Content Hub is the central place for managing and deploying content in Microsoft Sentinel, and partner solutions can also easily be deployed to your Sentinel instance from there. In general, Sentinel and Azure ecosystem provides plenty of options for integrating third-party solutions with Sentinel

A few examples are as follows:

- Sentinel integration with ServiceNow:

  Content Hub has a ServiceNow solution that provides the ability to retrieve incidents and create tickets for them in ServiceNow. It also provides the bi-directional sync option

- Integration with IBM Qradar:

  If your organization is using non-Microsoft SIEM tool and you want to send audit data into it, you can establish integration through Azure Event Hub.

- Send custom data to Sentinel:

  From the architecture point of view, Azure Log Analytics is underneath Sentinel. If you want to send custom data from your solution to Log Analytics and leverage the data in Sentinel this is possible through a MMA/AMA agent or via a REST API:

  - One example of this is the **Entra ID Security Config Analyzer** community project that leverages Azure Logic Apps to push data to an Azure Log Analytics custom table

  - More information about this solution can be found at `https://packt.link/jEGgq`.

Microsoft Defender XDR

Microsoft Defender XDR has similar features to Sentinel Content Hub. Here, you can find the Partner Catalog which details technology partners and professional services. From the Partner catalog you can easily find partners that provide product integrations and discover service offerings provided by leading service providers.

Besides that, Microsoft Defender XDR has APIs that support the automation of workflows and easy integration for third-party SIEM solution. At the time of writing, the Microsoft Defender XDR APIs are the following:

- Advanced Hunting API

- Incident API

- Streaming API

More info about Microsoft Defender XDR API can be found at `https://packt.link/nMQ1q`.

Microsoft Graph Security API

Finally, let's take a look at the Microsoft Security Graph API which has been available for years already. It provides a unified interface and schema for integrations for both Microsoft and partner solutions. The recommendation is to use the **Microsoft Graph Security API** when you want to build applications that do the following:

- Receives security alerts from several different solutions and consolidate as well as correlates alerts

- Gather information from services that are integrated with or are a part of Microsoft Defender XDR and investigate all occurrences and alerts

- Unlock contextual data to inform investigations

- Automate different tasks such as security tasks, processes, workflows, and more

- Forward threat indicators for personalized detections to Microsoft products

- Invoke actions to take in response to new threats

- Make security data visible to enable proactive risk management

The **Microsoft Graph Security API** provides several key features such as advanced hunting, alerts and incidents, attack simulation and training, eDiscovery, Information protection, Secure Score, and threat intelligence.

More information about the Microsoft Graph Security API can be found at `https://packt.link/aHme9`.

Case study analysis

In our case study analysis, High Tech Rapid Corp Solution's security and SOC teams emphasized the challenges they were having with their current **siloed architecture**. They also mentioned that they are suffering from alert fatigue in their SOC and lack full visibility into their environment. Also, because of the siloed architecture, investigation, mitigation and threat hunting are time consuming with the low number of resources they have available.

Transitioning to a modern **SOC** operations model can effectively address the challenges highlighted by the organization's security and SOC teams. The teams may operate considerably more productively by using automation and **Artificial Intelligence (AI)** to support investigations and other security-related duties by implementing a modern SOC operations and security architecture.

Implementing advanced threat detection and response technologies, coupled with automation, reduces alert fatigue and provides real-time insights, enhancing their overall visibility into the environment. Additionally, a modern SOC optimizes resource utilization through streamlined investigation, mitigation, and threat hunting processes, ultimately improving efficiency and responsiveness despite the limited resources of the organization.

Summary

In this chapter, we laid the groundwork for understanding SOCs, covering their essential roles, their importance, and their remarkable historical transformation. We also examined the differences between traditional and modern SOCs. Finally, we explored how the Microsoft unified XDR and SIEM solution enhances the SOC experience via its cost-saving potential and by enabling effective monitoring of your digital ecosystem.

These tools are very powerful together and when used correctly, they can really save the time required for investigations. In this book, we only scratch the surface, and we highly recommend that you explore all the features by yourselves to gain familiarity with the tools and all the possibilities they provide.

In the next chapter, we will cover some useful resources that can be leveraged to understand the XDR and SIEM stack and get more information about the topics covered throughout the book.

Further reading

Refer to the following links for more information about the topics covered in this chapter:

- Detect Changes in Azure Lighthouse Permission Delegations - `https://packt.link/blRsf`

- Best Practices for security teams and leaders - `https://packt.link/TsLcb`

- Security Operations Guide for Microsoft Defender for Office 365 - `https://packt.link/klcN4`

- Security Operations Guide for Microsoft Defender for Endpoint - `https://packt.link/Gq25P`

- Summarize incidents with Copilot for Security in Microsoft Defender XDR | Microsoft Learn - `https://packt.link/visV1`

- Microsoft Copilot for Security in advanced hunting | Microsoft Learn - `https://packt.link/mAmVD`

- Manage the deception capability in Microsoft Defender XDR | Microsoft Learn - `https://packt.link/y8Hl8`
- Overview of Microsoft Defender XDR APIs - `https://packt.link/oT7Kx`
- Use the Microsoft Graph Security API - `https://packt.link/Yc0or`
- Other security and threat protection APIs - `https://packt.link/cozUe`
- Microsoft Sentinel content hub catalog - `https://packt.link/Qbf2T`

5

Defend Attacks with Microsoft XDR and SIEM

In this chapter, we delve deeper into the Microsoft's unified XDR and SIEM detection capabilities and elaborate on how the security solutions can defend organizations from real-world attacks, as well as highlight some prevention strategies for them. In recent years, some of the attack scenarios have risen in popularity among adversaries. As a demonstration, we have selected a few of them to show you the power of Microsoft's unified XDR and SIEM solutions. The scenarios are as follows:

- Identity-based supply chain attack in a cloud environment
- **Business Email Compromise (BEC) attack**
- **Human-Operated Ransomware (HumOR)**

This chapter will cover the following main topics:

- An attack kill chain in XDR and SIEM
- Microsoft Defender XDR's automatic attack disruption
- Attack scenarios
- A case study analysis

An attack kill chain in XDR and SIEM

As we can see from *Figure 5.1*, Microsoft's security solutions provide comprehensive visibility for a wide range of attack techniques, including both external and internal threat scenarios. You can also see in *Figure 5.1* how the **Extended Detection and Response (XDR)** and **SIEM** solutions share signals between each other and work together to defend across common attack chains.

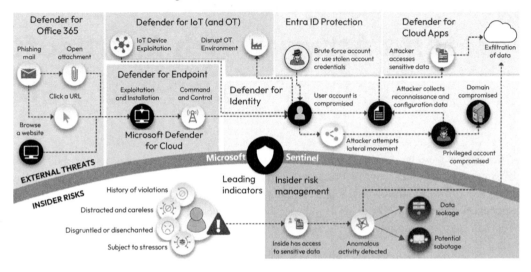

Figure 5.1 – An illustration of how XDR + Sentinel tools work together to keep organization secure

As we highlighted in *Chapter 3*, these capabilities can provide enhanced threat detections for organizations as well as automated investigation and response capabilities.

Identity threat detection and response

Identity Threat Detection and Response (ITDR) is a relatively new term that was invented to meet the need of having a security category in place to identify, reduce, and respond to potential identity-based threats. Based on Gartner, ITDR was one of the top security and risk management trends in 2022.

Microsoft ideology is to have an integrated partnership between the (previously divided) concepts **Identity and Access Management (IAM)** and **Extended Detection and Response (XDR)**. Here are the key areas that ITDR covers:

- **Secure access**: By following IAM and Microsoft Entra ID security best practices, such as deploying and configuring strong authentication methods, Conditional Access policies, and identity governance, organizations can reduce an environment's overall attack surface area while also providing needed context for security solutions, enabling them to detect possible breaches.

- **Threat-level intelligence**: By ingesting data from critical identity systems, such as on-premises Active Directory domain controllers, Microsoft Entra ID, underlying identity infrastructure such as **Active Directory Federation Service (AD FS)** and **Active Directory Certificate Services (AD CS)**, **Public Key Infrastructure (PKI)**, as well as third-party identity providers, SecOps teams can gain a full picture of an identity ecosystem, user behavior, and associated risks.

- **Automatic attack disruption**: The last piece of the ITDR puzzle is to automatically detect and stop ongoing lateral movement attacks with Microsoft Defender XDR's automatic attack disruption feature, by leveraging AI and machine learning models. The next section contains more information about attack disruption.

> **Note**
> Security analysts can now see the bigger picture of an attack by correlating identity data with other security signals, leading to more accurate and effective threat detection.

Microsoft Defender XDR's automatic attack disruption

Before going into attack scenarios, let us look at what **automatic attack disruption**. Microsoft Defender XDR, as well as other Microsoft security solutions, shares and correlates a huge number of signals daily. Automatic attack disruption was introduced initially in 2022, and the idea behind is to identify ongoing complex and sophisticated attacks with high confidence and execute mitigation actions automatically (containing compromised assets, such as identity and endpoints).

An overview of Microsoft Defender XDR's automatic attack disruption

Microsoft Defender XDR's automatic attack disruption mechanism leverages Microsoft AI models and threat research insights to detect possible attacks. One of the main advantages of using automatic attack disruption (compared to other XDR and SIEM solutions) is that the feature is built into the **Microsoft Defender XDR** platform. It's automatically enabled when solutions are deployed, but to make it work as intended (i.e., disrupt attacks), you need to make sure that prerequisites are met, which we will elaborate on in the next section.

> **How to configure automatic attack disruption**
> You will find detailed instructions at `https://packt.link/KvBR0`.

The automatic attack disruption feature leverages the full Microsoft Defender XDR security stack, and in a nutshell, the wider the Defender XDR deployment is, the more coverage you will get. The following list contains the items that need to be configured to fully utilize this feature in an environment:

- Deploy the entire **Microsoft Defender XDR** stack (MDE, MDO, MDI, and MDA).

- Automated response actions are key features in attack disruption. To leverage automated response actions, the following settings need to be configured:

  - **MDI**: Configure and enable an action account to an on-premises AD (follow the least privilege permissions principle)

  - **MDE**: It is recommended to configure the automation level as **Full - remediate threats automatically**, allowing Microsoft Defender XDR to automatically contain a device

  - **MDE**: Device discovery is set to standard

In October 2023, Microsoft announced capability for MDE to be able to automatically disrupt human-operated attacks, such as ransomware, early in the kill chain without needing to deploy any other features. With this new capability, full XDR deployment is not required, but it is still recommended because of enhanced protection for attack scenarios.

At the time of writing, the new MDE capability is included with MDE Plan 2 as well as Defender for Business standalone licenses.

If a human-operated attack is detected on a single device, the Microsoft Defender XDR attack disruption will simultaneously stop the campaign on that device and all other affected devices in the organization where the compromised user operates. In a nutshell, the mitigation ideology is the same, whether the full XDR deployment is in use or only MDE.

Here's some more information about MDE license plans:

- **MDE P1 and P2**: `https://packt.link/GmqA7`

- **Defender for Business**: `https://packt.link/jhyoV`

Automatic attack disruption key stages

Let's look at the different stages of attack disruption, starting with data collection:

- **Correlating signals**: Microsoft security solutions shares signals, events and alerts with each other, and the attack disruption leverages this collected data to identify a possible adversary high-confidence attack. Insights are collected from endpoints, identities, email (and collaboration tools such as Teams), and SaaS applications.

- **Identifying assets**: Attack disruption identifies assets managed by an adversary and used to spread an attack.

- **Automated actions**: Attack disruption automatically responds with actions across relevant Microsoft Defender products. Also, remember that the wider the deployment, the wider the coverage.

Available automated actions at the time of writing are as follows:

- **Contain device**: This action involves the automatic containment of a suspicious device to block any incoming/outgoing communication to/from the affected device.

- **Disable user**: The action is a MDI capability, and it requires having MDI deployed with **Action Account** configured. Disable user is an automatic suspension of a compromised account in an on-premises environment to prevent additional damage, such as lateral movement, malicious mailbox use, or malware execution.

- **Contain user**: The action automatically contains suspicious identities temporarily. By containing identities, organizations can block any lateral movement and remote encryption related to incoming communication with MDE onboarded devices in the early stages.

> **Note**
>
> Even though Microsoft Defender XDR's automatic attack disruption is fully automated, it doesn't mean that a security team doesn't need to investigate incidents.

Cyberattacks are evolving, becoming more sophisticated and frequent as well as faster, thus posing a threat to organizations of all sizes and industries. Microsoft Defender XDR's automatic attack disruption is a powerful feature that can help to enhance security, faster response times, and resiliency against attacks. To realize the difference it can make, see the following figures, which show defenses without attack disruption (*Figure 5.2*) and with attack disruption (*Figure 5.3*).

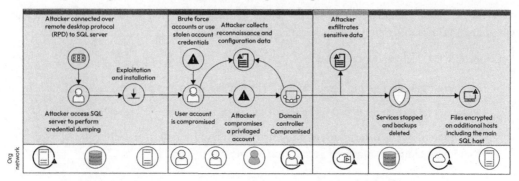

Figure 5.2 – Without Microsoft Defender XDR's automatic attack disruption in place

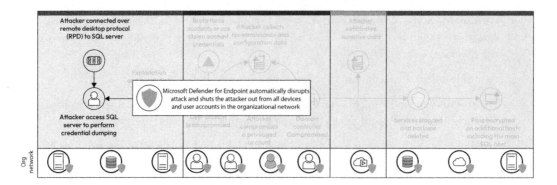

Figure 5.3 – With Microsoft Defender XDR's automatic attack disruption in place

As you can see from the preceding figures, there is a significant difference on capabilities if attack disruption is not configured with automated remediation. Keep in mind that the feature doesn't cover all the possible attack scenarios, but it covers some major ones.

Deception capability in Microsoft Defender XDR

Through its integrated deception capability, Microsoft Defender XDR effectively safeguards an organization's crucial assets by providing high-confidence detections of human-operated lateral movement, thereby preventing potential attacks.

Various attacks (such as ransomware and business email compromise) frequently exploit lateral movement, making early and definitive identification challenging. Defender XDR's deception technology, aligned with signals from Microsoft Defender for Endpoint, ensures robust and highly confident detections.

With the deception technology, SOC teams can get notification about a potential attack in the early stages and perform mitigation actions before it is successful.

Let's look at what decoys and lures are:

- Decoys are fake devices and accounts that pretend to belong to be part of an organization's network
- Lures are fake content placed on specific devices or accounts
- This content can be things such as documents, configuration files, or cached passwords – stuff that might tempt an attacker to read, steal, or mess with them

At the time of writing, two types of lures are available:

- **Basic lures**: These include planted documents, link files, and similar items that don't do much or interact very little with the customer environment
- **Advanced lures**: These involve planted content, such as cached credentials and interceptions, that actively respond or interact with the customer environment

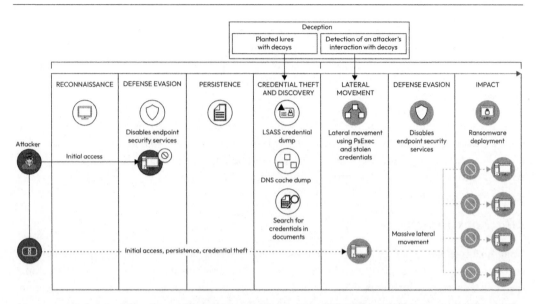

Figure 5.4 – Deception capability in Microsoft Defender XDR

Figure 5.4 illustrates how deception capability interrupts and identifies possible attacks with high-confidence detections of human-operated lateral movement.

More information on deception capability and its license and deployment requirements are available here: `https://packt.link/KZa9e`.

In the next section, we take a look at some popular attack scenarios and how Microsoft Defender XDR and Sentinel can help to detect the scenarios and mitigate them.

Attack scenarios

In this section, we will explore some of the common attack scenarios that have been increasing in recent years and how Microsoft's XDR and SIEM solutions can detect and remediate them.

An identity-based supply chain attack in the cloud

What's the definition of a supply chain attack? It is an attack that targets a trusted third-party vendor who provides critical supply chain services or software. In recent years, there has been a significant increase in security vulnerabilities related to cloud identities within the context of supply chain attacks (such as Solarigate).

Let's suppose an adversary can get access to a service provider environment by compromising the user entity. In this case, there are doors open to all client environments where the service provider provides services. To mitigate this, there are plenty of security measures that you could use on both the MSP/MSSP and client sides. However, many environments lack these safeguards, making them vulnerable to such attacks.

These identity-based supply chain attacks can cause significant damage to an organization's data, systems, and reputation. In this section, we will demonstrate how Microsoft's Defender for Cloud can be used to detect possible malicious activity coming from the service provider side, as well as how Azure Activity Log raw data can be used to detect against supply chain attacks, especially when Azure Lighthouse is used for delegations. This scenario will be discussed in more detail in *Chapter 9*, where we will discuss managed XDR and SIEM.

Attack description

Imagine a scenario where MSP/MSSP environment identities are not properly protected and an adversary compromises a service provider user entity. After compromising the service provider account (i.e., initial access), the next phase in the attack flow is reconnaissance, where the adversary identifies what permissions they gained and what they can do in the next attack. In *Figure 5.5*, you can see an example cloud identity-based supply chain attack flow. This attack belongs to the **Defense Evasion** category in the MITRE ATT&CK framework, which consists of techniques an adversary may use to evade detection or avoid other defenses.

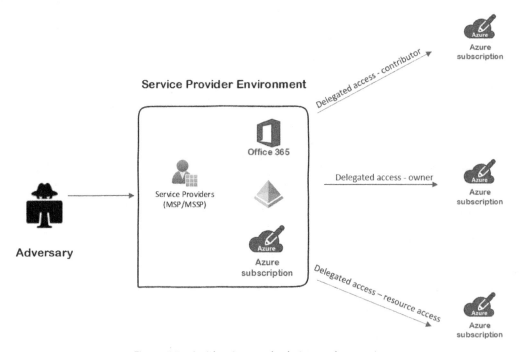

Figure 5.5 – An identity supply chain attack scenario

Detections

If an organization leverages **Microsoft Defender for Cloud** threat protection solutions (i.e., Defender plans) and especially Defender for **Resource Manager** (as shown in *Figure 5.6*), they can leverage new MDC detection capabilities especially for an identity-based supply chain attack scenario.

Figure 5.6 – An MDC enhanced plan configuration

This enhanced detection capability (i.e., an MDC alert, as shown in *Figure 5.7*) correlates events collected through **Azure Resource Manager** (**ARM**) and can identify possible suspicious activities coming from the MSP/MSSP side – that is, operations through delegated access. These activities are differentiated from member users' activities.

Figure 5.7 – An MDC delegated access from a suspicious proxy alert

Detecting possible adversary activities coming from the MSP/MSSP side is a bit tricky in a cloud environment. The reason is delegated access and how it works (i.e., a passthrough at the Azure RBAC level). When planning hypothesis and detection rules on this attack, you should also take into account that initial authentications are not seen on the customer tenant side. However, this doesn't mean that we would not be able to detect and see the activities; we just need some custom use cases and analytic rules.

MDC alone isn't enough in the MSP/MSSP Azure access scenario, and that's why we need to rely on Azure activity logs. It's worth mentioning that Microsoft has several partnership models that partners can use to manage customer environments, with different sets of permissions. We will not cover all the partnership models here, but some of the permission types make it possible to grant wide permissions to the customer environment.

The following query shows activities made by a user from an MSP/MSSP tenant towards a (customer) tenant. This query can be used as a starting point to investigate activities or create custom detection rules based on MSP/MSSP activity. The user (MSP/MSSP) sign-in activities are not shown in the customer tenant, but activities made through **Azure Resource Manager** (**ARM**) can be seen in it:

```
AzureActivity
| where TimeGenerated >= ago(1d)
| where ActivityStatusValue == "Success" or ActivityStatusValue
contains "Start"
| where OperationNameValue contains "WRITE"
| extend ['RBACRole'] = tostring(parse_json(tostring(parse_
```

```
json(Authorization).evidence)).role)
| extend ['RoleAssignmentScope'] = tostring(parse_json(tostring(parse_
json(Authorization).evidence)).roleAssignmentScope)
| extend ['Scope'] = tostring(parse_json(Authorization).scope)
| extend ['Message'] = tostring(Properties_d.message)
| extend ['Claims_authnmethodsreferences'] = tostring(parse_
json(Claims).["http://schemas.microsoft.com/claims/
authnmethodsreferences"])
| extend ['Claims_upn'] = tostring(parse_json(Claims).["http://
schemas.xmlsoap.org/ws/2005/05/identity/claims/upn"])
| extend ['Claims_tenantid'] = tostring(parse_json(Claims).["http://
schemas.microsoft.com/identity/claims/tenantid"])
| where ['Claims_tenantid'] != '<insert your tenant id here>'
| project TimeGenerated, Caller, CallerIpAddress,
['Message'], ['RBACRole'], ['Claims_authnmethodsreferences'],
['Claims_tenantid'], ['Scope']
```

Azure subscription access by MSP/MSSP is delegated through Azure Lighthouse, but if you are keen to find out MSP/MSSP sign-in activities and who accessed an Entra ID tenant through Microsoft Partner Center, you can find the relevant sign-in logs in Entra ID logs by using the **Cross tenant access type: Service Provider** filter, as shown in *Figure 5.8*. The same category contains other access types, such as B2B and Microsoft Support.

Date		Request ID		Username		Application		Status	IP address		Resource
⌄10/2/2023, 3:00:00 AM		8dba9a28-f9f5-4123-b315-150(		user_2ˮ		.	PCFulfillmentAppId		Success	8ſ		Microsoft Graph
10/3/2023, 12:11:00 AM		8dba9a28-f9f5-4123-b315-150(		user_		PCFulfillmentAppId		Success	8		Microsoft Graph
> 10/2/2023, 3:00:00 AM		75e9653c-85c1-4103-9c50-5b0		user_		.	Microsoft Partner Center		Success	8		PCFulfillmentAppId
> 10/1/2023, 3:00:00 AM		02f9878b-d826-4832-b370-7ae		user_		.	PCFulfillmentAppId		Success	8		Microsoft Graph
> 10/1/2023, 3:00:00 AM		f0214739-050a-484e-9f77-eb1f		user_2?(ᵉᵗᵃᵘᵇᵃᵘᵗᵘᵉᵗᵉᵘᵃᵉᵘˢᵉ…		Microsoft Partner Center		Success	8ſ		PCFulfillmentAppId

Figure 5.8 – Microsoft Entra ID sign-in logs using the Service provider filter

Mitigations

There are several security controls available for both sides, the service provider and the customer, and we will cover some of them in this section.

For the service provider

Follow **Cloud Solution Provider** (**CSP**) security best practices. The guidance applies to the MSP/MSSP scenario as well. You can find the full list of recommendations with detailed descriptions in the Microsoft Partner Center documentation here: `https://packt.link/h9RqX`.

Security best practices include a long list of recommendations, which we are not listing here, but let's highlight a few important ones:

- Use dedicated tenants and identities for managing customers

- Require a phishing-resistant multi-factor authentication mechanism, and harden your MSP/MSSP tenant Conditional Access policies

- Use **Privileged Access Workstations** (**PAWs**) when connecting to customer environments

- **Privileged Identity Management** (**PIM**) is a must, but consider using privileged access groups, if possible, in your scenario

- Leverage Microsoft Entra ID Protection (formerly Azure AD Identity Protection) to detect user risks (real-time and offline detections)

- Pay attention to security monitoring in an MSP/MSSP environment

For customer

Follow customer security best practices to harden your environment and to be able to monitor and detect suspicious activity in an environment. The following list highlights some of the most important recommendations (and you can find the full list of recommendations with detailed descriptions in the Microsoft Partner Center documentation: `https://packt.link/bkW15`):

- Require **multi-factor authentication** (**MFA**) in every scenario, and if possible, use phishing-resistant MFA

- Ensure you have a proper delegation model in place and that your organization follows a least privilege model

- Ensure your organization has security monitoring in place that takes into account privileged users, Entra ID activities, as well as Azure activities, enabling you to detect possible malicious activity in the cloud identity-based supply chain attack scenario

Besides the security recommendations, there are a few Azure Policy settings that we recommend implementing in the customer environment:

- Audit delegation scopes of a managing tenant

- Allow managing tenant IDs to onboard through Azure Lighthouse

With these policies, administrators on the customer side can audit the delegation scopes and limit the allowed delegations against their own tenants.

If you need to verify MSSP's permissions, they can be seen on the **Service providers** blade (in *Figure 5.9*) in the Azure portal.

M365x Sentinel Managed Service   ...

Details   **Role assignments**

Role assignments

The groups/users/service principals shown here from Azure Active Directory have access to your delegated resources.

3 items

Display Name	↑↓	Principal Id	↑↓	Role	↑↓	Access Type	↑↓	Multi-factor authentica...↑↓	Service Provider Appro..
LH Policy Automation Account				User Access Administrator ⓘ					
		555e1e19-93cd-44f5-9133-2d35789a30b6		Can assign access to: Contributor ⓘ Log Analytics Contributor ⓘ		Permanent		N/A	N/A
PAG - LH Azure Sentinel Contributor - Cus...		d1deab2f-6245-4bb3-98b0-15891916f867		Microsoft Sentinel Contributor ⓘ		Permanent		N/A	N/A
PAG - LH Azure Sentinel Responder - Cust...		9e45a635-f097-4321-8f6b-0578c841d1bb		Microsoft Sentinel Responder ⓘ		Permanent		N/A	N/A

Figure 5.9 – Service provider permissions in Azure

> **Note**
>
> When viewing role assignments for the delegated scope in the Azure portal or via APIs, customers won't see role assignments or any users from the service provider tenant who have access through Azure Lighthouse.

Business Email Compromise attack

In this section, we will focus on **Business Email Compromise** (**BEC**) attack. Let's start with the definition of a BEC attack. According to Microsoft, BEC attack is defined as follows:

> *"BEC is a type of cybercrime where the scammer uses email to trick someone into sending money or divulging confidential company info. The culprit poses as a trusted figure, then asks for a fake bill to be paid or for sensitive data they can use in another scam."*

BEC attacks are very popular among adversaries, and according to the Microsoft Threat Intelligence Cyber Signal report (published in May 2023), between April 2022 and April 2023, Microsoft Threat Intelligence detected and investigated 35 million BEC attempts with an adjusted average of 156,000 attempts daily. The report can be found at the following link: `https://packt.link/20OwX`.

Attack description

BEC starts typically with some form of phishing (MFA fatigue can be involved), and generally, lookalike tactics (e.g., user or domain impersonation) or "exact-domain spoofing" are used. The goal of this attack is to impersonate a trusted entity within an organization to mislead an employee into taking specific actions (e.g., financial transactions or sharing sensitive information).

Different types of BEC attacks include the following:

- Data theft
- CEO fraud

- Account compromise

- A false invoice scheme

- Lawyer impersonation

Figure 5.10 illustrates one example of a BEC attack flow, ranging from credential access to its impact.

Figure 5.10 – An example BEC attack flow

Detections

In a potential BEC type of attack, the attack kill chain consists of multiple workloads, as illustrated in *Figure 5.10*.

By leveraging Microsoft Defender XDR and SIEM, organizations would get protection for collaboration workloads, identities, devices, and data, which are all, or might be, used as detection mechanism in the BEC attack.

Microsoft Entra ID Protection provides protection against identity theft, such as token theft, or other possible malicious activities against a user entity. Together with Defender for Cloud Apps and Defender for Endpoint (which share signals with it) Entra ID Protection can detect malicious activities detected after the initial sign-in. This is called offline detection, which we discussed in detail in *Chapter 3*.

In addition, Microsoft Defender XDR's automatic attack disruption provides detection and automated mitigation in high-confidence attacks, as we described early on this chapter.

Figure 5.11 shows a BEC attack flow with related product alerts.

Figure 5.11 – A BEC attack flow that was prevented with Defender XDR
automatic attack disruption (with related product alerts included)

Microsoft Sentinel/BEC/financial fraud solutions

In September 2023, Microsoft published a Sentinel content hub solution containing analytic rules and hunting queries to help detect and investigate BEC attacks at different stages of the attack cycle, and across multiple data sources. The solution complements existing Microsoft Defender XDR detection capabilities and provides detection capabilities outside of Defender XDR solutions.

At the time of writing, it contains 7 analytic rules and 13 hunting queries that can be used for detection and hunting in Sentinel.

Severity	Name	Rule type	Data sources	Tactics	Techniques	Source name
Medium	IN USE Malicious BEC Inbox Rule	Scheduled	Microsoft 365 (formerly, Offic...	Persistence +1 ⓘ	T1098 +1 ⓘ	Business Email Compromise - Financial Fraud
Medium	Suspicious access of BEC related documents in AWS S3 buc...	Scheduled	Amazon Web Services	Collection	T1530	Business Email Compromise - Financial Fraud
Medium	Account Elevated to New Role	Scheduled	Azure Active Directory	Persistence	T1078	Business Email Compromise - Financial Fraud
Low	User Added to Admin Role	Scheduled	Azure Active Directory	Privilege Escalation	T1078	Business Email Compromise - Financial Fraud
Medium	Suspicious access of BEC related documents	Scheduled		Collection	T1530	Business Email Compromise - Financial Fraud
Medium	IN USE Privileged Account Permissions Changed	Scheduled	Azure Active Directory +1 ⓘ	Privilege Escalation	T1078	Business Email Compromise - Financial Fraud
High	IN USE Authentication Method Changed for Privileged Ac...	Scheduled	Azure Active Directory +1 ⓘ	Persistence	T1098	Business Email Compromise - Financial Fraud

Figure 5.12 – Sentinel BEC solution analytic rules

In *Figure 5.13*, there is a fusion incident that correlates Defender XDR signals with UEBA based on an entity, and it contains alerts from MDA, MDO, MDE, EIDP, as well as Sentinel, where BEC solution content (i.e., Sentinel analytic rules) has been leveraged.

Preview: Possible multistage attack activities detected by Fusion
Incident ID 3334

○ Refresh   🗑 Delete incident | ◉ Logs   📋 Tasks (Preview)   🗂 Activity log

ⓘ This is the new, improved incident page - **Now generally available**. You can use the toggle to switch back.

| High
Severity | ○ Active
Status | 👤 Unassigned
Owner | « |

Investigate in Microsoft Defender for Cloud Apps ☑

Workspace name
fetasentinel

Description
This Fusion incident triggered by our machine learning model correlates anomalous signals and suspicious activities that are potentially associated with multistage attacks on User: diegos@m3t............onmicrosoft.com and on IP: S............... We recommend that you investigate all alerts and/or anomalies included in this incident to understand the full chain of attack and take immediate actions to remediate.
Some alerts in this Fusion incident are converted from anomalies. You can view details in the Anomalies table using the following query: View anomalies in Log Analytics

Overview   Entities

Incident timeline

🔍 Search   🔽 Add filter

Sep 24
18:00:50   **UEBA Anomalous Failed Sign-in**
Informatio...   Detected by Microsoft Senti...   Tacti...   ...

Sep 24
16:23:31   **Suspicious inbox manipulation rule**
High   Detected by Microsoft 365 Defender   Tactics: ...

Sep 24
16:22:38   **Creation of forwarding/redirect rule**
Informa...   Detected by Microsoft Defender ...   Tac...   ...

Sep 24
16:20:58   **Suspicious inbox manipulation rule**
Hi...   Detected by Microsoft Defender for Cl...   Tact...   ...

Figure 5.13 – A Sentinel Fusion incident

A possible BEC attack is seen in both in Microsoft Defender XDR and Microsoft Sentinel as a multi-stage incident (or a Fusion incident) even Defender XDR's automatic attack disruption haven't detected and stopped the attack in this example incident. Keep in mind that it jumps into action only in attacks with high confidence. *Figure 5.14* contains an example Defender XDR multi-stage incident attack graph.

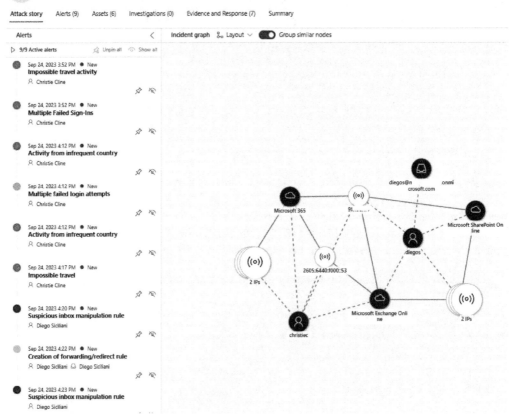

Figure 5.14 – Defender XDR – a possible BEC attack graph

Mitigations

Every organization wants to prevent a possible BEC attack before it occurs. To be able to prevent a BEC attack, it is recommended to follow the following security best practices:

- Consider having Microsoft Defender XDR solutions deployed to get signals from endpoints, identities, email, and data, as well as from cloud applications, as shown in *Figure 5.15*.

- Ensure policies are configured, and follow Microsoft best practices in MDO and MDA.

- Configure Microsoft Defender XDR's automatic attack disruption to be able to detect and automatically do mitigations.

- Configure Microsoft Sentinel's multi-stage attack detection (Fusion) and verify that it is enabled.

- Configure a Microsoft Sentinel/BEC/financial fraud content hub solution.

Figure 5.15 – Signals that were used to identify a real-world BEC attack

- Configure priority account protection for priority users, such as company executives and the VIP Users watchlist at Microsoft Sentinel.

- If your organization does not use **Microsoft Defender for Office 365**, verify that your email provides advanced phishing protection, business email compromise detection, internal email protection, and account compromise detection. We highly recommend using MDO to take advantage of its multi-layered email filtering stack with advanced tooling, protecting organizations against phishing attacks.

- In addition to email security policies, implement **DMARC** and **DKIM** to verify the sender's domain and prevent spoofing.

- Use Microsoft Entra ID's **Conditional Access (CA)** to require strong authentication from end users (MFA, and phishing-resistant MFA when possible):

  - Use **Continuous Access Evaluation (CAE)**, which revokes access in real time when changes in user conditions trigger risks, such as when a user's account is terminated, or the user moves to an untrusted location:

    - Verify that LOB and SaaS applications as well as used clients support CAE

    - Verify that CAE isn't disabled by CA policies

  - If custom CA policies aren't an option, leverage Microsoft-managed policies (licensed) or security defaults (free) to strengthen your identity posture

- Use Microsoft Entra ID Protection together with CA risk-based policies.

- Leverage user awareness and training – for example, Microsoft Defender XDR's Attack Simulator.

More information about BEC attacks and up-to-date threat intelligence from the Microsoft security blog is available here: `https://packt.link/QZm8F`.

Human-Operated Ransomware

The next popular attack scenario we will take a closer look at is ransomware attacks. Ransomware attacks have become one of the biggest security challenges for organizations today, and if successful, they can be costly to recover from. In the worst-case scenario, an entire environment needs to build from scratch.

Let's look at ransomware description.

A type of cyberattack known as ransomware, which is dangerous and encrypts or destroys files and folders, prevents the owner of the targeted device from accessing their data. The adversary then takes advantage of this situation by holding the company owner ransom for a decryption key to open the encrypted data. It is crucial to remember that, even in the event that money is paid, there is no guarantee that the hackers would uphold their half of the agreement and supply the key required to grant the business owner access again.

Ransomware attacks carried out by humans are more sophisticated and precise than conventional ransomware attacks. These targeted attacks, which are carried out by human attackers, make use of extensive understanding of typical system and security misconfigurations. Human-operated ransomware is persistent; it keeps changing to avoid being identified by anti-malware programs. Its adaptability allows it to live on the margins of an organization, ready to be unleashed when the moment is right.

Even though attacks are usually automated, "human-operated ransomware attacks" have increased in the past few years. In this scenario, it's a result of an active attack where an adversary deploys ransomware on critical data.

Attack description

As we can see from *Figure 5.16*, the typical human-operated ransomware attack has three phases:

- **Enter the environment**: The first phase is to get access to the environment, and different methods can be used here, such as different types of client attacks for data center-focused attacks. An alternative option is to buy access to target an organization from dark markets.

- **Traverse and spread**: In the second phase, the adversary gains a foothold in the environment and targets to gain administrative access on the environment.

- **Execute the objectives**: In the third phase, the focus is on causing business disruption by stealing data, encrypting (i.e., locking up) data, sabotage backup/recovery possibilities, and demanding money from the target organization.

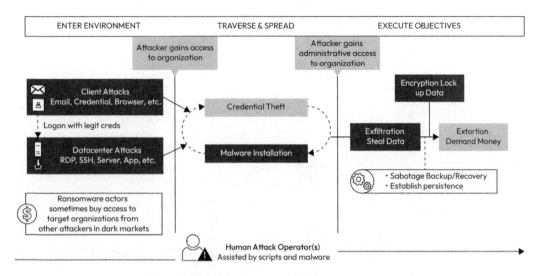

Figure 5.16 – A human-operated ransomware attack pattern

If you would like to test detection capabilities of possible ransomware attacks in your test environment, you can download ransomware files from GitHub (https://packt.link/wlF1A) to a device that is protected with Defender for Endpoint or another EDR+AV endpoint solution. This repository contains actual malware and ransomware, so do not execute any of these files on your PC unless you know exactly what you are doing.

An alternative approach is to use a ransomware simulator, provided my knowbe4 (https://packt.link/niGQa), which offers 24 ransomware scenarios and 1 crypto mining scenario to test.

Detections

The XDR stack is good at detecting threats, and Microsoft Sentinel complements them by providing additional capabilities. In *Figure 5.17*, you can see an example ransomware incident in Defender XDR. The incident contains a wide range of information that is helpful during an investigation, such as attack story, alerts, assets, investigations, evidence and response, and a summary.

In this example incident, you can also see that mitigations have already started (the device is isolated). Typically, SOC organizations have investigation playbooks that are followed during the incident response process. Even though playbooks would also be available, the highlighted section (on the bottom right) could bring additional value for an investigation in this type of attack. The available content is as follows:

- Ransomware playbook guidance by Microsoft
- A human-operated ransomware threat overview report

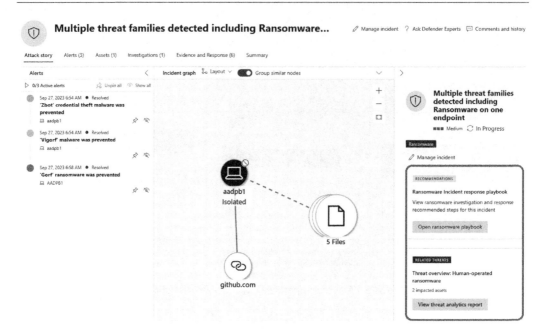

Figure 5.17 – Human-operated ransomware attack detection in Defender XDR

The same example incident overview page (entering by clicking – **View full details in the incident queue**) in Microsoft Sentinel is shown in *Figure 5.18*. Typically, an investigation starts from Sentinel, which summarizes the incident information and shows a timeline, entities, and similar incidents or top insights (UEBA), to name just a few features.

If you want to focus more on certain areas of an incident, you can add or remove alerts to and from the incidents. This feature brings additional flexibility to the investigation process and can also be automated (with Azure Logic Apps), based on the conditions.

In *Figure 5.18*, there are two sections highlighted. The Microsoft Defender XDR portal link in the top-left corner provides incident response for this example incident. Clicking the link will take you to the incident page in the portal. This could bring additional value in some scenarios – for example, if your organization does not ingest Microsoft Defender XDR solution raw data into Sentinel, you might want to finalize the investigation in the Defender XDR portal.

Another example is similar incidents. This feature can be useful if you want to focus on the bigger picture and would like to know whether there are any similar activities to the incident you are investigating. Identifying similar incidents relies on three key criteria: similar entities, rules triggered, and alert details.

Figure 5.18 – The ransomware incident investigation page in Sentinel

A HumOR attack is part of Microsoft Defender XDR threat analytics and is available for Microsoft Defender for Endpoint, as well as Microsoft Defender for Office 365 license holders. Here is a link to the threat analytics report in the portal: `https://packt.link/Sp1N2`.

The threat overview report provides information about the attack and additional information, such as related incidents as a combined view, impacted assets, endpoint exposure, and recommended actions to prevent similar incidents occurring in the future, as shown in *Figure 5.19*.

Threats > Threat overview: Human-operated ransomware

ⓘ Threat actor names are being updated in stages to align with the new Microsoft weather-themed naming taxonomy. Read How Microsoft names threat actors, for details.

Overview   Analyst report   Related incidents   Impacted assets   Endpoints exposure   **Recommended actions**

Perform these actions to address this threat and improve your overall posture. For a broader assessment and more recommended actions, view your secure score.

↓ Export

	Rank	Recommended action	Score impact	Points achieved	Status	Regressed	Have license?	Category	Product
☐	4	Ensure multifactor authentication is enabled for all users in administrative roles	+0.76%	0/10	◯ To address	Yes	Yes	Identity	Azure Active Directory
☐	5	Block executable files from running unless they meet a prevalence, age, or trust	+0.68%	0/9	◯ To address	No	Yes	Device	Defender for Endpoint
☐	6	Block Adobe Reader from creating child processes	+0.68%	0/9	◯ To address	No	Yes	Device	Defender for Endpoint
☐	7	Block credential stealing from the Windows local security authority subsystem	+0.68%	0/9	◯ To address	No	Yes	Device	Defender for Endpoint
☐	8	Block persistence through WMI event subscription	+0.68%	0/9	◯ To address	No	Yes	Device	Defender for Endpoint

Figure 5.19 – Human-operated ransomware threat overview report recommendations

Mitigations

The Defender threat analytics report states the following:

> *"While ransomware attacks have continued steadily and with increased impact, the attack techniques attackers use have not changed much over the years. A renewed focus on prevention is needed. Hardening against common threats can also help reduce alert volume and stop many attackers before they get access to networks."*

To prevent a ransomware attack in your organization, you need to build your defenses to protect multiple areas. If all the recommendations, or even the most critical ones, are implemented, an organization can protect itself not only from ransomware but also a wider range of attacks. Maybe the most important key takeaway from the Microsoft threat analytics report is that attackers need credentials to succeed in their ransomware attacks.

According to Microsoft's Threat Analytics report, this type of attack involves attackers compromising either domain administrator accounts or local administrator accounts on all machines throughout the network.

That being said, mitigation and prevention can be divided into the following most relevant sections (these are also seen in *Figure 5.19*). The list contains only some of the recommendations, and the full list for prevention activities is available at `https://packt.link/aRNU5` and `https://packt.link/aLA8h`.

The following are ways to prevent adversaries from entering an environment:

- **Enhance environment security posture and pay attention to remote access**:

  - It's crucial to enhance an environment security posture by securing Azure, multi-cloud, or hybrid environment workloads to prevent initial access from adversaries

  - Pay attention to user/device validation in an authentication process with Microsoft Entra ID CA policies, and deploy a VPN solution to protect remote connections if needed

  - Use cloud intelligence and solutions to protect and publish applications

  - Secure administrative connections to Azure resources (Azure Bastion or Entra Private Access are good candidates)

- **Collaborative workloads**:

  - Implement a modern email security solution (such as MDO) with proper security policies to a whole environment

  - Use **Attack Surface Reduction** (**ASR**) rules to block common attack techniques

- **Endpoints**:

  - Provide modern endpoint protection for all platforms.

  - Use ASR rules to block known threats, configure tamper protection, and enable "Block at first sight" in MDE.

  - Verify that network protection is enabled in your organization.

  - Adopt Windows Defender Application Control progressively, as it can help reduce security risks by limiting the apps that users can run and the code that runs in the kernel. It can also block unsigned scripts and **MS Installers** (**MSIs**), forcing Windows PowerShell to run in restricted mode.

  - Consider using web content filtering if you don't have a third-party solution in place that would do the same.

  - Apply security baselines to harden internet-facing workloads.

  - Pay attention to vulnerability management, keep software up to date, and fix vulnerable systems and protocols (i.e., isolate, disable, and retire).

    - Prioritize on-premises Active Directory updates (as soon as possible in phases)

  - Enforce device compliance (including a machine risk score) in CA policies.

  - Restrict access from BYOD devices with Intune MAM/MDM or an MDA session proxy.

- **Identities**:

  - Configure Microsoft Entra CA policies, and use strong authentication methods or passwordless sign-in for all users

  - Protect on-premises identities with cloud-powered intelligence, such as with Defender for Identity and Entra ID Password Protection

  - Use **Local Administrator Password Solution** (**LAPS**) or a similar solution to prevent lateral movement, using local accounts with shared passwords

The following are ways to prevent adversaries from escalating privileges:

- **A privileged access strategy**:

  - Enforce end-to-end security for admin portals using CA.

  - Deploy an XDR solution to protect and detect escalation attacks against identity systems:

    - XDR will also be able to detect and mitigate lateral traversal with compromised devices

  - It's important to protect admin accounts and prevent standing access to the environments. PIM that is time-based can be used to eliminate permanent access to Microsoft Entra ID and Azure resources:

    - Use **privileged access management** (**PAM**) to limit access to sensitive data or critical configuration settings

    - Consider using Entra ID authentication context, and enforce controls when activating privileged roles

- **Detection and response**:

  - With Microsoft's unified XDR and SIEM solutions, an organization gains visibility into an environment and can automatically stop a high-confidence attack, with Defender XDR's automatic attack disruption feature (when fully deployed)

  - Deploy Defender CSPM to gain valuable insights into your cloud security posture. Utilize attack path analysis, the cloud security explorer, and the ransomware dashboard workbook to pinpoint potential weak configurations and vulnerable resources, proactively mitigating security risks

  - Leverage MDA ransomware detection capabilities with automatic mitigation, out of the box policies, malware detection and potential ransomware activity.

  - Leverage Defender XDR's threat analytics reports to gain a deep insight of attack patterns, related incidents, impacted assets, endpoint exposure, and recommended actions

  - If you face a ransomware attack, follow the best practices on how to address containment, eradication, and how to recover from the attack

The following are ways to protect critical data:

- Identify the most critical system and perform regular backups. According to Microsoft threat analytics, analyze the five most important applications, which often fall into the following categories:

  - Identity systems

  - Human life

  - Financial systems

  - Product or service enablement

  - Security

- Besides taking backups, it's important to protect backups from sabotage.

- Do disaster recovery fire drills to test processes and backups properly. We have seen too many situations in the past where backups don't work when they are needed most.

- Data protection can be established by migrating data to cloud solutions, such as OneDrive and SharePoint, and leverage versioning and recycle bin capabilities.

- With controlled folder access (provided by MDE), valuable data can be protected from malicious apps and threats.

The following awareness training can help us prevent HumOR attacks:

- Last but not least, as stated earlier, attackers needs credentials to execute attacks, and that's why awareness training is important. With awareness training, end users get more information about real-world attacks and don't fall into traps too easily:

  - Options from Microsoft Defender XDR are attack simulation training or training campaigns

We strongly recommend that you read the Microsoft Learn page at `https://packt.link/HWZ6i` to learn more about how Microsoft Defender XDR can help detect human-operated ransomware.

> **Important**
> Early intervention prevents attackers from gaining a foothold and launching more disruptive attacks and cutting off attackers' access to credentials and network-connected devices cripples their ability to spread and buys precious time for SOC teams to neutralize the threat.

To recap, let's delve into the key takeaways from the attacks we explored in this chapter (see *Table 5.1*).

Attack	Detection - XDR-correlated alerts	Attack classification & compromised asset discovery	Disruption – Trigger automatic response
Supply Chain Attack	Delegated access related alerts in MDC. Suspicious Run Command invocation detected in MDC. Credentials to an OAuth app in XDR. Unusual ISP for an OAuth app in XDR. Suspicious Addition of an Exchange-related app. Azure VM Run Command related detections in Sentinel. Azure Portal Sign-in from another Azure Tenant.	Compromised user on CSP/MSSP side. Suspicious admin activities on customer environment	In general, automatic response depends on MSSP/CSP environment detection capabilities because initial attack happens on MSSP side.
BEC Attack	MFA Fatigue. Unfamiliar sign-in (Entra ID Protection alerts). Mailbox search for interesting mail threads. Creation of Inbox and forwarding rules. Sending emails with hijacking mail thread. Deleting sent mails from Sent folder.	Fraud attempt. Domain Spoofing. Domain Impersonation. Compromised user Compromised mailbox.	Automatic attack disruption acts as a guardian, identifying and stopping attacks swiftly by disabling compromised accounts. This prevents attackers from sending fraudulent emails and causing financial harm.
Human-Operated Ransomware Attack	There are many alerts that can be sign of a ransomware attack (here are few examples). Identity related detections: Password spray, numerous failed attempts, attempts to log on to multiple devices in a short period, multiple first-time logons, recently active user account. On-premises identity related detections raised by MDI. Phishing related detections raised by MDO. Malicious apps related detections raised by MDA or Application Governance. Endpoint related detections raised by MDE. IoT related detection raised by MDE.	Advanced aggregation and automated analysis of malicious activities like tampering, backup deletion, credential theft, lateral movement + more. Decodes the chain of attacks by tracing the malicious activity on devices back to its remote execution tactics, techniques, and procedures (TTPs).	Suspend/disable the compromised user account in Active Directory and Entra ID. Revoke any active sessions used by compromised account on protected devices. Contain device action involves the automatic containment of a suspicious device to block any incoming/outgoing communication to/from affected device.

Table 5.1 – Summary of all the three attacks discussed in this chapter

A case study analysis

As highlighted in the *Case Study* chapter, *High Tech Rapid Solutions* faced a BEC attack six months ago. One of the main reasons it was successful from an attacker point of view was security infrastructure consisting of disparate products that operate in isolation, resulting in limited visibility, fragmented threat intelligence, and inefficient incident response capabilities.

By implementing Microsoft's unified XDR and SIEM solutions, the company could address this security challenge. By utilizing Defender XDR and its security solutions, they would receive additional protection against a potential BEC attack in the future.

As with many known cyberattacks, a BEC attack usually starts with some form of phishing (reconnaissance first to get insights from a company), and the adversary tries to gain access (credentials) to the environment, as shown in *Figure 5.20*.

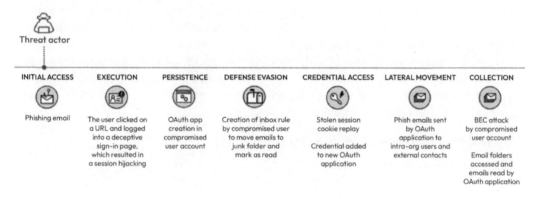

Figure 5.20 – A phishing email attack chain

For protection, a company should leverage Microsoft Defender XDR's automatic attack disruption, which adds enhanced protection against a BEC attack. To get the best possible coverage, they should deploy the whole Microsoft Defender XDR stack (MDE, MDO, MDI, and MDA), as highlighted in the *Microsoft Defender XDR's automatic attack disruption* section in this chapter.

A company should deploy Microsoft Defender XDR's deception capability in MDE, which we covered in the *Deception capability in Microsoft Defender XDR* section. By leveraging this feature, the company can detect possible attacks using lateral movement in the early stages.

Also, the company needs to verify that Office 365 has email filtering settings to ensure they block spoofed emails (spoofing protection), spam, and emails with malware, and they also need to verify that Defender for Office 365 (MDO) policies are properly configured to protect against BEC attacks.

They should also deploy Microsoft Entra ID Protection with auto-remediation configured to protect identities. Entra ID Protection can bring additional value because it also receives signals in some use cases from **Defender for Cloud Apps**. This will especially add enhanced protection in a BEC case.

By using auto-remediation (configured through Entra ID CA) end users can remediate possible risks themselves through MFA (a sign-in risk) or by a password change (a user risk). One consideration to add is requiring and configuring sign-in frequency in CA (re-authentication on every sign-in, or using hours or days as a parameter).

The latter methods has been challenging for hybrid users because if password change was initiated on-premises, **Microsoft Entra ID Protection** wouldn't have a clue about it and the risk wouldn't be auto-remediated. In September 2023, Microsoft announced a new capability (in preview at the time of writing) that allows user risk to be remediated when a password change is initiated on-premises.

In addition, Microsoft Sentinel acts as a BEC/financial fraud solution in a content hub that brings additional protection to this area if an organization wants to leverage Sentinel built-in content, instead of building detection rules on its own. At the time of writing, the solution contains several analytic rules and hunting queries that can be used to detect BEC attack-related activities. Sentinel has a built-in capability that leverages AI and ML mechanisms to detect multi-stage and fusion incidents. These enhanced capabilities, together with content hub solutions such as BEC, complement XDR detections and provides value to a company. Apart from detection, the company needs to have a strong focus on the mitigations and recommendations discussed throughout this chapter. We couldn't emphasize more how important a strong security posture is to prevent attacks. According to Microsoft's 2023 **Digital Defense Report** (MDDR), by applying minimum-security standards, it is possible to protect against over 99 percent of attacks. These are as follows:

- Enabling MFA (preferably phishing-resistant)
- Applying zero trust principles
- Using XDR and an antimalware solution
- Patching your workloads
- Protecting data

The same report highlights the good news about ransomware attacks. For organizations with a strong security posture, the likelihood of an attack succeeding is very low. Typically, an attack is stopped in the pre-ransom phase, with, on average, 2 percent of attacks progressing to a successful ransomware deployment.

Summary

In this chapter, we discussed three different attack scenarios that have increased worldwide in recent years. We have also seen how Microsoft unified XDR and SIEM solution can detect these attacks at a high level, providing recommendations to organizations on how to prevent them in the future. Attackers and defenders are constantly engaged in a game of cat and mouse, and attacks are constantly evolving. This means that organizations need to continuously develop their security monitoring strategies and approaches, detection techniques as well as enhance environment security posture to effectively defend the environment.

In the next chapter, we will discuss why it is important to fix misconfigurations and vulnerabilities, and how Microsoft's unified XDR and SIEM solution can help your organization do just that.

Further reading

For more information about the topics covered in this chapter, please refer to the following links:

- Configure automatic attack disruption capabilities in Microsoft Defender XDR | Microsoft Learn: `https://packt.link/8MfXR`

- Manage Microsoft-certified solution provider partner relationships | Microsoft Learn: `https://packt.link/IPUay`

- MSSP Access to Azure Sentinel and Defender XDR – Securing and Auditing: `https://packt.link/QmjQi`

- Detect Changes in Azure Lighthouse Permission Delegations: `https://packt.link/oIhym`

- Fortifying Your Defenses: How Microsoft Sentinel Safeguards Your Organization from BEC Attacks: Microsoft Community Hub: `https://packt.link/GaIK8`

- Stop BEC attacks with Microsoft's XDR: `https://packt.link/N8Myk`

- Advanced multistage attack detection in Microsoft Sentinel | Microsoft Learn: `https://packt.link/1op74`

- Configure multistage attack detection (Fusion) rules in Microsoft Sentinel | Microsoft Learn: `https://packt.link/OXy0G`

- Fortifying Your Defenses: How Microsoft Sentinel Safeguards Your Organization from BEC Attacks: Microsoft Community Hub: `https://packt.link/utUGZ`

- Detecting human-operated ransomware attacks with Microsoft Defender XDR | Microsoft Learn: `https://packt.link/svoWT`

- Responding to ransomware attacks | Microsoft Learn: `https://packt.link/TCe5g`

- 100+ Ransomware Attack Statistics 2023: Trends & Cost (getastra.com): `https://packt.link/ks6gg`

- Ransomware incident response playbook framework: `https://packt.link/xxmeO`

- Microsoft Digital Defense Report 2023: `https://packt.link/joTwA`

- Securing devices as part of the privileged access story: `https://packt.link/PdoKd`

6

Security Misconfigurations and Vulnerability Management

In this chapter, our initial focus will be on understanding security misconfigurations and vulnerabilities, exploring their implications for security incidents, and delving into the **vulnerability management framework**.

Subsequently, we will examine how Microsoft's unified XDR and SIEM solution can effectively tackle these challenges. Additionally, we will explore key considerations and the seamless integration of this solution with other tools.

In a nutshell, we will cover the following main topics:

- Introduction to security misconfigurations and vulnerabilities
- Vulnerability management framework
- How Microsoft's unified XDR and SIEM solution can help address these challenges
- Integration with other tools
- Case study analysis

Introduction to security misconfigurations and vulnerabilities

Misconfigurations and vulnerabilities are the biggest culprits that contribute to security incidents (see *Figure 6.1*). It's critical for any organization to monitor these issues and remediate them quickly as they are potential weaknesses that can be exploited by attackers. To mitigate both security misconfigurations and vulnerabilities, it is essential to regularly assess security, apply patches, configure systems securely, and follow best practices in setting up systems and networks. Both security misconfigurations and vulnerabilities can make systems and data vulnerable to attack. However, attackers often find it easier to exploit security misconfigurations because they do not require the attacker to have any knowledge of the underlying software.

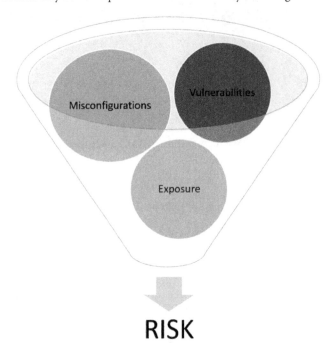

Figure 6.1 – Contributions to security risk

Security misconfigurations

A security misconfiguration is a weakness in a system or application that results from improper or incomplete security settings. This can include default settings that are not changed, open ports, improperly configured access controls, and unnecessary services running. Security misconfigurations can create security gaps that attackers can exploit to gain unauthorized access to systems and data. Security misconfigurations can arise from a variety of issues, such as human error, excess or unnecessary privileges, outdated software, unsupported systems, improper versioning, leaving out-of-the-box settings, inadequate security policies, lack of automation, and insecure services.

Finding and fixing security misconfigurations should always be a top cybersecurity priority. This is an ongoing process that can be automated. Security misconfigurations often create vulnerabilities, which are weaknesses in software or systems that can be exploited by attackers. For example, failing to update software and patch known security issues can create vulnerabilities. However, not all vulnerabilities are caused by misconfigurations; some are inherent to the software or system design.

Even if an organization has secured its endpoints, it must still regularly audit security controls and configurations to identify configuration drift. Organizations rapidly changing their digital estates to support their business needs, adopting new tools, applying patches, and so on, all of which can contribute to misconfigurations.

Vulnerabilities

Vulnerabilities are weaknesses in software, hardware, networks, or systems that attackers can exploit. They can be caused by coding errors, design flaws, or other problems in the technology itself. If exploited, these weaknesses can lead to security breaches or compromise the system's integrity, confidentiality, or availability.

Software and hardware vendors, as well as security researchers, are constantly working to identify, report, and fix vulnerabilities. Vulnerabilities are classified based on their impact, exploitability, and severity. Addressing vulnerabilities is essential for maintaining a secure environment and preventing potential security breaches.

> **Note**
> Security misconfigurations are mistakes made by humans when configuring software, hardware, or networks, while security vulnerabilities are weaknesses in the software itself.

Vulnerability management framework

Let us first understand what vulnerability management is and why we need a process to handle this.

Every organization should have a vulnerability management team and process in place. This process should be continuous, not only to detect risks and issues in the network but also to create a plan to prevent those vulnerabilities from causing future damage. Ideally, a good vulnerability management system combines technology and security experts to proactively detect and respond to security risks. The goal of vulnerability management is to find and fix known security weaknesses and to assess how well your IT organization can apply security patches within a set time limit.

Effective vulnerability management helps to improve your company's cybersecurity, reduce the risk of costly and damaging data breaches, and ensure compliance with security requirements and regulations. Unfortunately, most organizations, if not all, are failing to meet this standard. Therefore, it is important to adopt the right tool to address these challenges. In the next section of this chapter, we will discuss in detail how Microsoft's unified XDR and SIEM platform can help organizations in this area.

> **Note**
>
> Vulnerabilities extend beyond technology. Vulnerabilities can also stem from human behavior within the organization. We must consider the human element when addressing vulnerabilities.

We strongly recommend organizations perform a **vulnerability risk management assessment** and define a **vulnerability management strategy**, as discussed in *Chapter 8*.

Figure 6.2 – Vulnerability management framework

The specific steps involved in vulnerability management can vary depending on the framework an organization adopts, but here is a common vulnerability management framework (see *Figure 6.2*):

- **Discover**: The first and most important step in the vulnerability management process is to find all the potential vulnerabilities that may exist across your digital assets. This is usually done by using vulnerability scanners, which periodically scan all of your assets, such as endpoints, servers, firewalls, IoT devices, databases, cloud assets, on-premises assets, and containers (pretty much everything, depending on the type of scanners you install and configure). These scanners typically report the potential vulnerabilities with recommendations back to the portal such as Microsoft Defender XDR, which provides insights into the vulnerabilities.

- **Assess**: The assessment stage is another crucial step in vulnerability management, involving a comprehensive evaluation of discovered vulnerabilities. Few organizations combine this stage with the prioritization stage. This stage ensures that every device is secured with accuracy and efficiency. Relying on data from unreliable sources can lead to wasted time and resources due to false positives. Automated scans may not detect all vulnerabilities, so manual assessments by security experts are often necessary. Manual assessments involve in-depth analysis and may uncover vulnerabilities that are linked to other vulnerabilities. Remember that vulnerabilities extend beyond technology and exist within an organization's human element as well.

Assessing an organization's security posture is crucial for comprehending the current threat landscape, making informed decisions about vulnerability mitigation, and ultimately enhancing an organization's overall security posture. As discussed in *Chapter 8*, regular assessments are essential due to the ever-evolving nature of technology and cyber threats.

- **Prioritize**: Categorizing and prioritizing vulnerabilities is another essential and challenging phase of vulnerability management. The vulnerability management team must work with other stakeholders, such as business users, application owners, vendors, and other internal teams, to do this effectively. There are many factors to consider when prioritizing vulnerabilities, such as the potential business impact, severity, **Common Vulnerability Scoring System** (**CVSS**) score, asset exposure, threat context, organization goals, and risk tolerance.

Note

The CVSS score ranges from 0.0 to 10.0. Use the CVSS Version 4.0 Calculator to calculate the CVSS score (`https://packt.link/7gJC2`). The **National Vulnerability Database** (**NVD**) (`https://packt.link/nkBTV`) adds a severity rating for CVSS scores.

- **Remediate**: This stage usually has three core actions (remediate, mitigate, and accept risk), one of which is applied depending on the type of vulnerability you are dealing with and considering other factors at your organization level:

  - **Remediate**: Vulnerability remediation involves taking steps to fix the vulnerability, such as applying patches, closing vulnerable ports, or implementing a detailed process exception. Once organizations have prioritized risks and fully understand the vulnerabilities, they typically fix the flaws. This is generally the best course of action whenever possible, especially if the vulnerability is considered high-risk or affects a critical system or asset. Controls should be in place to ensure successful remediation, and progress should be documented.

  - **Mitigate**: In some cases, it may not be possible to fully remediate a vulnerability. In these cases, organizations may choose to mitigate the vulnerability instead. Mitigation involves implementing compensating controls to make it more difficult or even impossible for an attacker to exploit the vulnerability. These controls should be temporary and do not eliminate the vulnerability itself. However, they can provide organizations with time to develop a permanent solution and protect their systems in the meantime.

  - **Accept risk**: In cases where the likelihood of a vulnerability being exploited is very low, or where the cost of fixing the vulnerability is significantly higher than the potential damage caused by an exploit, an organization may choose to accept the risk and not take any action to address the vulnerability. This approach is particularly common for non-critical assets.

- **Verify**: After implementing mitigations, it is essential to verify their effectiveness. This may involve rescanning systems to confirm that vulnerabilities have been successfully addressed. This means not only verifying but also maintaining accountability and transparency across the organization.

- **Report**: Reporting is crucial throughout the entire vulnerability management process. This entails documenting findings, actions taken, and any lingering risks. Continuous monitoring is also essential to identify new vulnerabilities that may arise over time. Security teams can use this reporting to track vulnerability trends over time, provide risk reduction updates to management, and maintain compliance. Ideal solutions will integrate with IT ticketing systems and patch management to expedite information sharing between teams.

How can Microsoft's unified solution help to address this?

Now let's see how Microsoft's unified XDR and SIEM solution helps to deal with these misconfigurations and vulnerabilities.

This solution will address some of the common challenges organizations face without any additional vulnerability management tools, such as the following:

- How do I know which devices are compliant?

- How do I identify the misconfigurations in place and what are the recommendations?

- Which devices are vulnerable and how do I see the list based on the CVE?

- How do I get insights on the device exposure and how do I fix that?

- How can I monitor these activities continuously and automate most of them to eliminate manual work?

- What are the weaknesses that exist across my onboarded endpoints?

Microsoft Defender Vulnerability Management

First, let's start with **Microsoft Defender Vulnerability Management** (**MDVM**), which is deeply integrated into Microsoft Defender XDR (formerly Microsoft 365 Defender). It starts collecting the data from the moment you deploy a **Microsoft Defender for Endpoint** (**MDE**) agent as no special agent is needed. Depending on the type of license you have, the MDVM add-on and standalone options are available to start with the trail.

MDVM provides comprehensive visibility into your organization's assets, enabling you to identify, assess, and prioritize vulnerabilities across a wide range of devices, including Windows, macOS, Linux, Android, iOS, and network devices. By leveraging Microsoft's extensive threat intelligence, breach likelihood predictions, business context insights, and device assessments, MDVM rapidly and continuously prioritizes the most critical vulnerabilities on your most valuable assets, providing actionable security recommendations to mitigate risk and protect your organization (see *Figure 6.3*).

Figure 6.3 – MDVM's core features

MDVM's capabilities

MDVM's capabilities (see *Figure 6.3*) depend on the **operating system** (**OS**) and platform; refer to `https://packt.link/LryGE` to understand the capabilities per OS and platform.

Let's explore MDVM's capabilities:

- **Continuous asset discovery and monitoring**: Visibility is the cornerstone of any effective threat and vulnerability management solution. Without clear visibility, you can't effectively manage threats and vulnerabilities. As mentioned previously, MDVM works closely with MDE sensors without the need to deploy or configure another agent. Hence, this MDVM built-in and agentless scanner continuously monitors, collects, and reports the telemetry data to the Defender portal at `defender.microsoft.com` (formerly `security.microsoft.com`) from your devices in the organization even if the devices are not connected to the corporate network. This helps reduce the risk by identifying the vulnerabilities and misconfigurations.

  MDVM's continuous assets discovery and monitoring capability provides a comprehensive and consolidated inventory that provides a real-time, single-pane-of-glass view of your entire IT estates, such as applications, digital certificates, hardware, firmware, and even browser extensions for effortless monitoring and assessment.

  You can leverage the advanced vulnerability and configuration assessment tools available with MDVM, which helps you to understand and assess your cybersecurity exposure (the availability of these features depends on the type of licenses your organization has):

  - Security baseline assessment helps you to create a customized profile to assess and monitor your endpoints against industry-security benchmarks.

  - Visibility into software and vulnerabilities.

- Network share assessment helps you to identify internal network share vulnerabilities and provides actionable security recommendations.

- Authenticated scan for Windows helps you to regularly scan unmanaged Windows devices and also grants MDVM remote access to the devices.

- Threat analytics and event timelines. The event timeline helps you to understand fluctuations in the Secure Score and Exposure Score with the series of events that occurred.

- Browser extensions assessment helps you to identify the browser extensions installed across the organization with associated risk levels.

- Digital certificates assessment provides a list of digital certificates installed across your organization along with expiry dates and vulnerabilities or weaknesses related to these certifications.

- Hardware and firmware assessment provides insights into the hardware and firmware in your organization by system model, processor, and BIOS, along with the weaknesses, threat insights, and an exposed devices list.

- **Risk-based intelligent prioritization**: MDVM utilizes Microsoft's robust threat intelligence, business insights, breach predictions, and device assessments to promptly prioritize the most significant vulnerabilities within your organization. With a unified view of prioritized recommendations from various security feeds, alongside crucial details such as related CVEs and exposed devices, you can swiftly address the vulnerabilities posing the greatest risk to your most critical assets. If there is no official CVE-ID assigned to a vulnerability, the vulnerability name is assigned by MDVM.

  MDVM's risk-based intelligent prioritization capability prioritizes security recommendations by considering vulnerabilities that are currently being actively exploited in real-world scenarios and emerging threats posing the highest risk, keeping you ahead of the curve in safeguarding your systems.

  This capability also correlates vulnerability management and EDR data to pinpoint vulnerabilities being exploited in real-time attacks, allowing you to swiftly shut down breaches in progress for remediation and containment.

  Risk-based intelligent prioritization capability also helps to discover exposed devices harboring critical applications, confidential data, or high-value users, ensuring your most valuable assets are always under the strongest shield and remain consistently protected by the highest level of security.

- **Remediation and tracking**: MDVM reduces the cybersecurity risk by bridging the gap between security and IT teams to streamline workflows, prioritize, and conquer critical vulnerabilities and misconfigurations across your organization.

  Security and IT teams can work hand in hand with built-in workflows that streamline issue resolution. You can turn security recommendations into actionable tasks in Microsoft Intune with simple native integration and minimal effort.

Vulnerable applications for specific device groups can be blocked instantly to mitigate the risk.

Provides insights into other mitigations, such as configuration changes, to further reduce risk from software vulnerabilities.

Helps to track the progress and status of remediation efforts across your organization in real time.

The MDVM dashboard (see *Figure 6.4*) provides comprehensive insights, which is most important for security administrators and the security operations team, such as the Exposure Score, Secure Score, exposure distribution, top security recommendations, top remediation options, top events in the last seven days, and expiring certificates.

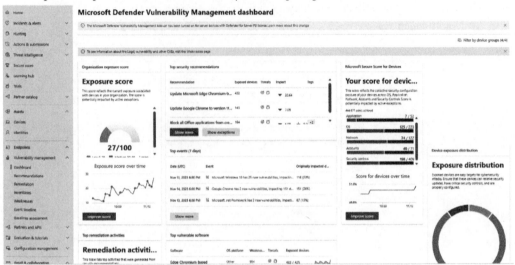

Figure 6.4 – MDVM dashboard

Tip

Boost efficiency and streamline vulnerability management by creating device groups for specific teams. This enables each team to focus on vulnerabilities relevant to their domain and responsibilities.

Exposure Score

The Exposure Score, which can be found on the MDVM dashboard (see *Figure 6.4*), plays a crucial role in evaluating your organization's vulnerabilities and understanding the current exposure of your devices to threats and vulnerabilities. Unlike the Secure Score, which will be discussed in *Chapter 7*, a low Exposure Score is favorable, indicating that your devices are less susceptible to attacks.

Gain insights into your organization's devices' exposure to threats and vulnerabilities through a comprehensive Exposure Score. Your score is determined by a combination of factors, including discovered device weaknesses, the severity of discovered vulnerabilities, the likelihood of your devices being compromised, the importance of these devices to your operations, and any relevant alerts associated with them. This Exposure Score is continuously calculated based on the telemetry data received by Defender sensors, and MDVM complements it with a set of recommendations prioritized based on the risk relative to your organization. The objective is to reduce your organization's Exposure Score by addressing the security configuration issues identified in the security recommendations. When you remediate these issues, it will enhance your overall security posture. Remember, your Exposure Score along with the Secure Score fluctuates based on the actions you consider under security recommendations.

Figure 6.5 – Exposure score on the MDVM dashboard

The Exposure Score is categorized into the following levels (see *Figure 6.5*):

- 0 –29: Low
- 30–69: Medium
- 70–100: High

The Exposure Score may fluctuate due to the release of new CVEs and security recommendations from Microsoft. The event timeline feature helps to track these changes and allows you to see what events caused your score to increase or decrease by hovering over the timeline within the MDVM dashboard.

While remediating vulnerabilities is essential, it does not guarantee complete protection, so it is crucial to stay vigilant against daily threats. Regularly monitoring your Exposure Score and promptly addressing vulnerabilities is crucial for maintaining a strong security posture. Once software weaknesses are identified, they are transformed into actionable recommendations and prioritized based on their potential impact on your organization's risk. The security recommendations page will display a prioritized list of actions, sorted by their potential impact on lowering your Exposure Score. Implementing these recommendations with high impact will significantly reduce your vulnerability to exploitation.

> **Note**
>
> Exposure Scores can be assessed by device groups, and the event timeline provides a clear picture of how different events are impacting the Exposure Score.

MDVM leverages its learning to deliver tailored insights based on the type of security recommendations, such as the following:

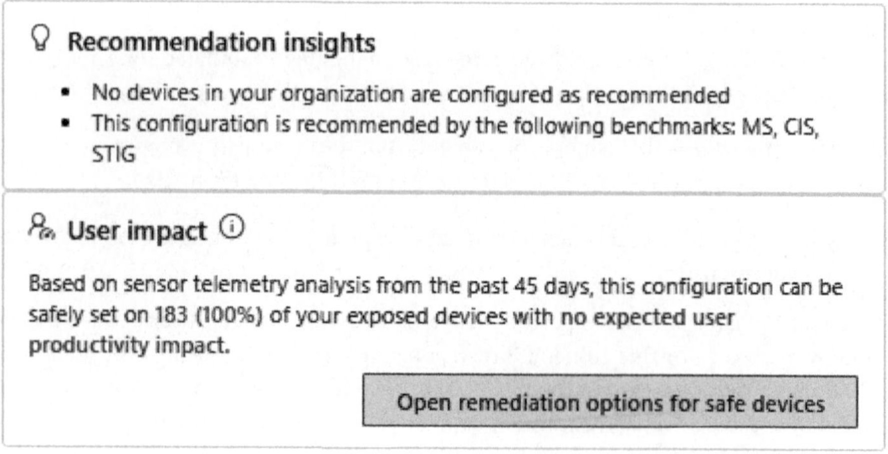

> ♡ **Recommendation insights**
>
> - No devices in your organization are configured as recommended
> - This configuration is recommended by the following benchmarks: MS, CIS, STIG
>
> 👥 **User impact** ⓘ
>
> Based on sensor telemetry analysis from the past 45 days, this configuration can be safely set on 183 (100%) of your exposed devices with no expected user productivity impact.
>
> [Open remediation options for safe devices]

Figure 6.6 – Sample insights from a specific security recommendation

Figure 6.6 illustrates a user impact insight derived from a recommended **Attack Surface Reduction (ASR)** rule security recommendation, based on telemetry data collected by Defender sensors.

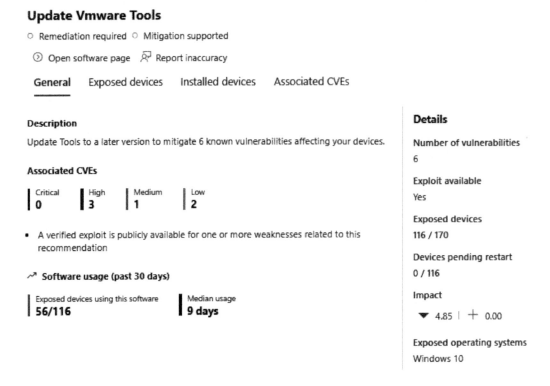

Update Vmware Tools

○ Remediation required   ○ Mitigation supported

ⓘ Open software page   ⚐ Report inaccuracy

General   Exposed devices   Installed devices   Associated CVEs

Description

Update Tools to a later version to mitigate 6 known vulnerabilities affecting your devices.

Associated CVEs

| Critical | High | Medium | Low |
| 0 | 3 | 1 | 2 |

• A verified exploit is publicly available for one or more weaknesses related to this recommendation

↗ **Software usage (past 30 days)**

| Exposed devices using this software | Median usage |
| **56/116** | **9 days** |

Details

Number of vulnerabilities

6

Exploit available

Yes

Exposed devices

116 / 170

Devices pending restart

0 / 116

Impact

▼ 4.85 | ＋ 0.00

Exposed operating systems

Windows 10

Figure 6.7 – Sample insights from a specific security recommendation

As illustrated in *Figure 6.7*, this security recommendation highlights outdated software versions that require updates, along with the number of exposed devices using those versions over the past 30 days.

There are many other valuable insights you can get from these security recommendations. Other important ones are breach insights (⟠) and threat insights (◎) (see *Figure 6.8*):

•   A highlighted breach insights (associated public exploits) icon indicates a vulnerability within your organization.

•   When the threat insights icon (possible active alerts) is highlighted, it alerts you to the presence of known exploits for this vulnerability in your organization. Mousing over the icon reveals additional information about the threat. This includes whether it is part of an exploit kit or linked to specific advanced persistent campaigns or activity groups and, if available, a link to a **threat analytics** report containing news, disclosures, or security advisories related to zero-day exploitations.

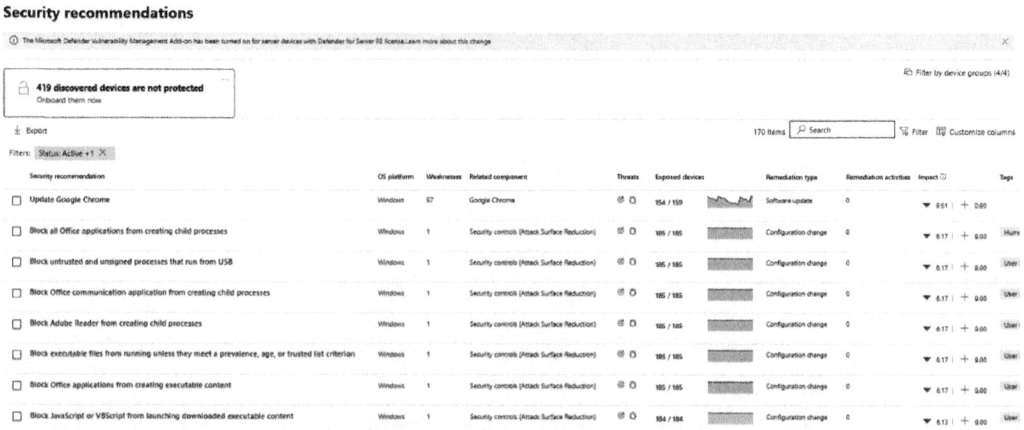

Security recommendations

Figure 6.8 – Security recommendations

The **Impact** column (see *Figure 6.8*) shows how much your Exposure Score and Security Score could improve by applying a recommended action. Focus on addressing vulnerabilities that will significantly reduce your Exposure Score and increase your Secure Score for devices. The potential reduction in your Exposure Score is displayed by a down arrow icon such as ▼ 6.17 and a projected increase to your Secure Score for devices is displayed with a plus icon such as ➕ 9.00.

Microsoft Defender for Cloud

Building on the capabilities discussed in *Chapter 3*, Microsoft unified XDR and SIEM Solution extends its vulnerability management to multi-cloud, hybrid cloud, and on-premises workloads such as servers, virtual machines, Kubernetes, containers, databases, APIs, app services, and DevOps. Microsoft Defender for Cloud provides a simple and fast deployment process for this comprehensive protection.

Defender for Cloud provides various vulnerability scanning options (see *Figure 6.9*), such as MDVM, which is natively integrated and uses MDE sensors in the background for telemetry data. You can choose to deploy the built-in Qualys vulnerability scanner, or you can **Bring Your Own License (BYOL)** and deploy a Qualys or Rapid7 vulnerability scanner you have licensed separately. At the time of writing, Qualys vulnerability scanning is still available in MDC, however its retiring soon in March 2024 and you can find more information at `https://packt.link/jAi3i` and `https://packt.link/j1cZe`.

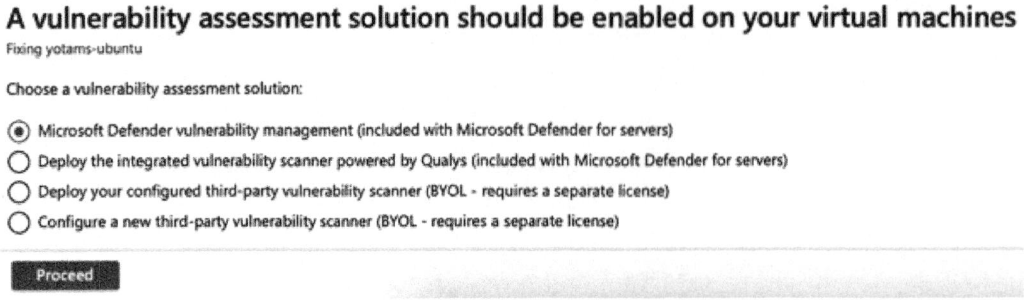

A vulnerability assessment solution should be enabled on your virtual machines

Fixing yotams-ubuntu

Choose a vulnerability assessment solution:

- (•) Microsoft Defender vulnerability management (included with Microsoft Defender for servers)
- ( ) Deploy the integrated vulnerability scanner powered by Qualys (included with Microsoft Defender for servers)
- ( ) Deploy your configured third-party vulnerability scanner (BYOL - requires a separate license)
- ( ) Configure a new third-party vulnerability scanner (BYOL - requires a separate license)

[Proceed]

Figure 6.9 – Onboard MDVM

Defender for Cloud simplifies agent installation (such as **Azure Monitor Agent**) by automatically deploying them to existing and new machines when you enable the relevant plan on that subscription. Leveraging agentless technology, Defender Cloud Security Posture Management provides a holistic perspective of your cloud security posture, attack path analysis, vulnerability scanning, and sensitive data discovery without installing agents.

> **Note**
>
> The choice between agent-based and agentless security solutions depends on your specific needs and environment. Both have advantages in different scenarios and should be considered on a case-by-case basis.

Refer to this comprehensive guide on agent-based and agentless cloud protection: https://packt. link/5p4Oi. This will help you better understand Microsoft Defender for Cloud agent-based versus agentless security.

Attack path analysis identifies and prioritizes the most critical security issues in your environment based on their exploitability and potential impact. Defender for Cloud helps you understand the potential attack paths that attackers could use to breach your environment and highlights the security recommendations you need to address to mitigate those risks. Refer to the *Microsoft Defender for Cloud* section in *Chapter 3* to understand these capabilities from a misconfiguration and vulnerabilities perspective.

Defender for Cloud also helps in discovering misconfigurations in **Infrastructure as Code (IaC)**, and at the time of writing, Microsoft Defender for Cloud supports **Azure DevOps**, **GitHub** (Free, Pro, Team, and Enterprise cloud), and **GitLab** environments. Refer to https://packt.link/7b6Ih to learn more details about these capabilities.

The cloud security explorer is another powerful Defender for Cloud capability that helps you proactively identify potential security risks in your **multi-cloud environments**. Its graph-based queries and query builder allow your team to proactively search for and address threats based on your specific organizational context.

Microsoft Sentinel

While many organizations rely on tools such as ServiceNow and **Azure Logic Apps** to automate vulnerability management tasks, some are increasingly turning to **Microsoft Sentinel** for its seamless integration with Defender solutions. This allows for even greater automation and efficiency in addressing vulnerabilities.

Here are a few use cases where using Microsoft Sentinel can significantly enhance the effectiveness of the vulnerability management team:

- Alert the team about critical vulnerabilities and implement necessary measures to mitigate threats

- Bring MDVM vulnerability data into Microsoft Sentinel and create insightful workbooks and custom detections

- Correlate vulnerabilities with other data stored in Microsoft Sentinel, such as security events and other third-party tools being used

- Automate manual tasks related to the vulnerability management process in many ways, such as using Logic Apps or integrating with ServiceNow

Microsoft Copilot for Security

Microsoft Copilot for Security is a generative AI-powered security solution, and its goal is to enhance security outcomes quickly and efficiently, boosting Defender's abilities and effectiveness. At the time of writing this book, Copilot for Security is an **Early Access Program** (**EAP**).

There are a few ways Copilot for Security can be very beneficial to the vulnerability management team when addressing misconfigurations or vulnerabilities:

- Copilot for Security simplifies vulnerability management by letting users ask the tool about potential risks in their tech stack.

- You can get up to compliance standards fast with Copilot for Security's automated audits and expert remediation guidance. This can save you time as there is no need to carry out manual auditing or find remediation guidance.

- Copilot for Security can scan your endpoints and servers for outdated software, matching it to known vulnerabilities in real time, and can generate remediation steps to mitigate the risks. While MDE already performs vulnerability detection and mitigation tasks, the integration of Copilot for Security means it can now automatically generate remediation steps, perform complex risk mitigation tasks, and even apply patches without any user interaction. This will significantly improve your security posture by lowering your Exposure Score and raising your Secure Score.

- Copilot for Security's **vulnerability impact assessment promptbook** helps you quickly assess any vulnerability. It checks whether the vulnerability is publicly known, exploited, or used by attackers and offers recommendations for addressing or mitigating the threat, summarized in a concise executive report. You can also develop your own custom promptbook(s) depending on the need.

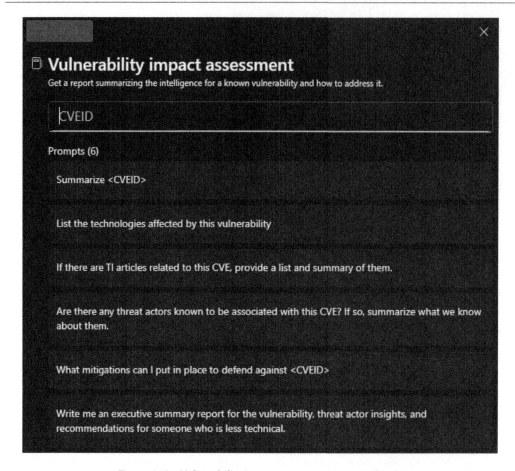

Figure 6.10 – Vulnerability impact assessment promptbook

- The Copilot for Security embedded experience within Microsoft Defender XDR (formerly Microsoft 365 Defender) offers advanced hunting capabilities. It assists vulnerability management teams in further investigation by enabling them to analyze data within tables through natural language to the Defender XDR KQL plugin, which can assist the team by generating KQL queries. Teams can leverage Copilot for Security's flexibility to build custom plugins, skills, and skillsets to enhance their security posture.

> **Note**
>
> **Managed Security Service Providers (MSSPs)** working with organizations can gain access to their Copilot for Security capabilities, allowing them to collaborate seamlessly with your security team.

Refer to Microsoft's Copilot for Security documentation | Microsoft Learn at `https://packt.link/A27MZ` and `https://packt.link/3mWDx` to learn more about Microsoft Copilot for Security.

Integration with other tools

The unified XDR and SIEM solution from Microsoft seamlessly integrates with any tool, be it Microsoft or non-Microsoft, as long as it supports API integration.

ServiceNow integration

The Microsoft unified XDR and SIEM solution seamlessly integrates with ServiceNow, empowering customers to streamline their security workflow and prioritize critical remediation efforts. By connecting their ServiceNow instance to their Defender environments, users can automatically generate and manage ServiceNow tickets (linked to specific recommendations) directly within Microsoft Defender and Sentinel tools. This integration leverages the **ITSM (incident management)** module within ServiceNow, ensuring that security incidents receive prompt attention and resolution.

Refer to these links for guidance on ServiceNow integrations with some Microsoft tools:

- ServiceNow integration with Microsoft Defender for Cloud: `https://packt.link/oCNT1`
- Microsoft Sentinel incident bi-directional sync with ServiceNow: `https://packt.link/pUJFA`

Intune/MDE remediation (native integration capability)

Integrating Intune with MDE unlocks powerful threat and vulnerability management capabilities. MDVM, which works with MDE, identifies weaknesses, and Intune allows you to quickly remediate them, streamlining the process and reducing risk across your environment. This risk-based approach prioritizes critical weaknesses, enabling you to focus your efforts on the most critical threats, ultimately improving your organization's security posture.

Refer to this helpful resource for guidance on integrating Intune and MDE to effectively remediate vulnerabilities: `https://packt.link/UcJgk`.

API integrations and automation

Custom security dashboards and reports can be developed with MDVM APIs to gain deeper insights into potential threats and vulnerabilities while simplifying your security team's workflow. You can also leverage these APIs to integrate MDVM with other solutions in your environment.

Refer to `https://packt.link/pXM9J` for the list of available vulnerability management APIs.

Here are a few articles on how you can build powerful reports with these APIs:

- How these MDVM APIs can boost and customize your vulnerability management program: `https://packt.link/REEx0`

- Create custom reports using Microsoft Defender ATP APIs and Power BI – Microsoft Community Hub: `https://packt.link/Nf0ba`

- Create a dashboard and automate with Power Automate: `https://packt.link/FQ2CN`

Tools such as Power Automation and Logic Apps can be leveraged along with the advanced hunting schema (vulnerability management tables) to generate notifications (via email, Teams, Slack, and so on).

Case study analysis

Now let's look at some of the security challenges High Tech Rapid Solutions Corp is facing as mentioned in the case study at the beginning of this book:

- There is a lack of visibility of internet-exposed digital assets and potential threats. By leveraging the Cloud Security Explorer feature, the team can identify internet-exposed assets with vulnerabilities. Also, once deployed, MDE sensors offer a comprehensive device inventory, giving teams a clear picture of their devices.

- The SOC team is noticing too many incidents and is confident that handling certain vulnerabilities would fix these incidents and reduce the number of incidents/alerts, but they are struggling to gain visibility of the vulnerabilities.

    This unified solution can help in many ways:

    - As a first step, Defender for Cloud and MDE provide comprehensive insights on misconfigurations and vulnerabilities

    - Integrating with tools such as Intune, ServiceNow, and Logic Apps can streamline vulnerability identification and remediation

    - Teams can leverage the flexibility of workbooks to develop custom reports that address their unique needs and objectives

- Management is increasingly concerned about the SOC team's inability to promptly address vulnerabilities and misconfigurations, attributed to the absence of a defined process and a dedicated vulnerability management team.

    There are many ways Microsoft's unified XDR and SIEM solution can address these challenges, such as the following:

    - Providing comprehensive insights into misconfigurations and vulnerabilities

    - MDE integration with Intune can help automate some of the remediation activities

    - Microsoft Sentinel with ServiceNow's ITSM module integration, which supports bi-directional sync, can significantly reduce the team's manual tasks

- The team can leverage Microsoft Sentinel features such as playbooks to automate vulnerability management-related activities, utilize workbooks for reporting and email notifications/reports, or drop messages to Teams groups

- Microsoft Copilot for Security can assist and guide the team in identifying misconfigurations and vulnerabilities quickly, along with security recommendations

- High Tech Rapid Solutions Corp's SecOps teams have been struggling to identify possible attack paths to cloud resources.

  High Tech Rapid Solutions Corp's SOC/vulnerability management team can use the Attack Path Analysis feature, which provides insight into potential exploit paths attackers might utilize to compromise your environment.

Summary

This chapter emphasized the crucial role of monitoring security misconfigurations and vulnerabilities, showcasing how Microsoft's unified XDR and SIEM solution, as well as the core capabilities of MDVM, tackles these challenges and strengthens your security posture. Additionally, we explored the importance of tracking the Exposure Score for devices and highlighted key integrations.

In the next chapter, we will dive into the Secure Score and the calculations behind it and discover how continuous monitoring strengthens your security posture.

Further reading

Refer to the following for more information about the topics covered in this chapter:

- *2022 Top Routinely Exploited Vulnerabilities* | CISA: https://packt.link/0CpzX

- *NSA and CISA Red and Blue Teams Share Top Ten Cybersecurity Misconfigurations* | CISA: https://packt.link/nsTtj; PDF version: https://packt.link/LIePP

- Microsoft Defender Vulnerability Management documentation | Microsoft Learn: https://packt.link/vVtJa

- *Compare Microsoft Defender Vulnerability Management plans and capabilities* | Microsoft Learn: https://packt.link/WMAmU

- National Vulnerability Database: The NVD is a United States government database that stores vulnerability management information based on standards, and it uses the **Security Content Automation Protocol** (**SCAP**) to present this data: https://packt.link/j3qB6

- *Common Vulnerability Scoring System SIG*: https://packt.link/B35XQ

- Common Vulnerability Scoring System calculator: https://packt.link/m2l9U or https://packt.link/dfcAo

- CVE Program website: https://packt.link/k8Ul8

- *Known Exploited Vulnerabilities Catalog* | CISA: https://packt.link/ZKm5S

7

Understanding Microsoft Secure Score

Based on **Microsoft Digital Defense Report** (**MDDR**) 2023, the top four threats and attack vectors were identity attacks, ransomware encounters, targeted phishing, and **business email compromise** (**BEC**) attacks. In all these scenarios, the better the environment security posture is, the lower the likelihood of an attack succeeding. Also, in cloud environment breaches, some of the common factors are misconfiguration, mismanaged credentials, and insider theft.

Security posture management is a broad topic that is related to environmental footprint. Even though **Microsoft Secure Score** does not cover all the possible scenarios related to environment posture management, by leveraging it, organizations can enhance security and manage the built-in controls from supported workloads.

This chapter will cover the following main topics:

- What is Microsoft Secure Score?
- Understanding your score – how are scores calculated?
- How to access and improve findings
- Integrations
- Case study analysis

What is Microsoft Secure Score?

Microsoft Secure Score helps organizations assess their cloud environment's security posture and pinpoint areas for improvement, based on Microsoft's best practices. The Secure Score baseline is based on common attack vectors that Microsoft observes across the threat landscape, as well as the security standards and frameworks in the industry based on supported applications. Microsoft maintains the baseline and is updating it regularly to reflect the latest threats and mitigations.

Let's start delving deeper into Microsoft Security Score by going through some variations of it. If you are familiar with Secure Score, you might have seen it in different Microsoft security solutions such as MDC, Entra ID, and Microsoft Defender XDR. Secure Score can be found (or some variation of it) in the following solutions:

- **Microsoft Defender Extended Detection and Response (XDR)** – Microsoft Secure Score.

- Microsoft Defender for Cloud – Azure secure score.

- Microsoft Entra ID – identity secure score.

- Defender for Endpoint – device score and exposure level. Details on Threat and Vulnerability dashboard in Microsoft Defender XDR portal.

- Microsoft Purview Compliance portal – compliance score.

- Defender for Cloud Apps – Cloud Discovery where each application has risk score.

Why do we need to monitor Secure Score?

Monitoring your Microsoft Secure Score is important for several reasons. Firstly, it provides an objective assessment of your current security level, allowing you to compare it with industry standards and that of your peers. Secondly, it helps you keep track of your security progress over time (history graph), enabling you to measure the impact of security improvements. Thirdly, Secure Score offers actionable recommendations tailored to the environment. In addition, Microsoft is constantly improving the solution and adding more controls to it, as well as covering more solutions that are supported, such as SaaS applications. Lastly, it can be beneficial in demonstrating compliance status with regulatory standards.

Azure secure score in MDC

Let's look at different types of secure score available in the Microsoft cloud ecosystem. As you can see from the preceding list, there are several variations of secure score in the cloud environment. The first instance of secure score we investigate is in Azure, to be precise, in MDC.

The MDC secure score provides a comprehensive view of the security state across all clouds (including multi-cloud scenarios), as well as in hybrid resources as seen in *Figure 7.1*. It supports several regulatory compliance frameworks (including custom standards/recommendations) that can be used to measure security status in the environment.

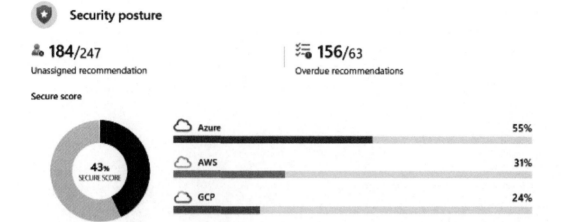

Figure 7.1 – Multi-cloud environment Secure Score in MDC

The full list of available regulatory standards is available in Microsoft Learn (`https://packt.link/t7aNe`).

By default, the following regulatory compliance standards are available in MDC for supported workloads:

- For Azure subscriptions:

  - **Microsoft cloud security benchmark** (**MCSB**): This is assigned by default. This is the Microsoft-authored, cloud-specific guidelines for security and compliance best practices based on common compliance frameworks.

- For AWS accounts:

  - **AWS Foundational Security Best Practices standard**: This is automatically assigned by default. This is the AWS-specific guideline for security and compliance best practices based on common compliance frameworks.

- For GCP projects:

  - **GCP Default standard**: This is assigned by default.

The foundation for the MDC Secure Score in Azure is the Azure Policy engine, which is used underneath the hood to measure security controls and their statuses. The standards you assign to your environment can be managed as initiatives in Azure Policy. An initiative is a collection of multiple policies that are grouped together. The MCSB Azure Policy initiative compliance status can be seen in *Figure 7.2*.

Figure 7.2 – MCSB Azure Policy initiative

With AWS and GCP, MDC scanning works differently, and it uses direct API query resources several times per day. More details on how these work and how to configure them are available at https://packt.link/x1Fx9 (for AWS) and https://packt.link/e1kBM (for GCP).

Security controls in MDC

Regulatory standards (such as MCSB) recommendations are grouped into **security controls**. These controls are shown in the MDC **Recommendations** blade as a logical group of recommendations, such as **Remediate vulnerabilities**, which show vulnerable attack surfaces against your resources.

Name ↑↓	Max score ↓	Current score ↑↓	Potential score ... ↑↓	Status ↑↓	Unhealthy resources	Insights
› Enable MFA	10	10.00 ▮▮▮▮▮▮▮▮▮▮		Completed	0 of 2 resources	
› Secure management ports	8	8.00 ▮▮▮▮▮▮▮▮		Completed	0 of 8 resources	
∨ Remediate vulnerabilities	6	1.41 ▮▮▮▮▮▮	+ 10%	Unassigned	6 of 8 resources	
Machines should have a vulnerability assessment sol...				Unassigned	2 of 8 virtual machines	⚡
Machines should have vulnerability findings resolved				Unassigned	4 of 8 virtual machines	
Machines should have secret findings resolved				Completed	0 of 6 virtual machines	🔖

Figure 7.3 – Security recommendations in MDC

If you are addressing your vulnerabilities and trying to improve your score, it is important to know that your score improves only when you remediate all the recommendations for a single resource within a control.

Furthermore, it's important to note that only the built-in recommendations within the default initiatives affect the MDC secure score. Additionally, recommendations labeled as **preview** (marked with 🔖) aren't included in the calculations of the environment secure score. An example of this is seen in *Figure 7.3*.

> Tip
>
> Customization of security recommendations is available in MDC. You can disable recommendations and exclude individual resources from a recommendation. We suggest tailoring recommendations to align more closely with your organization's specific security requirements.

Identity secure score in Entra ID

The identity secure score is a representation of identity security posture recommendations and is found in the Entra ID portal (in *Figure 7.4*). Most of the recommendations are also found in Microsoft Secure Score (Defender XDR portal), which has more granularity for managing the recommendations.

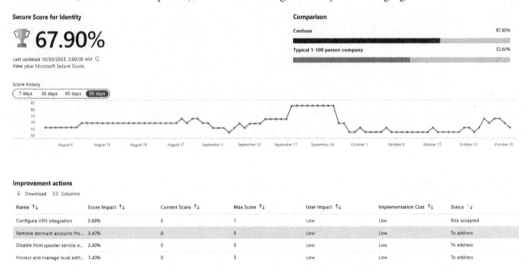

Figure 7.4 – Security recommendations in MDC

Microsoft Entra has also recommendations in the **Tenant overview** blade. These recommendations include identity secure score recommendations and are seen in the **Microsoft Entra overview** blade. Recommendations do not have points, but identity secure score controls have points, as shown in *Figure 7.5*.

It might be a bit confusing to find different secure scores in several places and many might be wondering how all the recommendations should be managed. What is the best practice for controlling all the recommendations and mitigation actions for the controls?

Figure 7.5 – Microsoft Entra recommendations

To address this challenge, our recommendation is to use Microsoft Secure Score in the Microsoft Defender XDR portal and MDC Secure Score for managing security posture controls and recommendations in your environment. These solutions provides wider coverage and more granularity for managing the controls.

Microsoft Secure Score in Microsoft Defender XDR

Microsoft Secure Score in the Defender XDR portal addresses the following areas:

- It evaluates and reports the current state of the organization's security posture based on Microsoft's recommendations.

- It enhances security measures by enhancing discoverability, visibility, guidance, and control.

- It compares with benchmarks and establishes **key performance indicators** (**KPIs**).

Microsoft Secure Score

Overview   Recommended actions   History   Metrics & trends

Microsoft Secure Score is a representation of your organization's security posture, and your opportunity to improve it.

Applied filters:

Your secure score   Include ⌄

Secure Score: 44.06%

129.1/293 points achieved

100%

50%

0%

09/17 09/24 08/31 09/07 09/14 09/21 09/28 10/05 10/12 10/19 10/26 11/02 11/09 11/14

Breakdown points by: Category   ⌄

Identity   42.79%

Data   55.56%

Apps   43.95%

■ Points achieved   ■ Opportunity

Actions to review

Regressed ⓘ	To address ⓘ	Planned ⓘ	Risk accepted ⓘ	Recently added ⓘ
0	**45**	**0**	**0**	**0**

Recently updated ⓘ

0

Top recommended actions

Recommended action	Score impact	Status	Category
Ensure that intelligence for impersonation protecti...	+2.73%	○ To address	Apps
Move messages that are detected as impersonated ...	+2.73%	○ To address	Apps
Enable impersonated domain protection	+2.73%	○ To address	Apps
Set the phishing email level threshold at 2 or higher	+2.73%	○ To address	Apps
Enable impersonated user protection	+2.73%	○ To address	Apps
Enable Azure AD Identity Protection sign-in risk pol...	+2.39%	○ To address	Identity
Enable Azure AD Identity Protection user risk policies	+2.39%	○ To address	Identity
Ensure multifactor authentication is enabled for all ...	+3.07%	○ To address	Identity

Figure 7.6 – Microsoft 365 Secure Score

The **Microsoft Secure Score** landing page (seen in *Figure 7.6*) shows the overall status of the environment secure score by percent based on the data collected from different data sources. The main categories in the secure score are **Apps**, **Data**, **Device**, and **Identity**, which can be used for filtering and managing recommendations. During the last years, Microsoft has added more and more solutions to Secure Score and, at the time of writing, it supports the following products:

- App governance
- Microsoft Entra
- Citrix ShareFile
- Microsoft Defender for Endpoint
- Microsoft Defender for Identity
- Microsoft Defender for Office

- DocuSign

- Exchange Online

- GitHub

- Microsoft Defender for Cloud Apps

- Microsoft Purview Information Protection

- Microsoft Teams

- Okta

- Salesforce

- ServiceNow

- SharePoint Online

- Zoom

As we can see from the list, the coverage is wide and provides recommendations for both first- and third-party applications.

> **Note**
>
> The recommendations won't cover all the attack surfaces associated with each product, but they are a good baseline.

SaaS security posture management

Let's look at the new approach Microsoft has taken in terms of security recommendations. **Defender for Cloud Apps** (**MDA**), which we covered in *Chapter 3*, provides protection and controls for SaaS applications. By integrating a SaaS application into MDA, organizations will get additional protection (threat protection layer) for the application, as well as visibility and the possibility of leveraging MDA session proxy for advanced scenarios. In addition, posture information is synced from the application to MDA and is seen in the secure score.

MDA provides a security configuration assessment for the integrated SaaS applications once you have integrated the application into MDA. The only prerequisite is that you need to have a proper MDA license in place.

More information about MDA SaaS security posture management is available at Microsoft Learn (https://packt.link/FbVlb).

Security posture assessments in MDI

As we described in *Chapter 3*, MDI fulfills visibility in the ecosystem by monitoring on-premises **Active Directory (AD)** signals to identify and detect advanced threats, users, and devices to spot suspicious activities.

In addition, MDI provides security posture assessments from on-premises AD environments. In terms of security posture assessments, MDI provides information for known exploitable components, misconfigurations, and vulnerabilities, as well as recommendations on how to mitigate the findings. These reports are built-in features and made possible through data collected by the MDI sensor. At the time of writing, the available reports are as follows:

- Domain controllers with a Print Spooler service available
- Dormant entities in sensitive groups
- Entities exposing credentials in clear text
- Microsoft LAPS usage
- Legacy protocols usage
- Riskiest **lateral movement paths (LMPs)**
- Unmonitored domain controllers
- Unsecure account attributes
- Unsecure domain configurations
- Unsecure Kerberos delegation
- Unsecure SID History attributes
- Weak cipher usage

MDI reports are available in Microsoft Secure Score, located in the Defender XDR portal, as can be seen in *Figure 7.7*.

Microsoft Secure Score

Overview   Recommended actions   History   Metrics & trends

Actions you can take to improve your Microsoft Secure Score. Score updates may take up to 24 hours.

⬇ Export   19 items 🔍 Search   ⛛ Filter ☰ Group by

Filters: Product: Defender for Identity ✕

	Rank	Recommended action	Score impact	Points achieved	Status	Regressed	Have license?	Category	Product	Last synced
☐	1	Resolve unsecure domain configurations	+0.39%	0/5	○ To address	No	Yes	Identity	Defender for Identity	11/1/2023
☐	2	Remove dormant accounts from sensitive groups	+0.39%	0/5	○ To address	No	Yes	Identity	Defender for Identity	11/1/2023
☐	3	Protect and manage local admin passwords with Microsoft LAP	+0.39%	0/5	○ To address	No	Yes	Identity	Defender for Identity	11/1/2023
☐	4	Resolve unsecure account attributes	+0.39%	0/5	○ To address	Yes	Yes	Identity	Defender for Identity	11/1/2023

Figure 7.7 – MDI recommendation in Microsoft Secure Score

Recommendations for devices

The secure score for devices is divided into several locations. It is found in Microsoft Secure Score as well as in **Threat and Vulnerability Management** (**TVM**). Even though recommendations for devices are visible in Microsoft Secure Score, those cannot be managed from Microsoft Secure Score (see *Figure 7.8*). The recommendation for devices needs to be addressed in Defender XDR and TVM, which we are addressing more closely in *Chapter 6*.

Block Adobe Reader from creating child processes

○ To address

Go to threat and vulnerability management to take action ⬩ Manage tags

General   Exposed entities   Implementation

Description

Attack Surface Reduction (ASR) rules are the most effective method for blocking the most common attack techniques being used in cyber attacks and malicious software.
This ASR rule prevents Adobe Reader from creating additional child processes.

This security control is only applicable for machines with Windows 10, version 1903 or later.
Through social engineering or exploits, malware can download and launch additional payloads and break out of Adobe Reader.

Implementation status

6/6 exposed devices

Details

Points achieved   0 / 9

History
0 events

Category
Device

Product
Defender for Endpoint

Figure 7.8 – Sample device recommendation in Microsoft Secure Score

Now that we have gone through the most important variations of Secure Score, it's time to look at how scores are calculated in Secure Score and how organizations can address the recommendations.

Understanding your score – how are scores calculated?

In a nutshell, Secure Score serves as a metric for assessing an organization's security posture, where a higher score signifies a lower level of risk. The overall score, which is a representation of an organization's security posture, is shown on the **Overview** page on the left (breakdown points by category). For example, in *Figure 7.9*, you can see the overall score (51.58%) from the Microsoft Defender XDR portal. The score is presented as a percentage, but points are also visible, which can be used to identify where you are (667.6/1,275 points achieved).

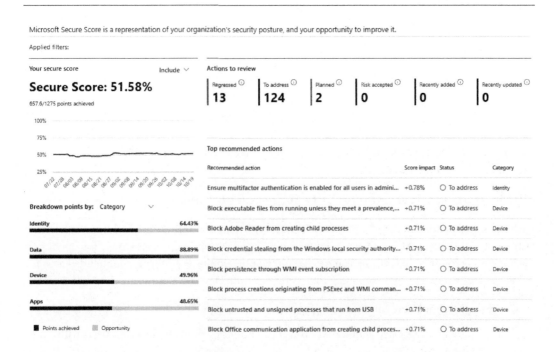

Figure 7.9 – Overall Secure Score blade in the Microsoft Defender XDR portal

Let's look at how scores are calculated in Azure (MDC secure score) with the following example. As we can see in *Figure 7.10*, there is one Azure control (**Remediate vulnerabilities**) in MDC that has a total of 78 resources with a current score of 0.31 and a max score of 6.

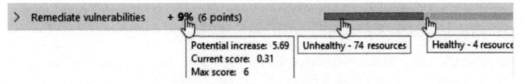

Figure 7.10 – Secure Score measurement

As we can see from *Figure 7.10*, in **Remediate vulnerabilities**, the max score is 6 points (which is set by the importance and controls list, and the score is dynamic and might change as the product grows). The control has 78 resources in total behind the scenes, which means that one individual resource can increase/decrease a score by 0.0769 points.

The max score can be divided by the number of healthy (4) + unhealthy resources (74). Then, the formula will be 6/78=0.0769.

By multiplying 0.0769 with healthy resources, we can get the current score (0.0769*4=0.31).

The potential increase is 6-0.31=5.69, which means a potential increase of 9%.

The formula for the security control current score calculation is seen in *Figure 7.11*.

$$Current\ score = \frac{Max\ score}{Healthy + Unhealthy} \times Healthy$$

Figure 7.11 – Secure Score formula

Secure Score in Microsoft Defender XDR and identity score in Entra ID follow the same pattern even though they have some variations.

Microsoft Secure Score and Identity Score calculations

Each suggested action is worth 10 points or less, and the majority of these are evaluated in a binary fashion. If you implement the Secure Score recommended action, such as creating a new policy or turning on a recommended setting, you receive 100% of the points. For other recommended actions, points are granted as a proportion of the total configuration. Here are some examples:

- **Example from Microsoft Secure Score**:

    For example, a suggested action states you get 10 points by protecting all your users with MFA. If you have protected 50 out of 100 total users, your score for this action will be calculated as 5 points (50 protected / 100 total * 10 max points = 5 points).

- **Example from Identity Score**:

    For example, if the recommendation states that there's a maximum increase of 10.71% if you protect all your users with MFA and you have 5 out of 100 total users protected, you're given a partial score of around 0.53% (5 protected / 100 total * 10.71% maximum = 0.53% partial score).

Azure secure score calculation – single subscription

Score calculation for a single subscription is the same as with the data connector (AWS and GCP), and the same formula is being used. In *Figure 7.12*, you can see the formula as well as example scores from an Azure environment with a secure score of 68% (33.33 / 49 x 100 = 68).

$$Secure\ score\ for\ a\ subscription = \frac{\sum current\ scores\ for\ all\ conrols}{\sum maximum\ scores\ for\ all\ controls} \; x\ 100$$

68%
Secure score ⓘ

10/39
Active recommendations

0 Attack path
We didn't find attack paths in your environment. Learn more >

🔍 Search recommendations

Recommendation status == **None** ✕   Severity == **None** ✕   Resource type == **None** ✕

Environment == **Azure** ✕   ⚡ Add filter

Show my items only

∧ Less

⊘ Name ↑↓	Max score ↑↓	Current score ↑↓	Potential score increase ↑↓	Status ↑↓	Unhealthy resources
> Enable MFA	10	10.00 ▮▮▮▮▮▮▮▮▮▮		● Completed	0 of 1 resources
> Secure management ports	8	8.00 ▮▮▮▮▮▮▮▮		● Completed	0 of 2 resources
> Remediate vulnerabilities	6	0.00 ▮▮▮▮▮▮	+ 12%	● Unassigned	2 of 2 resources
> Apply system updates	6	6.00 ▮▮▮▮▮▮		● Completed	0 of 2 resources
> Encrypt data in transit	4	4.00 ▮▮▮▮		● Completed	0 of 4 resources
> Manage access and permissions	4	4.00 ▮▮▮▮		● Completed	0 of 9 resources
> Enable encryption at rest	4	0.00 ▮▮▮▮	+ 8%	● Unassigned	2 of 2 resources
> Restrict unauthorized network access	4	1.33 ▮▮▮▮	+ 5%	● Unassigned	2 of 6 resources
> Enable endpoint protection	2	0.00 ▮▮	+ 4%	● Unassigned	2 of 2 resources
> Enable auditing and logging	1	0.00 ▮	+ 2%	● Unassigned	18 of 18 resources
> Enable enhanced security features	Not scored	Not scored		● Unassigned	2 of 5 resources
> Implement security best practices	Not scored	Not scored		● Unassigned	2 of 11 resources
> Remediate security configurations	Not scored	Not scored		● Completed	0 of 2 resources
> Apply adaptive application control	Not scored	Not scored		● Completed	0 of 2 resources
> Protect applications against DDoS attacks	Not scored	Not scored		● Completed	0 of 2 resources

Figure 7.12 – Azure secure score for single subscription

Azure secure score calculation – multiple subscription

Score calculation differs from a single subscription (or connector) in that weight is included in the calculation. The weighting of subscriptions and connectors is dynamically established by MDC, considering factors such as the quantity of resources involved. The calculation of the current score for each subscription or connector mirrors that of a single instance, with the subsequent application of weights as specified in the equation.

In *Figure 7.13*, you can see both the formula and example score calculation in a multiple-subscription or connector situation.

$$Secure\ score\ multiple\ subscription = \frac{\sum(subscription\ score\ x\ subscription\ weight)}{\sum Weights\ for\ all\ subscriptions}\ x\ 100$$

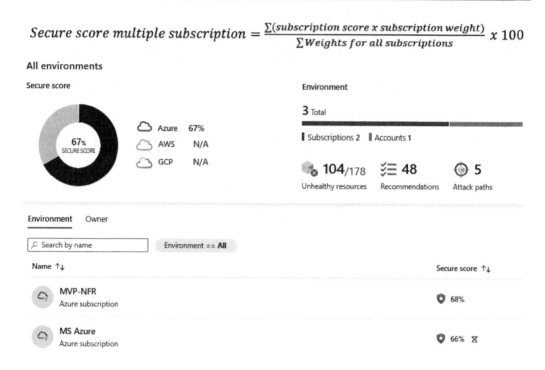

Figure 7.13 – Azure secure score for multiple subscriptions

Now that we know how scores are calculated, in the following section, we will look at how we can assess and improve the findings raised by Microsoft Secure Score.

How to assess and improve findings

Now that we know how the score is calculated, it's time to look at how you can address the scores and enhance security posture in the environment. The most important task is to define a strategy and success criteria for improving scores. The following list names a few different approaches:

- Some organizations aim to attain the highest achievable score
- Some organizations are content with achieving a score somewhere in the middle
- Some organizations may prioritize addressing their top five items based on categories
- Some organizations focus only on items that demand minimal effort
- Some organizations don't use secure scores at all for managing recommendations

As we can see, there is no silver bullet or strategy that fits all organizations. Approaches and responsibilities need to be clear so that organizations can address recommendations effectively and improve their environmental security posture.

Addressing findings

In the following example, we are using Secure Score in Microsoft Defender XDR.

The overall page shows the overall status of your environment, actions to review, and the comparison between organizations with a similar size. Scores can also be filtered, which is useful if you would like to see the overall situation by category, and it gives a better understanding of which area might be lacking as well as which of the areas are in good condition. In *Figure 7.14*, we can see that the **Data** protection is in the best shape and the **Apps** area needs the most improvements.

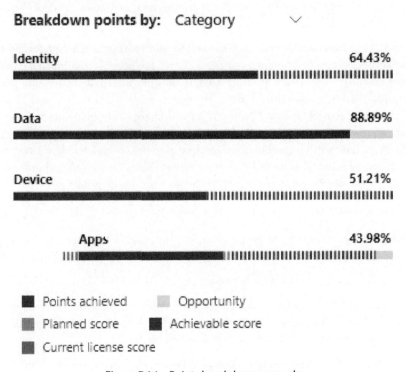

Figure 7.14 – Points breakdown example

The **Recommended actions** blade has all the recommendations listed with their statuses, as seen in *Figure 7.15*. How many recommendations you can see depends on your license levels. At the time of writing, there are multiple products that feed data into Secure Score, such as Entra ID, MDE, MDI, Exchange Online, and SharePoint, to name a few.

Microsoft Secure Score

Overview   **Recommended actions**   History   Metrics & trends

Actions you can take to improve your Microsoft Secure Score. Score updates may take up to 24 hours.

⤓ Export   232 items   🔍 Search   🏷 Filter

	Rank	Recommended action	Score impact	Points achieved	Status	Regressed	Have license?	Category	Product	Last synced	Microsoft update
☐	1	Ensure multifactor authentication is enabled for all users in administrative roles	+0.78%	0/10	○ To address	Yes	Yes	Identity	Azure Active Directory	10/18/2023	None
☐	2	Block executable files from running unless they meet a prevalence, age, or trus	+0.71%	0/9	○ To address	No	Yes	Device	Defender for Endpoint	10/20/2023	None
☐	3	Block Adobe Reader from creating child processes	+0.71%	0/9	○ To address	No	Yes	Device	Defender for Endpoint	10/20/2023	None

Figure 7.15 – Secure Score recommendations

> **Note**
>
> At the time of writing this book, not all recommendations are available in certain regions. Also, the number of recommendations you see in the portal depends on your licenses and deployed solutions.

When you open **Recommended actions** in **Microsoft Secure Score**, you can see relevant information about the action, including a description, implementation status, possible user impact, implementation guidance, and control status (such as completed, to address, alternate mitigation, planned, risk accepted, or mitigated through a third-party). The recommended actions are ranked based on the number of points left to achieve (see *Figure 7.15*), the difficulty of implementation, the impact on users, and the complexity of the action. The highest-ranked actions have many points remaining, are easy to implement, have a low impact on users, and are simple to complete. Managing controls from the **Microsoft Secure Score** window and changing statuses affects the overall environment score, and in *Figure 7.16*, we can see the completed control state with maximum points gathered.

The available action statuses for the controls are as follows:

- **To address**: You agree that the proposed course of action is important, and you plan to take it in the future. This also applies to actions that are partially completed, but not yet finished.

- **Planned**: There are plans in place to implement the recommended security control.

- **Risk accepted**: An organization has the option to either accept the associated risk or the residual risk and abstain from implementing the suggested action. When selecting **Risk accepted** in the control panel, Secure Score doesn't give you any points.

- **Resolved through a third party and resolved through alternate mitigation**: A third-party application, internal tool, or piece of software has already handled the recommended action. You will still receive the points associated with the action, and your score will better reflect your overall security posture. However, Microsoft will not be able to see whether the action has been fully implemented.

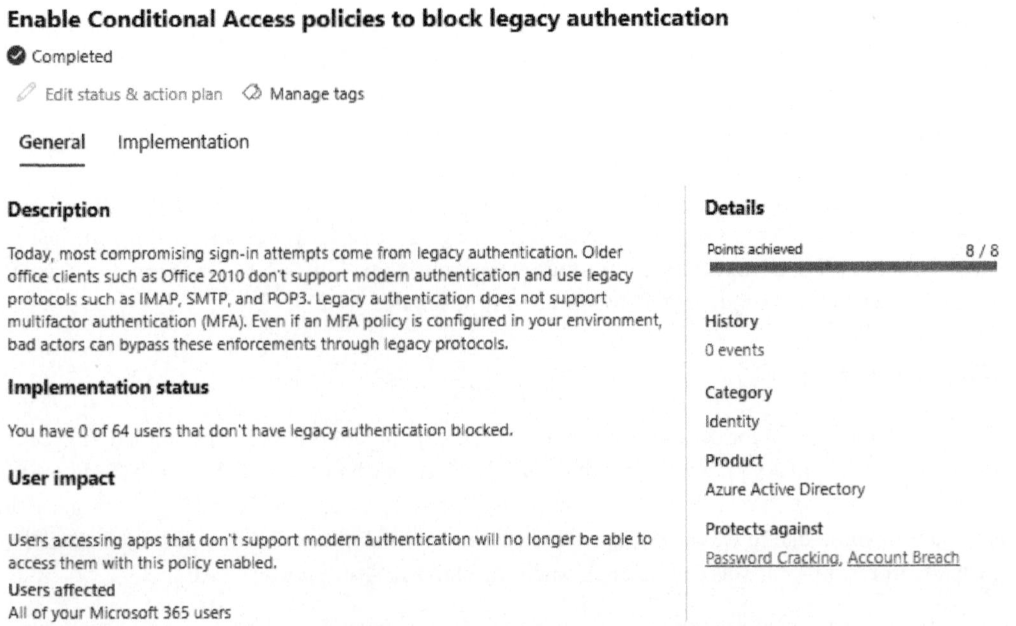

Enable Conditional Access policies to block legacy authentication

✅ Completed

✏ Edit status & action plan   ⊘ Manage tags

General   Implementation

Description

Today, most compromising sign-in attempts come from legacy authentication. Older office clients such as Office 2010 don't support modern authentication and use legacy protocols such as IMAP, SMTP, and POP3. Legacy authentication does not support multifactor authentication (MFA). Even if an MFA policy is configured in your environment, bad actors can bypass these enforcements through legacy protocols.

Implementation status

You have 0 of 64 users that don't have legacy authentication blocked.

User impact

Users accessing apps that don't support modern authentication will no longer be able to access them with this policy enabled.

Users affected
All of your Microsoft 365 users

Details

Points achieved   8 / 8

History
0 events

Category
Identity

Product
Azure Active Directory

Protects against
Password Cracking, Account Breach

Figure 7.16 – Completed control state in Microsoft Secure Score

In Secure Score across Microsoft solutions, changing control statuses has the same effect even though actions are named differently.

For example, if you use alternative mitigation for the **Ensure multifactor authentication is enabled for all users in administrative roles** control and change the status of the control to **Resolved through alternative mitigation** as seen in *Figure 7.17*, it will affect your overall secure score by raising points, and the higher the points, the better the security. The impacts of these actions on the overall score can vary between controls.

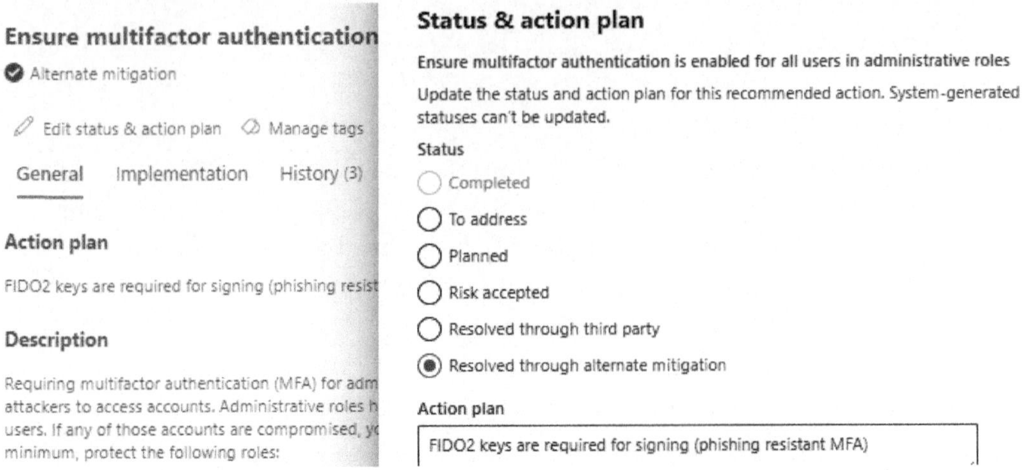

Ensure multifactor authentication

✅ Alternate mitigation

✏ Edit status & action plan   ⊘ Manage tags

General   Implementation   History (3)

Action plan

FIDO2 keys are required for signing (phishing resist

Description

Requiring multifactor authentication (MFA) for adm
attackers to access accounts. Administrative roles h
users. If any of those accounts are compromised, y
minimum, protect the following roles:

Status & action plan

Ensure multifactor authentication is enabled for all users in administrative roles

Update the status and action plan for this recommended action. System-generated statuses can't be updated.

Status

◯ Completed

◯ To address

◯ Planned

◯ Risk accepted

◯ Resolved through third party

◉ Resolved through alternate mitigation

Action plan

FIDO2 keys are required for signing (phishing resistant MFA)

Figure 7.17 – Configuring alternative mitigation in Secure Score

As we have seen in this chapter, secure scores are found in several portals, and when organizations are planning to leverage one, it is essential to plan the integrations, which we look at in the following section.

Integrations

By combining secure score information with other security data sources, organizations can gain deeper insights and better manage their overall security posture, as well as be able to track the history related to secure score changes. For continuous export and reporting, Secure Score provides various mechanisms that can be used. Let's address these in the next section.

MDC secure score

MDC provides an option for continuous export of different content types (recommendations, secure score, alerts, and regulatory compliance) to external sources such as SIEM, SOAR, or ITSM systems through Event Hubs. There is also an option to use Azure Log Analytics as an export target if an organization would like to export data to a dedicated Log Analytics or Sentinel instance instead as we can see in *Figure 7.18*. This can be established through the Azure portal or API.

API methods provide flexible options for data querying, enabling organizations to create a customized reporting system to monitor the changes in your secure scores over time.

Learn more about the MDC secure score API and how to leverage it at the following link: `https://packt.link/0N04v`.

Also, refer to `https://packt.link/tVSmg` for GitHub-based tools for working programmatically with secure score.

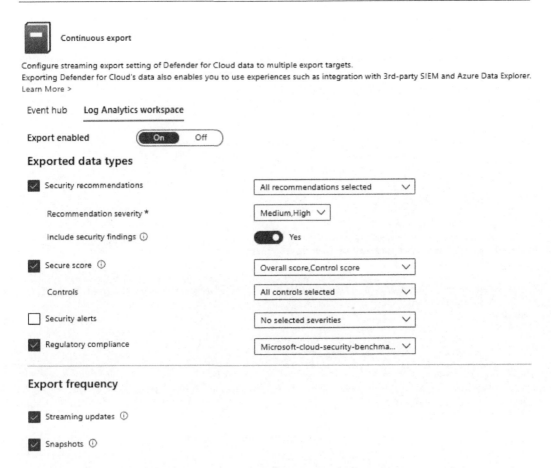

Figure 7.18 – MDC continuous export configuration

Even though MDC provides a possibility to leverage Azure Workbooks for data visualization, it might be that the compliance team doesn't have access to all the needed data. In this scenario, exporting data to a dedicated Sentinel or Log Analytics instance provides a way to leverage Azure Workbooks for compliance data visualization, as seen in *Figure 7.19*.

Figure 7.19 – Compliance data visualization in Azure Workbooks

Microsoft Secure Score

Microsoft Secure Score provides a manual export option from the portal (in the **Recommendations** blade), and if an organization would like to export data to external sources, there is an API (secureScores) that can be used. An export example can be seen in *Figure 7.20*.

```
    },
    {
        "controlCategory": "Apps",
        "controlName": "aad_admin_consent_workflow",
        "description": null,
        "score": 5,
        "implementationStatus": "Admin consent workflow is: ",
        "scoreInPercentage": 100
    },
    {
        "controlCategory": "Apps",
        "controlName": "aad_managed_approved_public_groups_only",
        "description": null,
        "score": 0,
        "implementationStatus": "Groups are set as private or approved as public confiruation is: ",
        "scoreInPercentage": 0
    },
    {
        "controlCategory": "Apps",
        "controlName": "intune_mobile_password_requirement",
        "description": null,
        "score": 0,
        "implementationStatus": "Mobile devices to have a password configuration is: ",
        "scoreInPercentage": 0
    },
```

Figure 7.20 – secureScores API export

Now you know how secure scores work in a nutshell and how organizations can address the scores and improve environment security posture status. Let's turn our focus to a fictional company and their challenges, as well as how Microsoft Secure Score could help them strengthen their environment configurations.

Case study analysis

As we highlighted in the *Case Study* chapter, *High Tech Rapid Solutions* has identified several security challenges they would like to address in their environment. Based on MDDR 2023, 99% of the attacks would be prevented by implementing a few fundamental security hygiene practices, which are as follows:

- Enable MFA
- Apply Zero Trust principles
- Use XDR and antimalware
- Patch your systems
- Protect data and prevent data leaks

This is also related to a strong security posture. Based on the same report, the successful ransomware attack likelihood is very low if an organization has a strong security posture. Typically, these attacks are stopped in the pre-ransom phase. This is where Secure Score can help High Tech Rapid Solutions.

As stated earlier, the secure score recommendations won't cover all the attack surfaces associated with each product, but they are a good baseline. If the company leverages both the MDC secure score and Microsoft Secure Score, they have a solid baseline for Azure and Microsoft Defender XDR workloads. By doing so, they will address one of the challenges: regulatory compliance. On the Azure side, they can leverage one of the existing frameworks (MSCB, CIS, ISO 27001, etc.) or create a custom framework standard that fits their needs.

Something we would like to highlight here is the use of internal cybersecurity experts or work with third-party security experts (vendors), which will be discussed in detail in *Chapter 9*. High Tech Rapid Solutions has a major transformation planned in which the technology platform will be changed. This will require skilled cybersecurity experts to join the company or work with vendors who can help them reach their goals. Technology provides great opportunities, but it is also constantly evolving, and High Tech Rapid Solutions needs internal experts to lead and drive the transformation in the organization.

Summary

In this chapter, we have covered Microsoft Secure Score and its variations around the cloud ecosystem. We also described how organizations can address secure score findings and strengthen the environment's security posture and what the benefits would be in doing so.

In the next chapter, we will discuss various assessments and implementation strategies for XDR and SIEM solutions. We will also cover what factors to consider when planning to deploy these solutions and provide an example of an implementation roadmap.

Further reading

Refer to the following links for more information about the topics covered in this chapter:

- Microsoft Secure Score | Microsoft Learn (`https://packt.link/2eHRy`)
- Microsoft Entra recommendations | Microsoft Learn (`https://packt.link/4j0zw`)
- Microsoft Digital Defense Report and Security Intelligence Insights (`https://packt.link/Awscb`)
- Defender for Cloud – GitHub programmatic remediation tools (`https://packt.link/84nGC`)
- Microsoft Secure Score API (`https://packt.link/cxTer`)

Part 3 – Mastering Microsoft's Unified XDR and SIEM Solution – Strategies, Roadmap, and the Basics of Managed Solutions

This part guides you through key assessments, strategies, and managed service options to smoothly adopt and implement this unified security solution. We emphasize the importance of starting with a thorough assessment and a clear strategy to maximize the benefits of XDR and SIEM. Additionally, we explore the basics of managed security services in the Microsoft ecosystem, focusing on the generic **Managed Security Services Provider (MSSP)** framework and some useful resources.

This part has the following chapters:

- *Chapter 8, Microsoft XDR and SIEM Implementation Strategy, Approach, and Roadmap*
- *Chapter 9, Managed XDR and SIEM Services*
- *Chapter 10, Useful Resources*

8

Microsoft XDR and SIEM Implementation Strategy, Approach, and Roadmap

In this chapter, we will focus on various assessments and strategies to adopt and implement Microsoft's unified XDR and SIEM solution. We will delve into the significance of initiating this process with an assessment and a well-defined strategy before embracing the unified XDR and SIEM solution. Furthermore, we will delve into how these assessments and strategies can contribute to cost reduction for organizations while simultaneously strengthening their defenses against potential **cyberattacks**.

In a nutshell, we will cover the following main topics in this chapter:

- Understand why we need assessments and strategies before we adopt or implement Microsoft's unified XDR and SIEM solution

- Various assessments and strategies to be considered before we adopt or implement the unified solution

- Implementation approach and roadmap

XDR and SIEM assessment and implementation strategy

It is important to assess your organization's current **security posture** and develop a clear strategy before adopting the Microsoft unified XDR and SIEM solution. This preparatory step will help you to identify any gaps in your security, understand your specific needs, and determine the best way to implement the solution. Once you have completed the assessment, you can develop a strategy (or strategies) to address any weaknesses and to ensure that the solution is used effectively.

The question arises: which of these two should we pick – assessments or strategies? Both are essential for the successful adoption of the unified solution. Security assessments help you to understand the current state of your security and identify the areas where the solution can provide the most benefit.

Strategies help you to plan for implementation and to ensure that the solution is used in a way that meets your organization's specific needs.

Ultimately, the best approach (if it can be adopted) is an iterative one. Conduct an initial assessment to identify your organization's needs, then develop a strategy for implementing the solution. As you implement the solution, continue to monitor your security posture, re-assess the strategy, and adjust your strategy as needed (see *Figure 8.1*).

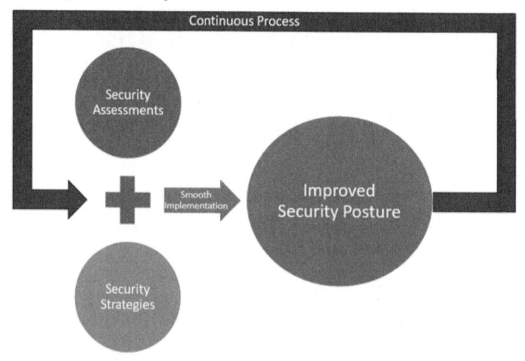

Figure 8.1 – Improved security posture

Security assessments

Now, let's look at some common assessments to assess your environment's **security posture** before you adopt or implement Microsoft's unified XDR and SIEM solution. These assessments are typically carried out either internally by your own team or by engaging professional companies specializing in these domains. The right assessment for you will depend on your organization's situation, security posture, and requirements.

Here are some common questions about assessments:

- Do I really need to start with an assessment? Why do I need to?

- Which assessment is right for me?

- How many assessments should I choose?

- In what order should I conduct the assessments?

There are no easy answers to these questions, as the best approach will vary depending on your organization's specific needs. It is possible to conduct and implement multiple security assessments before defining a clear strategy or approach to adopting or implementing the unified solution.

If you are unsure of how to start assessing your security posture, we recommend starting with a high-level assessment. This will give you a broad overview of your security and help you to identify any major areas of concern. Once you have identified your major areas of concern, you can conduct more detailed assessments to better understand the specific risks and **vulnerabilities** facing your organization or other details you are looking for.

It is important to continuously reassess your security posture to ensure that your organization is still protected from the latest **cyber threats**. The **threat landscape** is constantly evolving, and new risks and vulnerabilities are emerging all the time. Additionally, your security strategy may need to be updated to reflect changes in your organization or the threat landscape.

Security strategies

As mentioned in the previous section, it is important to define, plan, and implement strategies based on the outcomes of your **security assessment(s)**. Like assessments, multiple strategies can be considered depending on your organization's specific requirements and needs.

Ideally, your strategies should include some of the following:

- **Clear direction and goals**: What do you want to achieve with Microsoft's unified XDR and SIEM solution?

- **Implementation plan**: How do you implement the solution?

- **Security monitoring**: How are you going to monitor the solution to ensure that it is working effectively?

- **Measurable success**: How will you measure the success of your adoption or implementation?

- **Maintenance**: How will you maintain the solution over time?

- **Risk planning**: How will you mitigate the risks associated with adopting or implementing the solution?

- **Training:** How do you ensure the team's readiness and the effectiveness of their training plan?

Now let's look at some of the assessments and strategies we can consider before we adopt Microsoft's unified XDR and SIEM solution:

- **Piloting strategy**: This is one of the most common strategies many organizations adopt and start with. Start by implementing the solution for a subset of users or devices. Do not try to implement the solution across your entire organization all at once; we always recommend you start with piloting the solution. Learn about the tool's features, capabilities, prerequisites, potential roadblocks, pros, and cons. This will help you to leverage the tool's capabilities to the fullest and ensure that it is a good fit for your organization.

  Evaluate and test the tool's recommendations within your organization. Potential conflicts or risks concerning other internal tools/applications may arise due to the tool's configuration, which varies for each customer. There is no one-size-fits-all solution, so it is important to pilot the tool with a small subset of users or devices before implementing it across your entire organization.

  Here are some additional benefits of piloting the tool with a small subset of users or devices:

  - It allows you to identify any potential problems with the tool before rolling it out to your entire organization

  - It helps to identify all the prerequisites needed and reduce the potential business downtime later

  - It also identifies the training needs for your employees on how to use the tool before they start using it in a production environment

  - It allows you to gather feedback from your employees on the tool and to make any necessary adjustments before rolling it out to your entire organization

  - In certain cases, this can also help to do a side-by-side comparison with the existing tool

  Let's take a look at an example.

  Piloting **Microsoft Defender for Endpoint** (**MDE**) requires a well-defined plan.

  The following are the high-level steps:

  - Start with exclusions on both sides (MDE and your non-Microsoft AV/EDR solution). This will prevent the two solutions from interfering with each other.

  - Never start by uninstalling the non-Microsoft EDR solution and then installing MDE. This will leave your endpoints unprotected.

  - Use the MDE client analyzer to identify any gaps in the prerequisites. Address these gaps before onboarding pilot devices to MDE.

  - Simulate a test incident to make sure that devices have been onboarded successfully.

  - Review your existing rules in your non-Microsoft solution. Map these rules to MDE features or migrate them to MDE.

- Verify the status of MDE to make sure that it is either in passive or EDR block mode. Microsoft recommends enabling EDR block mode to allow MDE to block malicious behaviors detected after a breach.

- Slowly deploy ASR rules and other ASR capabilities in audit/warn mode. Once you are satisfied with the results, you can gradually transition to block mode.

- Consider uninstalling the non-Microsoft solution once MDE is fully deployed and operational.

Refer to `https://packt.link/fDVIu` for more details on the piloting or migration.

> **Note**
>
> Piloting the Microsoft unified XDR and SIEM solution can help you identify any gaps in the product compared to non-Microsoft solutions. Assessing these gaps is important, but we recommend that you always consider the holistic benefits of the solution rather than just the individual benefits of each product.

- **Licensing assessment and strategy**: This assessment and strategy can be part of or combined with other strategies, such as cost reduction, **Return on Investment** (**ROI**), and gap analysis strategies. Before adopting Microsoft XDR, it is important to have a licensing strategy in place. Microsoft XDR is a suite of security products and services that require a variety of licenses. The specific licenses you need will depend on your organization's specific needs and requirements.

  Typically, organizations adopt this strategy in cases such as the following:

  - When organizations are planning to buy licenses for Microsoft 365 E5 or A5, or when they are upgrading their licenses from Microsoft 365 E3 to E5 or A3 to A5, they try to get the most out of the tools that come with those licenses.

  - Another scenario is a company that has Microsoft 365 E3 or A3 licenses and is planning to replace its other non-Microsoft solutions with the Microsoft unified XDR and SIEM solution. However, this is part of a multi-quarter or multi-year roadmap, and the company does not want to upgrade its licenses immediately

    For example, if the company only plans to replace its non-Microsoft EDR solution in the current fiscal year, it might make sense to temporarily purchase MDE P2 licenses and then slowly transition to Microsoft 365 E5 or A5 licenses. This means that the company can start using the Microsoft unified XDR and SIEM solution without having to upgrade its licenses immediately. This can be a cost-effective option for companies that are not ready to upgrade their licenses all at once. However, some of the features or tool's capabilities will be limited until they upgrade their licenses

    If a company is using Microsoft 365 E3 or A3 licenses and does not plan to acquire or upgrade to E5 or A5 licenses, but they are interested in one of the advanced features of the XDR solution, they can purchase an individual license for that tool. For example, they could purchase a license for MDE P2 or the MDVM add-on.

- **ROI assessment and strategy**: This strategy will help the organization ensure that their security investments are worthwhile and deliver measurable value. Typically, before implementing this strategy, organizations conduct a current state assessment to review their existing security posture and use that as a baseline for comparison. After adopting the Microsoft unified XDR and SIEM solution, they conduct an ROI assessment to ensure that their security-related investments are justified and delivering the expected value by comparing the current state to the baseline.

  ROI = [Net Benefits - Total Cost of Ownership (TCO)] / TCO

  Take the following examples:

  - Organizations that are currently using a non-Microsoft SIEM and are planning to replace it with Microsoft Sentinel should calculate their ROI based on the following factors:

    - **Existing spending budget:** Includes the cost of the non-Microsoft SIEM, as well as the cost of integrating it with other security tools.

    - **Migration cost:** This is the cost of migrating data and configuration from the non-Microsoft SIEM to Microsoft Sentinel, as well as additional cost spending for the side-by-side implementation during the migration

    - **Maintenance cost:** Includes the cost of maintaining Microsoft Sentinel, as well as the cost of maintaining any integrations with other security tool

      To calculate the ROI, organizations can compare the **Total Cost of Ownership** (**TCO**) of their current non-Microsoft SIEM solution to the TCO of Microsoft Sentinel. The TCO should include all the costs associated with the solution, such as licensing, ongoing developments, integrations, maintenance, support, and training.

  - Organizations that are currently handling incident remediation manually and are considering adopting Microsoft Sentinel SOAR can expect to significantly reduce their costs. The TCO for the manual incident remediation should include the resource cost, training, and business impact or risks during remediation and use this as a baseline and comparison against the cost of adopting Microsoft Sentinel (which includes onboarding, migration if applicable, maintenance, training, resource costs, and licensing).

- **Gaps assessment and strategy**: This assessment allows you to identify the gaps in your security posture, address them by implementing security tools, and come up with a strategy to address them. You can also combine this strategy with other strategies, such as licensing strategies, to leverage your existing licenses by adopting the tools that are part of them. Once you have identified the gaps, prioritize them based on the risk they pose to your organization and develop a plan to address those gaps to harden the attack surface.

Take the following examples:

- If you have a Microsoft 365 E5 or A5 license and do not have a detection tool to detect advanced attacks in a hybrid environment, these strategies can help you to identify the gaps and adopt the MDI tool that is part of your existing license.

- If your current email security solution does not cover Safe Links and Safe Attachments, you should consider using **Microsoft Defender for Office 365 (MDO)** to implement these policies for Teams, OneDrive, and SharePoint. You do not have to replace your current email security solution if you are happy with it or need time to replace it. You can use MDO as an additional layer of security and apply the Safe Links and Safe Attachments policies to specific users. However, we recommend that you eventually replace your current email security solution with MDO, as it offers significant benefits, such as holistic security, XDR integration with auto disruption capabilities, and native benefits.

- **Cost reduction assessment and strategy**: This assessment is very useful when you need to reduce costs immediately without compromising on security. It is often combined with other assessments, such as licensing assessments, ROI assessments, and outsourcing assessments, to develop a well-defined strategy with a potential roadmap that can contribute to cost reduction. This process can also identify and eliminate unnecessary security-related spending apart from prioritizing your security needs.

The following are some examples:

- Organizations with Microsoft 365 E5/A5 licenses who are heavily using non-Microsoft solutions such as EDR, **Cloud Access Security Broker (CASB)**, and office protection solutions may benefit from this assessment to reduce costs by replacing those solutions with MDE, MDA, and MDO, which are included in those licenses.

- Organizations that are using a non-Microsoft SIEM and investing time and money in building and maintaining integrations between the SIEM and other security tools can use this assessment and strategy to eliminate most of the manual integration effort and maintenance by adopting or implementing the Microsoft unified XDR and SIEM solution.

Few organizations are now conducting AI assessments as part of their cost-reduction efforts. They are exploring ways to reduce costs by adopting AI, such as investing in Copilot for Security, which can significantly reduce SOC budgets and improve response times to security incidents.

- **Integration assessment and strategy**: This assessment and strategy can be very helpful for organizations that are dealing with a large number of data sources, non-Microsoft tools, and infrastructure challenges such as firewalls and disconnected/isolated networks. This assessment can provide high-level insights and validate the Microsoft unified XDR and SIEM solution, including how to adopt it, when to adopt it, and the prerequisites for data integration, data ingestion, tools, and so on, then help with defining the strategy. It also helps the organization to identify and address any potential performance or scalability issues associated with implementing the solution and estimating the costs of implementing, migrating (if applicable), and maintaining the solution.

Take the following example.

An organization wants to implement MDE, MDO, and MDI as soon as possible, but they do not have the budget or resources to adopt all of the solutions at once. They also want to continue using their non-Microsoft SIEM system for the next few years.

This integration assessment can help the organization to identify the data integration requirements that they will need to address in order to make these different systems work together. This includes identifying the integration requirements for MDE, MDO, and MDI to integrate with their non-Microsoft SIEM system, ticketing systems (such as ServiceNow and Jira), and threat intelligence platforms.

- **Security monitoring assessment and strategy**: This assessment helps organizations understand and evaluate their security monitoring and incident response capabilities. It is important to conduct this assessment on a regular basis, as in threats and attacks are constantly evolving, and organizations need to adapt their security posture accordingly. This assessment will give you the opportunity to understand what is currently being monitored, gaps in your security monitoring and incident response capabilities, challenges, strengths and weaknesses in your security posture, how to detect and respond to security incidents more effectively, and so on. It will also provide guidance on developing a strategy to address the challenges identified.

Take the following examples:

  - If your organization's SOC team is struggling to analyze threat actors and respond to security incidents in a timely manner, this security monitoring assessment can help you identify these challenges and develop a strategy to adopt **Microsoft Defender for Threat Intelligence (MDTI)** to integrate with Microsoft Sentinel for gathering threat intelligence to improve your threat analysis.

  - This assessment can help organizations to reassess their SOC maturity level before considering options to reduce the cost of Microsoft Sentinel. For example, organizations could build a security data lake with **Azure Data Explorer (ADX)** and redirect certain logs there instead of to the Log Analytics workspace. This would allow the SOC team to access the logs at the security data lake when needed. However, this type of architecture requires a mature SOC team.

If an organization is struggling to handle its security incidents and respond to them in a timely manner, and its SOC team is constantly looking for guidance, then considering Copilot for Security will significantly improve the SOC team's performance.

- **Outsourcing assessment and strategy (for example, MDR or MXDR)**: This assessment and strategy helps organizations to identify their core strengths and weaknesses and the tasks they can outsource to professional companies when they do not have the resources, bandwidth, or knowledge to handle them. This is sometimes also executed as a shared model (not 100% outsourced), where both the organization and the professional company are responsible for these tasks.

Conducting this assessment and defining a strategy before adopting the Microsoft unified XDR and SIEM solution will help the organization in the following ways:

- This assessment and strategy can help organizations to identify the tasks that they can outsource to professional companies, which can save time and money.

- It provides organizations with a high-level estimate of the costs associated with implementing and using the Microsoft unified XDR and SIEM solution.

- It also helps organizations decide when and how to adopt the Microsoft unified XDR and SIEM solution, based on their specific needs and requirements.

- Organizations will be able to develop a plan for implementing the Microsoft unified XDR and SIEM solution that is tailored to its specific needs of what needs to be outsourced.

This will be discussed in more detail in *Chapter 9*.

- **Vulnerability management assessment and strategy**: Many organizations adopt this assessment and strategy because it can help them identify and address **misconfigurations** and **vulnerabilities**, which can expose their systems to cyberattacks and data breaches. As digital estates and needs expand, it is becoming increasingly difficult for organizations to manage all of their misconfigurations and vulnerabilities. This can lead them to adopt multiple vulnerability tools, which can be time-consuming and expensive to integrate. Even after doing so, organizations may still lack a comprehensive and unified view of their security posture.

This assessment and strategy can help organizations to identify these areas and eliminate the need for multiple tools by adopting the Microsoft unified XDR and SIEM solution. This unified solution provides comprehensive visibility into an organization's security posture and can help to identify and address misconfigurations and vulnerabilities.

Here are a few examples:

- This assessment and strategy can help organizations that are using multiple vulnerability tools for their on-premises, multi-cloud, Kubernetes endpoints, and servers to replace those tools with **Microsoft Defender for Cloud** (**MDC**) and MDE. MDC and MDE can identify misconfigurations and vulnerabilities, and they provide a comprehensive unified view. Both tools are part of the Microsoft unified XDR and SIEM solution.

- This assessment and strategy can also help organizations identify the manual processes or custom integrations they need to implement to identify and handle misconfigurations and vulnerabilities. MDE supports direct integration with Intune. You can take advantage of MDE's threat and vulnerability management capabilities and use Intune to remediate endpoint weaknesses identified by MDE.

Security misconfigurations and vulnerability management were discussed in detail in *Chapter 6*.

- **Vendor evaluation assessment and strategy**: Many organizations choose to combine this assessment and strategy of evaluating the Microsoft unified XDR and SIEM solution with a pilot strategy. This allows them to validate whether the solution is a good fit for their organization currently, or whether they need to wait and adopt it in the future. While Microsoft's unified XDR and SIEM solution is a good fit for most customers, there may be a few situations where they would need to wait or choose a non-Microsoft solution. We encourage you to focus on the overall benefits of a holistic approach to security, rather than comparing individual products. This will help you to improve your overall security posture.

  If you are considering a non-Microsoft XDR and SIEM solution for a specific division, be sure to review the *How to choose the right XDR and SIEM tool* section in *Chapter 2*.

  Here are some specific examples of situations (apart from budget) where an organization might need to wait or choose a non-Microsoft XDR and SIEM solution:

  - Organizations that are still maintaining older versions of Windows servers or endpoints may need to consider a different solution, as these versions are not supported by MDE. But we highly recommend upgrading these older versions of Windows for better protection.

  - Organizations with strict **compliance requirements** regarding data storage may need to consider a different solution if the Microsoft unified XDR and SIEM solution does not support storing data in the required region. They can use a local solution for that subset of data until the regional storage option is available.

- **Zero Trust assessment and strategy:** The Zero Trust security assessment is one of the most common assessments used today. It is an essential step before implementing the Zero Trust security model. It helps organizations establish a strong security foundation based on the principles of least privilege, continuous monitoring, and continuous improvement to protect against modern cybersecurity threats.

  This assessment helps organizations evaluate their security posture to identify the gaps where they can improve it to align with the Zero Trust security model. We discussed the importance of zero trust in security operations in *Chapter 1*. This may require extensive team efforts, as the assessment will touch on all of the Zero Trust pillars, such as identity, endpoints, data, apps, infrastructure, and network (see the *Zero Trust pillars* section in *Chapter 1*).

- **Security risk assessment and strategy**: This assessment helps organizations to understand their security posture, including risk score, security risks, gaps, threats, defects, and vulnerabilities. It also helps them to prioritize these risks based on their budget and risk tolerance. The goal of the assessment is to identify potential threats and vulnerabilities and develop strategies to mitigate them. We encourage organizations to conduct this security risk assessment on a regular basis to analyze their potential risks, reassess their strategies, and make informed decisions about security investments.

Take the following examples:

- Organizations that are adopting the Microsoft unified XDR and SIEM solution and are concerned about their internal resources and skills can mitigate this risk by considering managed services such as managed EDR, managed XDR, and managed Sentinel.

- This assessment can help organizations identify the potential risks of not capturing reconnaissance and lateral movement activities on-premises and define a strategy to implement MDI.

- Organizations sometimes conduct penetration testing, also known as pen testing, to simulate cyberattacks and identify vulnerabilities. Pen testing uses the same tools and techniques that malicious actors use to find and exploit vulnerabilities. This helps organizations to understand their risks and areas where they need to improve their security posture.

- Similar organizations also conduct cyber resiliency assessments as part of their security risk assessments to understand their risk factors. A cyber resiliency assessment is a comprehensive evaluation of an organization's ability to withstand and recover from a cyberattack. It assesses the organization's security posture, incident response plan, and business continuity plan to identify areas for improvement. This helps organizations to understand the areas they need to focus on, how to increase resilience to cyberattacks, and more.

Before diving into the implementation, it's crucial to consider these key assessments and strategies for adopting Microsoft's unified XDR and SIEM solution. Remember, some of these assessments should be repeated periodically post-deployment to ensure continuous improvement. Now, let's explore the implementation process and key considerations for a smooth transition.

Implementation approach and roadmap

XDR is a platform that involves using a collection of products, rather than a specific product. EDR is one of the most important products for XDR, as it provides the foundation for XDR's capabilities. Endpoints are involved in most security incidents, especially attacks on high-value assets such as servers. Phishing emails and compromised identities are frequently used by attackers to gain access to applications and steal sensitive data.

Forrester, a leading cybersecurity research firm, has stated in one of their reports that *"good XDR lives and dies by the foundation of good EDR"* and *"EDR is dead. Long live XDR."* This highlights the importance of EDR to XDR and the fact that XDR is the next evolution of EDR. In other words, you need to start with EDR before you can implement XDR. EDR is the foundation of XDR, and it is essential for detecting and responding to threats on endpoints.

When implementing this Microsoft unified XDR and SIEM solution, organizations may face some of the following challenges:

- Conflicts with the existing or changing landscape, where organizations may still be using legacy tools that are difficult to integrate with XDR.

- Handling different log sources, data types, and formatting issues. XDR systems need to be able to collect and analyze data from a variety of sources, including endpoints, networks, and cloud environments. This data can be in different formats, and XDR systems need to be able to normalize it before it can be analyzed.

- Organizations with multiple tenants may have specific needs to implement XDR in a way that supports each tenant's unique security requirements.

- Organizations might face challenges with compliance requirements and regional restrictions, as XDR solutions need to comply with all applicable regulations and meet any regional restrictions that may be in place.

- Cost-effectiveness. Even though there are many benefits to XDR, XDR can be a significant investment apart from the ongoing investments in the security area, but it is important to choose a solution that is cost-effective for the organization.

- Unsupported software and infrastructure. Organizations with incredibly old or unsupported versions of their software or infrastructure may have difficulty implementing XDR.

- Organizations with complex security controls can face challenges with integrations, as XDR solutions need to be able to integrate with existing security controls, which can be complex.

- Skill gaps and budget issues. Organizations may not have the necessary skills or budget to implement and manage an XDR solution.

- Organizations might face challenges meeting some of the prerequisites for this Microsoft unified solution, so it's always a good practice to verify the prerequisites using Microsoft-recommended tools such as MDE Client Analyzer, the sizing tool for MDI, and the **Office 365 Advanced Threat Protection Recommended Configuration Analyzer (ORCA)** tool.

Adoption order

The order in which you adopt the Microsoft unified XDR and SIEM solution will vary depending on your organization's specific needs. However, we recommend that you consider conducting some of the security assessments mentioned previously and developing a strategy for adoption before you begin implementing XDR, SIEM, and managed services.

As we mentioned before, EDR is the foundation for XDR. However, the order in which organizations adopt EDR and XDR depends on their immediate needs, gaps, budgets, and priorities. If you have not already set up Microsoft Defender XDR components, Microsoft recommends enabling them in the order shown in *Figure 8.2*.

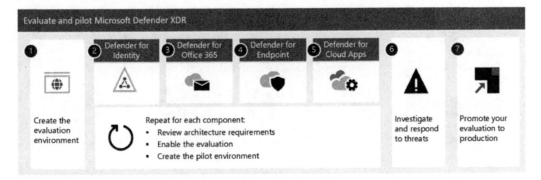

Figure 8.2 – Microsoft's recommended order of enabling Microsoft Defender XDR components

This order is commonly recommended because it provides the most value as quickly as possible, based on the effort required to deploy and configure each capability. For example, MDO can be configured more quickly than enrolling devices in MDE.

> **Note**
>
> You should prioritize the XDR components based on your business needs, and you can enable them in a different order if necessary. To understand your needs and priorities, we strongly encourage you to conduct some of the assessments discussed in this chapter, such as a security gaps assessment, cost reduction assessment, and security risk assessment.

Right after implementing these individual defender solutions, you can consider extending its capabilities to on-premises, multi-cloud, and IoT environments by adopting MDC and Microsoft Defender for IoT (see *Figure 8.3*). Organizations can implement multiple defender solutions at the same time, depending on their budget and resources. It may take months or even years to implement all of Microsoft Defender's capabilities, depending on the complexity of your current security posture.

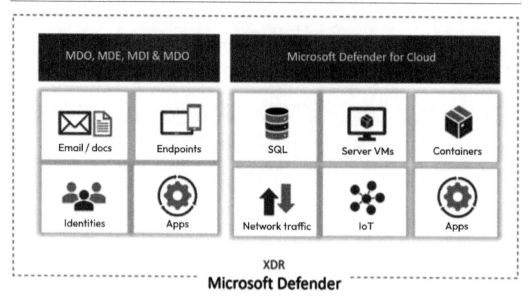

Figure 8.3 – High-level Microsoft Defender coverage

Please see Microsoft's documentation for instructions on how to set up XDR tools `https://packt.link/9p0Kg`.

When it comes to implementing Microsoft Sentinel, you do not have to wait until you complete the adoption of XDR; you can start onboarding Microsoft Sentinel from day one, along with the Defender products. There are different ways to implement it as mentioned below, depending on the specific needs of the organization; each approach has its challenges. We need to consider these challenges and develop a strategy for a successful rollout of SIEM and SOAR, here are some of the implementation approaches:

- A greenfield implementation of Microsoft Sentinel when there is no existing SIEM or SOAR, which means Sentinel would be the first SIEM and SOAR solution implemented in the organization.

- Organizations can consider implementing Microsoft Sentinel as a side-by-side SIEM. This means they will have two SIEMs running simultaneously, but they will forward security incidents from one SIEM to the other, depending on their needs, and rely on one of their SOAR platforms for automation. This approach will allow organizations to take advantage of the benefits of Microsoft Sentinel, such as native integration with other Microsoft security products and cloud-native architecture.

  Here are the possible scenarios with recommendations from Microsoft when using two SIEMs:

  - Moving logs from Microsoft Sentinel to your legacy SIEM – not recommended

  - Moving logs from your legacy SIEM to Microsoft Sentinel – not recommended

  - Using Microsoft Sentinel and your legacy SIEM side by side as two separate solutions – not recommended

- Sending alerts and enriched incidents from Microsoft Sentinel into your legacy SIEM – suboptimal

- Sending alerts from your legacy SIEM to Microsoft Sentinel – recommended

- Organizations looking to replace their existing SIEM (legacy SIEM or modern non-Microsoft SIEM).

  Here are the steps you would follow at a high level:

  - Onboard Microsoft Sentinel.

  - Implement **Out-of-the-Box (OOTB)** cloud-native connectors.

  - Send alerts and enriched incidents from Microsoft Sentinel into your legacy SIEM until you complete the migration and the SOC team is mature enough to handle Microsoft Sentinel or you establish a managed SOC service.

  - Focus on migrating your data sources, rules, TIs, reports, and other components from your non-Microsoft SIEM to Microsoft Sentinel.

  - Migrate your historical data for compliance requirements.

  - Define and implement a strategy to make Microsoft Sentinel as primary SIEM and also define strategy for data retention and archiving.

  - Sunset the non-Microsoft SIEM after testing and monitoring for a certain period.

Tip

We highly recommend tracking your migration with the Microsoft Sentinel Deployment and Migration workbook. Refer to `https://packt.link/TXOQv` for more details on how to deploy and use it.

Also, keep in mind that migrating from a non-Microsoft tool to Microsoft Defender solution is not the same as a greenfield implementation. Organizations need to have a well-defined migration strategy and plan in place.

We strongly recommend following Microsoft's migration guides. See the following:

- Microsoft's documentation for migrating from a third-party protection service or device to MDO: `https://packt.link/SXnMp`

- Microsoft's documentation for migrating from a non-Microsoft solution to MDE: `https://packt.link/O1DxS` and `https://packt.link/M38zo`

- Microsoft's documentation for migrating from a third-party SIEM to Microsoft Sentinel: `https://packt.link/XklZI` and `https://packt.link/Pm998`

Managed service options are also available, so you don't have to wait until you have completely implemented all of the products in the unified solution. In some cases, considering managed services early can be beneficial for your team, as they allow you to rely on the expertise of professional companies for security monitoring. This can free up your team to focus on the implementation or on establishing internal SOC operations. *Figure 8.4* shows the three major stages of the adoption order.

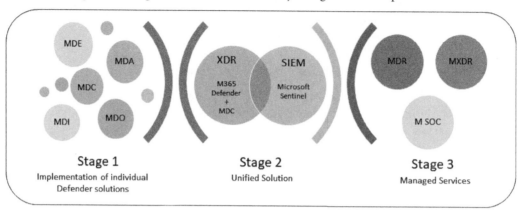

Figure 8.4 – Microsoft unified XDR and SIEM solution – implementation

As a best practice, always start with small sample (such as endpoints for MDE, Apps for MDA, etc) and gradually roll out to large subsets, no matter what product you are implementing. Also, adopting certain features can take a couple of months, to minimize the business impact and risks; hence, start with audit mode where applicable then slowly transition into warn mode or block mode depending on the requirements, for example, **Attack Surface Rules** (**ASRs**), network protection, and controlled folder access in MDE.

Figure 8.5 shows a sample implementation plan with high-level activities. Some of these activities may vary depending on the product, but most of them follow a similar implementation approach. We recommend that you refer to the Microsoft Learn documentation for each of these products for more information on required prerequisites, migration approaches, feature and security control adoption, and side-by-side approaches.

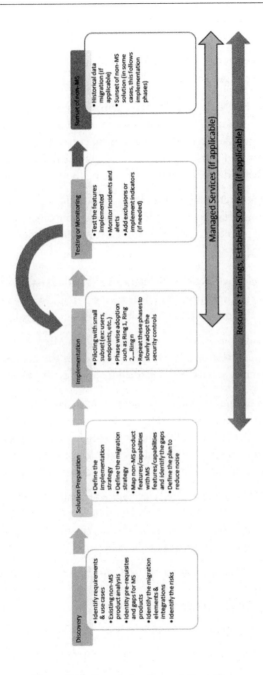

Figure 8.5 – Sample implementation plan

To ensure your Microsoft unified XDR and SIEM solution delivers its full potential, let's dive into these critical post-deployment considerations.

What's next?

There are certain things we need to consider after implementing this Microsoft unified XDR and SIEM solution, and here are a few:

- **Data retention/archival**: Data retention and archival are essential activities for all organizations. They help to protect against data loss and ensure compliance with regulations. However, it is important to configure data retention and archival correctly to avoid unnecessary costs. The cost of data retention and archival depends on several factors, including the amount of data to be retained, the retention period, and the storage method.

   When configuring data retention and archival, organizations should consider their compliance requirements and business needs. For example, some companies are required to maintain logs for a certain period of time in order to comply with regulations.

   Take the following examples:

   - Microsoft Sentinel provides access to interactive data for two years and archival data for up to 12 years. This can be configured directly from the portal. However, depending on your needs and budget, there are other options available, such as archiving data to Blob storage or ADX.

   - Microsoft Defender XDR data can be ingested into Microsoft Sentinel or other storage options mentioned previously for future reference, as the default data retention period is limited. For example, MDE data is retained for 180 days by default.

- **Continuous features update**: Microsoft is constantly investing in improving its products to protect against cyber threats. As a result, it is important for organizations to develop a process for reviewing new features and additions to the Microsoft XDR and SIEM unified solution, assessing the impact on their security posture, and prioritizing and implementing those features that are most important to their needs (budget versus security needs).

- **Managed services**: Managed security services are typically provided by security experts 24/7. They continuously monitor and analyze data to help organizations improve their security coverage against threats. These services include security monitoring, threat detection, training, investigation, remediation, and hunting.

   Managed security services are a good option for organizations with skills gaps or that need to rely on experts. They can be outsourced on an individual basis, depending on your specific needs. This can be a significant cost-effective option for many organizations.

   Take the following examples:

   - If you don't have the resources or expertise to monitor your endpoints internally, consider **managed EDR** services. You can also consider **managed XDR** services for your unified XDR solutions and managed Sentinel for your SIEM solution.

- When you are adopting a Microsoft unified XDR and SIEM solution and replacing all of your non-Microsoft solutions, it is sometimes wise to consider managed services for the solutions as you deploy when you have limited resources and skill gaps and need to rely on cybersecurity experts for some time. For example, as soon as you complete replacing your non-Microsoft EDR solution with MDE, you can onboard managed EDR services. Then, you can focus on replacing other areas, such as non-Microsoft email security, with MDO.

  Gradually, you can switch to managed XDR services as you keep adopting the unified XDR solution and then managed Sentinel if you have onboarded it. This way, your team can continue focusing on other priorities, such as replacing non-Microsoft solutions with the Microsoft unified XDR and SIEM solution. This will also give you the opportunity to train your team and establish internal teams to manage these solutions in the future.

  This will be discussed in more detail in *Chapter 9*.

- **Cyber insurance**: Cyber insurance is an insurance policy some organizations have started considering that provides financial compensation to businesses who have suffered a cyberattack. This includes the cost of recovering from data breaches, defending against cyberattacks, and dealing with business interruptions. Cyber insurance is an important part of any organization's risk management strategy and worth considering for businesses of all sizes, but especially small businesses.

  Which type of cyber insurance policy is right for you will depend on your business's specific needs. There are many different companies that offer cyber insurance, so it is important to compare policies and choose one that fits your budget and needs.

  Cyber insurance is not a replacement for strong cybersecurity measures. However, it can help businesses to recover from cyberattacks and minimize business disruption.

  Participating insurers now use Microsoft Secure Score to provide posture-based rates to small and medium-sized businesses; hence, the higher the Secure Score, the better rate you can expect. We discussed Microsoft Secure Score in detail in *Chapter 7*.

- **Microsoft Secure Score**: Microsoft Secure Score is a measure of an organization's security posture. It is important to monitor your Secure Score regularly and review the recommendations that Microsoft provides to reduce your attack surface. This was discussed in detail in *Chapter 7*.

Case study analysis

Now let's look at some of the challenges High Tech Rapid Solutions Corp is facing as mentioned in the case study at the beginning of this book.

Management has initiated cost reduction strategies across the organization and allocated limited funds to the security team, asking them to reduce their costs and headcount and submit an ROI for any proposals, but at the same time asking them to enhance the security.

The assessments mentioned in this chapter, such as the cost reduction assessment, ROI assessment, and licensing strategy assessment, can provide valuable insights to management before making any decisions. The cost reduction assessment can identify the areas where costs can be reduced or adjusted, the ROI assessment can help to determine the ROI from adopting this Microsoft unified XDR and SIEM solution, and the licensing strategy assessment can help management to understand the most cost-effective option to adopt this unified XDR and SIEM solution.

The existing security team is not ready to adopt new technologies and needs training and guidance for the new initiatives.

High Tech Rapid Solutions Corp can easily assess whether their current infrastructure is ready for the Microsoft unified XDR and SIEM solution by conducting a vendor evaluation assessment. Additionally, piloting an assessment and strategy can help them to deploy this solution for a small subset and test it.

The SOC team has limited resources, which is leading to challenges in triaging, investigation, and remediation. These delays are being escalated to senior management. Also, the SecOps team doesn't have enough knowledge about the Entra ID application consent framework and how new and existing application registrations and permissions should be evaluated.

Outsourcing assessment and strategy can help management identify gaps in areas within the organization and consider managed services by outsourcing to MSSPs until their team has the necessary training and maturity to handle the solution themselves.

The CISO is concerned about ongoing attacks, such as ransomware and BEC attacks.

This security challenge can be addressed with some of the assessments discussed in this chapter, such as the following:

- Vulnerability assessment can help the team to identify potential misconfigurations and vulnerabilities in their systems and networks. This information can then be used to develop a strategy to address those issues.

- Gaps assessment helps the team to identify the weaknesses within their security posture and potential risks and develop plans to address them.

- Security monitoring assessment can help the SOC team identify gaps in their current security monitoring and develop strategies to address those gaps with Microsoft Sentinel SIEM and SOAR automation.

- Zero trust assessment can help the team assess each zero trust pillar mentioned in *Chapter 1*, identify gaps and risks in their security posture, and develop a strategy to adopt the zero trust security model.

- Additionally, management can consider outsourcing assessment to identify the weak areas as part of the risk management strategy and consider managed services such as managed EDR, managed XDR, and managed Sentinel.

Summary

This chapter highlighted the importance of evaluating and planning before adopting the Microsoft unified XDR and SIEM solution. We also discussed common security assessments and strategies to be considered before adopting this Microsoft unified solution. We also covered the typical implementation roadmap for the Microsoft unified XDR and SIEM solution. Finally, we discussed some of the considerations after implementing this unified solution.

In the next chapter, we will discuss managed services for XDR and Sentinel and how these services can benefit organizations with a skills gap and a need to rely on experts or professional services.

Further reading

For more details on the topics covered in this chapter, please refer to the following links:

- *CISOs are struggling to get cybersecurity budgets: Report*: https://packt.link/wJROk. In a climate of budget cuts, it is essential for CISOs to carefully select the right tools and develop a robust plan. The assessments and strategies discussed in this chapter can be invaluable in ensuring that the budget is used effectively.

- Security Operations Self-Assessment Tool | Microsoft Security: https://packt.link/MncO8

- Microsoft Secure Score assessment: https://packt.link/v4tIz

- Microsoft Security Blog | Digital Security Tips and Solutions: https://packt.link/vScsq. Provides up-to-date information on security threats, best practices, and so on.

- The **Microsoft Security Assessment Tool** (**MSAT**) is a risk assessment application designed to provide information and recommendations about best practices for security within an **Information Technology** (**IT**) infrastructure. Download the MSAT from the official Microsoft Download Center: https://www.microsoft.com/en-au/download/details.aspx?id=12273

- What's new in Microsoft Defender XDR | Microsoft Learn: https://packt.link/jrsyL

- What's new in Microsoft Sentinel | Microsoft Learn: https://packt.link/d02UY

- Microsoft Digital Defense Report – *Building and improving cyber resilience, Executive Summary*, October 2023: https://packt.link/pTDAK

- Microsoft Digital Defense Report – *Building and improving cyber resilience*, full report, October 2023: https://packt.link/QI5mq

- Cyber insurance guidance from National Cyber Security Centre: https://packt.link/IM9Ge

- Microsoft 365 licensing guide by Aaron Dinnage: https://packt.link/TZtIT

- Evaluate and pilot Microsoft Defender XDR: https://packt.link/xW8DL

Managed XDR and SIEM Services

In the fast-paced world of cybersecurity, staying ahead of the game is no easy feat. That's where in-house cybersecurity operations or managed services come into play. These aren't just nice-to-haves—they're must-haves if an organization wants to protect itself from an increasing number of attacks.

The following topics are covered in this chapter:

- Overview of managed services
- The generic **managed security services provider** (MSSP) framework in the Microsoft ecosystem
- Pros and cons of having in-house cybersecurity operations or managed services

Managed services overview

Let's dive into the details of managed services and explore what they offer.

Managed services is a term that is commonly used to describe a subscription-based approach that enables businesses to assign particular tasks or services to an outside partner. These service providers— also referred to as MSSPs in the cybersecurity domain—take on the duty of supplying, managing, and maintaining the assigned service. Managed services in the field of cybersecurity typically entail contracting with a specialized vendor to handle **Security Operations Center** (SOC) functions.

Next, we cover some of the typical services that are provided by MSSPs. It's understandable that the services MSSPs provide vary between providers, but the next section contains some common and well-known services that MSSPs typically provide to organizations.

Security services

According to *Gartner MSSP Market Guide 2022*, the services between MSSPs can vary a lot but there are some commonalities in terms of security services. Here are some of these services, which are provided as continuous or as consultancy type of services:

- **Managed detection and response (MDR)**: This service provides 24/7 monitoring of and response to security incidents. MDR or **managed extended detection and response (MXDR)** is typically provided.

  MDR is a service offering that combines human knowledge with advanced technologies to provide continuous, round-the-clock (24/7) monitoring, threat detection, incident response, and overall management of security tools and processes. MDR typically covers organization networks, endpoints, and cloud environments but coverage might differ between service providers. It also uses **threat intelligence (TI)** and threat hunting to find and stop attacks faster and has been typically focused on **Endpoint Detection and Response (EDR)**.

  MXDR is an upgraded version of MDR that extends coverage to more areas of an organization's attack surface and combines several technologies and functionalities. In order to provide a comprehensive and cohesive view of the security posture, MXDR services include proactive threat hunting, incident response, remediation, and enhancing environment security posture. Its main objectives are to increase the speed and effectiveness of threat detection and response procedures while reducing the complexity and expense of managing a variety of instruments.

  The main difference between MDR and MXDR is the scope of protection. MXDR offers a more comprehensive and holistic view of your environment, while MDR typically focuses on the core components of an organization's infrastructure. Both solutions can help you improve environment security posture, prioritize incidents, respond faster, and manage vulnerabilities.

- **TI services**: As we have elaborated throughout the book, TI plays a very important role in modern **security operations center (SOC)** operations. Typically, a TI service collects, analyzes, and shares data on potential threats and vulnerabilities.

  Drawing from diverse sources, including open intelligence and proprietary feeds, these services provide detailed insights into **indicators of compromise (IoCs)**, tactics, and procedures used by threat actors. SOC teams can leverage this information to predict and proactively address future threats, offering both tactical and strategic intelligence.

  - **Tactical TI**: This provides details about current threats and incidents.
  - **Strategic TI**: This provides details about broader trends, threat actors, and long-term security planning.

  These facilitate collaborative information sharing and the delivery of customized reports that provide actionable insights and recommendations. By leveraging these reports, organizations can understand the potential impact and further strengthen their defenses.

  By using TI services, organizations can strengthen their cybersecurity posture, respond more effectively to threats, and make informed decisions to protect their sensitive information and digital assets.

- **Security posture management**: Environment security posture management is the service that aims to ensure that infrastructure and applications are configured and maintained according to the best security practices (such as continuous posture management and **threat and vulnerability management (TVM)**).

  The cloud environment and its features are constantly evolving, which means that you need to keep up with the latest updates and changes. If you don't, you may expose your cloud assets to new vulnerabilities or miss out on new security capabilities.

  Attacks are also evolving as threat actors use sophisticated techniques and tools to exploit environments, especially cloud environments. For example, they may leverage misconfigurations, compromised credentials, or serverless functions to gain access to organization data or resources.

  Security posture management is often neglected as many organizations focus more on security monitoring and incident response. However, these reactive measures are not enough, and it is necessary to adopt a proactive approach that continuously assesses and improves an organization's security posture.

- **Co-managed detection**: Especially in larger organizations, there might be both in-house and outsourced security operations in place. This model is called a **hybrid approach** to security operations, where the MSSP works alongside the organization's internal security team. A good example of this is a scenario where the MSSP handles 24/7 security monitoring and deeper investigations (tier-3 operations) are done by an in-house security operations team.

- **Security assessments**: As we elaborated in *Chapter 8*, a security assessment strategy is extremely important. It is important to continuously reassess your organization's security posture to ensure that your organization is still protected from the latest cyber threats. The **threat landscape** is constantly evolving, and new risks and vulnerabilities are emerging all the time. Additionally, your security strategy may need to be updated to reflect changes in your organization or the threat landscape.

  Also, it's important to perform a security assessment of the major platforms you are using through a cycle that is convenient for your organization. For example, when was the last time your organization performed a deep-dive **Microsoft Entra ID** or **Azure** platform assessment?

- **Digital forensics and incident response (DFIR)**: DFIR services are a subset of cybersecurity services that assist organizations in discovering, containing, and recovering from security incidents as well as gathering, evaluating, and storing digital evidence in order to combat cyberattacks. Together with associated proactive and reactive security services, a DFIR service usually provides a combination of **digital forensics (DF)** and **incident response (IR)** capabilities. Even though a DFIR service is typically provided as on demand, it's a crucial service to have alongside continuous 24/7 security monitoring and other services that MSSPs provide to their clients.

- **Application SOC (AppSOC)**: In recent years, concerns have been arising about application security posture management in organizations. MSSPs have created a service around this need called AppSOC, whose main idea is to focus on application security and provide continuous monitoring around this domain as well.

- **Tech maintenance and advisory support**: If the MSSP is using modern security solutions, maintaining infrastructure takes less time than compared to solutions that are monitoring it by themselves. Security technology maintenance and management still play a crucial role on the MSSP side. Constant service development, for example, in the scope of MDR/XDR is needed for the service to be up to date and for the MSSP to be able to detect and mitigate constantly evolving threats. At the same time, advisory consulting is needed to understand the newly released features, their impact, and the adoption strategy.

- Also, there are still servers to maintain. Even though modern SIEM would be used (Sentinel, etc.), you need Syslog forwarder servers to ingest data from custom Linux-based log sources that don't provide REST API connection methods.

How to select a provider

In *Chapter 8*, we covered *Outsourcing Assessment and Strategy*, which helps organizations to identify their core strengths, weaknesses, and the tasks they can outsource to professional companies when they do not have the resources, bandwidth, or knowledge to handle them. This assessment along with the strategy is a very important phase in selecting the correct MSSP provider as an outsourcing partner.

The assessment outcome might also be that you want to build and maintain SOC functions as in-house operations, but it can be challenging, especially for **small and medium-sized businesses (SMBs)**. That's why some organizations opt to outsource their SOC to a third-party provider that offers SOC and other services as a managed service. But is outsourcing SOC or other functions a good idea? What are the benefits and drawbacks of having an outsourcing partner providing SOC as a managed service?

Some of the key areas to focus on when selecting the correct outsourcing partner are as follows:

- Choose a service provider that tailors its solutions to your specific requirements.

- Select a cybersecurity provider with a demonstrably successful track record in delivering high-quality services. Carefully review their experience, credentials, and customer testimonials to verify their capacity to address your company's security needs. While established firms abound, the burgeoning cybersecurity market also boasts smaller organizations capable of providing robust solutions. Consider all options, regardless of size, to secure the optimal partner for your data protection efforts.

- When choosing a supplier, prioritize transparency and clear communication regarding their processes, pricing, and service guarantees. Ensure you fully understand what your payment covers and establish clear expectations for reporting, response times, and preferred communication channels.

- To ensure continuous protection against cyberattacks, which can strike at any moment, especially outside business hours, it's critical that the supplier offers 24/7 response and monitoring services. This allows for swift identification and mitigation of risks.

- It's essential to verify the provider's compliance with applicable regulations such as GDPR, HIPAA, PCI DSS, and NIS2, which are crucial for your industry and region to protect your data and avoid legal or financial consequences.

- Seek a provider equipped with the latest TI capabilities to monitor evolving threat groups and their infrastructure. Implementing a **Threat Intelligence as a Service (TIaaS)** solution, as discussed earlier, would offer deeper strategic understanding and guidance.

- Remember, security comes at a cost. While managed security services (including SOC) can be expensive, prioritizing value is key. Carefully weigh the prices and service offerings from various vendors to find the perfect fit for your security requirements and budget limitations.

Pros and cons of using managed services

Some might say that there is no perfect service or solution and that every approach has its pros and cons. The following section contains some of the benefits of having a managed security service provider providing continuous managed services.

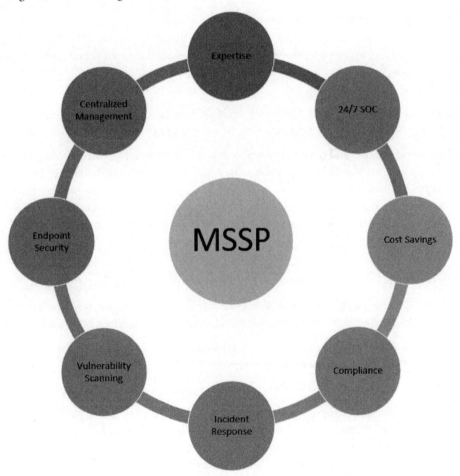

Figure 9.1 – Some of the benefits of the MSSP model

Let's start with the positives (see *Figure 9.1*):

- **Expertise**: An outsourcing partner has a team of experienced and certified professionals who specialize in cybersecurity, and have the skills and knowledge to handle various types of threats and incidents. MSSPs are also leveraging TI data, whose importance we have highlighted throughout the book.

- **24/7 security monitoring**: MSSPs monitor client environments 24/7, which ensures that incidents are investigated immediately, no matter when they happen. MSSPs also leverage automation and orchestration, which speeds up the investigation process.

- **Cost savings**: Outsourcing cybersecurity-related services, such as the SOC, can help reduce costs. Outsourcing can eliminate the need for costs associated, for example, with infrastructure, licenses, and staffing.

- **Development**: MSSPs continually advance their entire security stack, environment, and detection technologies to be able to detect the latest threats and attack vectors impacting their clients. The ongoing development is seamlessly integrated into the service price, providing advantages compared to in-house operations, where similar advancements can often incur significant development costs.

- **Focus on core competencies**: Outsource your SOC to a dedicated **MSSP**, allowing your internal teams to breathe easy and concentrate on their core business functions.

- **Security evaluation and compliance support**: With the expertise MSSPs have, they can provide security assessments of client environments, which it's important to do on a regular basis (see *Chapter 8* for more details). Also, many organizations need to meet regulatory compliance standards, such as PCI DSS, HIPAA, GDPR, NIST, ISO 27001, and NIS2, which MSSPs can help an organization achieve in order to measure their compliance status.

Here are the negatives of MSSPs:

- **Dependency**: Organizations rely heavily on the service provider to fulfill essential security needs.

- **Costs**: While organizations can save on costs by outsourcing security services, it's important to note that there may be additional services that could potentially elevate monthly expenses.

- **Integration challenges**: Integration with existing systems and processes can be challenging, depending on the provider's tools.

- **Customization limitations**: There is a limited scope for tailoring services to specific requirements.

- **In-house specialists and service owners**: Defining security specialists and service owners within a client organization is important as it brings notable benefits. This approach ensures clear accountability, effective communication, and more efficient decision-making processes. Especially in smaller organizations where dedicated security teams might be lacking, this may affect decision-making and present a challenge.

- **Vendor lock-in**: If the MSSP is providing services at the top of the modern solutions, it's relatively easy to change service providers, but changing vendors is another challenge. Migration from vendor to vendor can be costly and time-consuming depending on many factors.

In summary, the choice between different security services provided by MSSPs and which provider to select as an outsourcing partner depends on the organization's specific requirements, resources, and risk tolerance. Outsourcing services offers several benefits but it comes with considerations regarding costs, dependency, and the need for careful integration with existing IT environments.

Generic MSSP framework in the Microsoft ecosystem

Let's familiarize ourselves with Microsoft partnership models and basics. Microsoft partners can have different permission types depending on the partnership model that is used. Some of these permission types grant quite wide permissions to the customer environments. The full list of different permission types for partners can be found in the Microsoft Learn article at the following link: `https://packt.link/APXTm`. Some of these permissions are outlined in the following list:

- **Delegated Administration Privileges (DAP)**

  These are for partners that manage services for your organization or school. In Microsoft Entra ID, the partner has a Global Administrator permission.

  DAP has had issues from a security point of view in the past and nowadays Microsoft does not grant DAP for new customer creation. Instead, GDAP is granted when a new customer tenant is created.

- **Granular Delegated Admin Privileges (GDAP)**

  These are the same as DAP, but the permissions are more limited. The idea is to follow the least privilege principle to execute the needed tasks. For example, partners managing Azure don't receive Global Administrator permissions to customer tenants automatically.

- **Reseller**

  Partners who sell and manage Microsoft products to your organization or school.

- **Reseller and delegated administrator**

  Partners who sell and manage Microsoft products to your organization or school.

- **Partner**

  Granular access privilege granted to a partner account, allowing them to manage other Microsoft services on your behalf.

- **Advisor**

  Authorized partners have the ability to reset user passwords and address support inquiries.

- **Microsoft Products and Services Agreement (MPSA)** partner

  If you've collaborated with multiple companies through the MPSA program, you can grant them access to each other's purchase records.

- **Line-of-business (LOB)** partner

  Trusted partners can develop, submit, and manage line-of-business applications tailored to your organization's needs.

As we can see from the preceding list, there are plenty of different ways to grant permissions for a service provider to customer environments. Besides that, some of the models also grant permissions to the Azure environment or give a possibility to do so.

> **Important**
> DAP, which is used on the CSP model, is on the sunset path, and GDAP is the way to go.

Let's now turn our attention to the MSSP framework and examine the common solutions utilized by MSSPs to maintain the security of their client's environments.

Azure Lighthouse

Azure Lighthouse is a service that enables MSPs/MSSPs to deliver managed services to their customers at scale. With Azure Lighthouse, service providers can access and manage multiple customer subscriptions from a single portal, using delegated access and identity management (RBAC passthrough). This reduces the complexity and overhead of managing multiple tenants and improves the efficiency and security of service delivery. In general, MSSPs mainly use Azure Lighthouse for managing multiple Azure environments. This approach is great from a productivity point of view but can have significant security challenges depending on how the service provider environment is configured and hardened.

If you compare, for example, GDAP and Azure Lighthouse, the latter adds more granularity for managing the permissions and doesn't require a similar partnership to GDAP (the latter requires a reseller partnership).

Microsoft Entra ID

Even though Azure Lighthouse plays a central role in an MSSP scenario, Microsoft Entra ID plays a vital role as well. Typically, users from an MSSP organization are invited to the client organization tenant where they appear as guest users. Then these users can be granted Entra ID roles that can manage Microsoft 365 services such as Microsoft Defender XDR.

> **Note**
> Azure Lighthouse can grant access only to Azure roles and guest users can be granted both Entra ID and Azure roles.

Read more about Azure and Entra ID role differences at the following link: `https://packt.link/MV0vC`.

Figure 9.2 shows an example of MSSP architecture where the following components are in place:

- Dedicated MSSP tenant

- Two client tenants

- Azure Lighthouse for managing Azure resources on client environments

- Entra ID B2B access

- **Multi-tenant** management for managing Microsoft Defender XDR

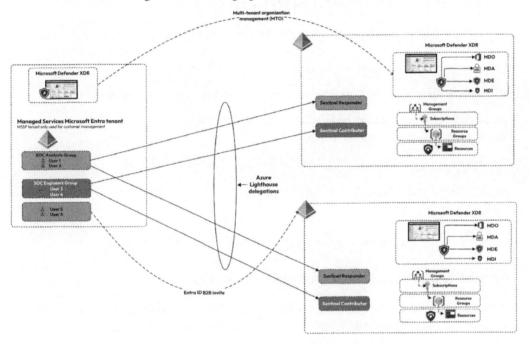

Figure 9.2 – An example of an MSSP architecture in the Microsoft ecosystem

Multi-tenant management in Microsoft Defender XDR

Multi-tenant management is a new feature that addresses the complexity of managing multiple tenants in a Defender XDR context. Before multi-tenant management, SOC teams needed to jump between Defender XDR portals (new authentication) if they switched tenants, which was time consuming and reduced efficiency.

Multi-tenant management provides a single unified view for all client tenants a user has access to. By leveraging multi-tenant management capabilities, SOC teams can speed up the investigation process across multiple tenants and can perform advanced hunting across multiple tenants.

The available content at the time of writing this book is as follows:

- **Incidents**: Incidents can be managed across tenants.

- **Alerts:** Alerts can be managed across tenants.

- **Advanced hunting and custom detection rules**: Hunting queries can be run across tenants.

- **Devices**: Devices can be seen across tenants.

- **TVM**: TVM information can be seen across tenants.

- **Tenant settings**: You have the ability to manage tenants.

Prerequisites for multi-tenant management

To leverage multi-tenant management for managing tenants and Microsoft Defender XDR content, you need to establish access through GDAP or Entra ID B2B as well as the necessary permissions to manage the content in the Defender XDR context.

If GDAP is the chosen approach, then these can be set from the Microsoft Partner Center.

Entra ID B2B Guest accounts can be established, for example, by leveraging Entra ID Access Packages or cross-tenant synchronization capabilities.

More information about the GDAP and B2B approach is available at the following links:

- GDAP (`https://packt.link/kZEgT`)

- Entra ID B2B (`https://packt.link/LVqAG`)

- Cross-tenant synchronization capabilities (`https://packt.link/8SfeQ`)

Content management in an MSSP scenario

Content management can be one of the challenges in an MSSP scenario where a service provider is managing tens, or even hundreds, of customer environments and content on them.

Microsoft's ecosystem has rich APIs that can be leveraged for content management, especially in a scenario where the full Microsoft stack is not used. If the MSSP utilizes the Microsoft stack, Sentinel **Workspace Manager** can be used for content management. By leveraging the Workspace Manager, MSSPs can manage and push content to customer environments.

In *Figure 9.3*, you can see possible Workspace Manager architectures. The simplest one is a direct link where the MSSP controls all member workspaces through one central workspace.

In the co-management model, more than one central workspace may manage member workspaces. This benefits greatly if a shared responsibility model is used between customer organizations and MSSPs.

The N-tier model supports more complex scenarios where a central workspace controls another central workspace.

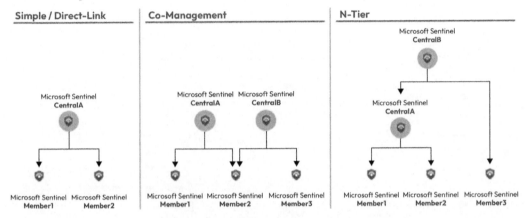

Figure 9.3 – Example MSSP in the Microsoft ecosystem

At the time of writing this book, the following content types are available and supported by the Workspace Manager:

- Analytics rules
- Automation rules (excluding Playbooks)
- Parsers, saved searches, and functions
- Advanced hunting and livestream queries
- Workbooks

In *Figure 9.4*, you can see an example of a direct-link Workspace Manager architecture in place where content is managed in the central workspace and pushed to member workspaces.

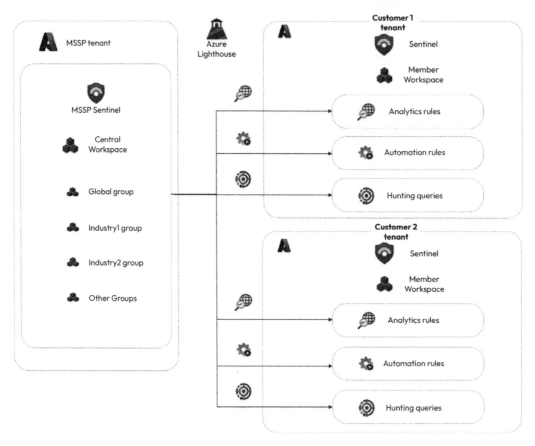

Figure 9.4 – Example Sentinel Workspace Manager architecture

Content management is a crucial part of MSSP-managed environments. They have multiple customers to manage and content needs to be delivered to the environment efficiently and confidently. The solutions we described here are leveraged in typical Microsoft reference architecture but, as we highlighted, there are many different providers on the market as well.

Case study analysis

In this case study analysis, the main challenges raised by the fictitious company, High Tech Rapid Solutions Corp, were siloed architecture and lack of visibility of the environment. Some challenges and concerns were raised by the current security team, which are summarized in the following list:

- The existing security team is struggling to adopt new technologies and there is a skill gap.

- There are limited funds available (reduced costs) and at the same time, the security posture should be developed further.

- The SOC team doesn't have active security monitoring or posture management solutions for on-premises and at the same time, they have limited visibility of the environment.

The company will have its own security team in the future but because of the challenges mentioned previously, it would be beneficial to outsource some of the services to an MSSP and focus on the core functions. One approach could be a shared model where responsibilities are shared between the MSSP and the High Tech Rapid Solutions Corp security team.

This kind of approach would address the visibility issues in the cloud, on-premises, and in the IoT/OT environment. By using an MSSP team, the company would greatly benefit from their expertise and knowledge in the cybersecurity domain and would also be able to have long-needed TI data included in their security monitoring approach, as well as cutting-edge and constantly developing tools and services.

Alright, that wraps up the *Case study analysis* section. As highlighted throughout the book, these tools that are part of Microsoft Unified XDR and SIEM are very powerful together and, when used correctly, they can really save your time and dramatically improve your security posture. In this book, we only scratched the surface by covering a few use cases with the fictional organization High Tech Rapid Solutions Corp and we highly recommend that you explore all the features by yourselves to become more familiar with the tools and all the possibilities they provide.

Summary

In this chapter, we discussed managed services at a high level and elaborated on the typical services that MSSPs are offering to their customers. We also went through tips for selecting a service provider for your security services as well as the pros and cons of having one in place. From a technical point of view, we covered typical MSSP architecture in the Microsoft ecosystem, but real-world implementations vary, as do the services provided, between MSSPs.

In the next chapter, you will find references for useful resources that delve deeper into the topics covered in earlier sections.

Further reading

Refer to the following links for more information about the topics that are covered in this chapter:

- Manage Microsoft-certified solution provider partner relationships | Microsoft Learn (`https://packt.link/frWor`)
- What is Azure Lighthouse | Microsoft Learn (`https://packt.link/SdLWJ`)
- GDAP introduction | Microsoft Learn (`https://packt.link/19o0y`)
- Microsoft Sentinel Workspace Manager | Microsoft Learn (`https://packt.link/Pb9Om`)

- Cloud Solution Provider (CSP) security best practices | Microsoft Learn (`https://packt.link/tstkE`)

- Customer security best practices | Microsoft Learn (`https://packt.link/9uPhu`)

- MSSP Technical Playbook (`https://packt.link/941ZH`)

- Manage multiple Microsoft Sentinel workspaces with workspace manager | Microsoft Learn (`https://packt.link/6ct7K`)

- Provide managed security service provider (MSSP) access | Microsoft Learn (`https://packt.link/1Rg3m`)

- Professional services supported by Microsoft Defender XDR | Microsoft Learn (`https://packt.link/5cD4a`)

10
Useful Resources

In this chapter, we will cover some of the useful resources that can be leveraged to understand the big picture and get more information about the topics covered throughout the book.

This chapter will cover some of the useful resources for the following:

- Microsoft's Unified **extended detection and response** (**XDR**) and **security information and event management** (**SIEM**) resources
- Some of the non-Microsoft XDR and SIEM solutions
- Some of the well-known managed XDR and managed SOC providers
- Cybersecurity industry reports
- Some useful community and third-party resources such as blogs, training, GitHub resources, and books

Microsoft Unified XDR and SIEM Solution resources

Microsoft's integrated XDR and SIEM are strategically designed to strengthen your organization's security stance. Some key components of these resources are outlined in the following sections.

Microsoft Defender XDR

As part of Microsoft's XDR suite, Microsoft Defender XDR delivers unified security across various critical fronts, encompassing endpoints, email, collaborative tools, and cloud applications. See the following for more on Microsoft Defender XDR:

- *A day in the life of a Defender Experts for XDR analyst* (`https://packt.link/x6nqx`)
- *Evaluate and pilot Microsoft Defender XDR* (`https://packt.link/D5hxX`)
- *Integrating Microsoft Defender XDR into your security operations* (`https://packt.link/tW26F`)

Microsoft Sentinel

- *Best practices for Microsoft Sentinel* (https://packt.link/AfWek)
- *Plan your migration to Microsoft Sentinel* (https://packt.link/VOOCT)
- Microsoft Sentinel migration tracker workbook (https://packt.link/FluHu)

Microsoft Defender for Identity

- *Deploy Microsoft Defender for Identity with Microsoft Defender XDR* (https://packt.link/WWb0C)
- *Plan capacity for Microsoft Defender for Identity deployment* (https://packt.link/8s4ry)
- *Design your Microsoft Sentinel workspace architecture* (https://packt.link/rWZ9P)

Microsoft Defender for Office

- *Microsoft Defender for Office 365 Security Operations Guide* (https://packt.link/zTZte)
- *Migrate from a third-party protection service or device to Microsoft Defender for Office 365* (https://packt.link/guEUd)
- *Recommended settings for EOP and Microsoft Defender for Office 365 security* (https://packt.link/jtAa1)
- *Set up an evaluation or trial in audit mode* (https://packt.link/Yv78g)

Microsoft Defender for Endpoint

- Enable access to Microsoft Defender for Endpoint service URLs in the proxy server (https://packt.link/FPEkK)
- *Migrate to Microsoft Defender for Endpoint from non-Microsoft endpoint protection* (https://packt.link/ziFoz)
- *Performance analyzer for Microsoft Defender Antivirus* (https://packt.link/kD7Jo)
- *Run the client analyzer on Windows* (https://packt.link/3zgvs)
- *Validate connections between your network and the cloud* (https://packt.link/F7yow)

Microsoft Defender for Cloud Apps

- *Lifecycle management strategy in Defender for Cloud Apps* (`https://packt.link/90g4o`)

- *Best practices for protecting your organization with Defender for Cloud Apps* (`https://packt.link/aUVZO`)

- *Top 20 use cases for Defender for Cloud Apps* - `https://packt.link/NRFL1`

Microsoft Defender for Cloud

- Microsoft Defender for Cloud's overview page (`https://packt.link/UMRnK`)

- The Microsoft Defender for Cloud community repository (`https://packt.link/6KO1A`)

- *New Ransomware Recommendation Dashboard in Microsoft Defender for Cloud* (`https://packt.link/9nABh`)

Non-Microsoft XDR and SIEM solutions

Many companies offer XDR and SIEM solutions that are not from Microsoft. Some of the most well-known providers are listed in the following sections.

XDR solutions

- Palo Alto Networks Cortex XDR (`https://packt.link/XIDcR`)

- CrowdStrike Falcon XDR (`https://packt.link/y5ORu`)

- Elastic Security for XDR (`https://packt.link/T8Neh`)

- Rapid7 InsightIDR (`https://packt.link/wStEp`)

- SentinelOne Singularity XDR (`https://packt.link/0a8oM`)

- Sophos Intercept X XDR (`https://packt.link/oh8Eq`)

- Trend Micro Vision One XDR (`https://packt.link/DZwGb`)

SIEM solutions

- ArcSight (`https://packt.link/fvvZM`)

- Chronicle SIEM (`https://packt.link/zFYoa`)

- Elastic Security (`https://packt.link/ruTK8`)

- IBM Security QRadar (`https://packt.link/6NEba`)

- LogRhythm (`https://packt.link/WaxYu`)

- Rapid7 InsightIDR (`https://packt.link/Tl2Je`)
- Securonix (`https://packt.link/HR99T`)
- Splunk (`https://packt.link/aaJ4k`)

Managed XDR and managed SOC providers

Several companies offer high-level expertise and services in managing XDR and SOC operations. Some of the reputable names in this field include the following:

- Microsoft (`https://packt.link/dn2re`); you can also find professional services supported by Microsoft Defender XDR at `https://packt.link/t2wZ5`
- Avanade (`https://packt.link/qnq4z`)
- BlueVoyant (`https://packt.link/wtRFb`)
- Wortell Protect (`https://packt.link/xuHPv`)
- Wipro (`https://packt.link/GfdTp`)
- Mandiant (`https://packt.link/vQ2Ds`)
- Glueckkanja (`https://packt.link/VsNVo`)
- Netox (`https://packt.link/cAHMV`)
- Rapid 7 (`https://packt.link/E0gdq`)
- Securonix (`https://packt.link/z8Uow`)
- SentinelOne (`https://packt.link/dkn2N`)
- Sophos (`https://packt.link/y86Q1`)
- Accenture (`https://packt.link/ZSXW9`)
- IBM Security (`https://packt.link/bMnTF`)

Cybersecurity Industry Reports 2023

Several research firms offer insightful reports on cybersecurity, exploring its trends, challenges, and promising opportunities. Here are a few examples:

- **Microsoft – Digital Defense Report**: This is an effective resource for businesses who are looking to improve their cybersecurity posture. The report provides a comprehensive overview of the current threat landscape and offers practical recommendations for how to mitigate risks (`https://packt.link/WJXUP`).

- **Palo Alto – the State of Cloud-Native Security Report**: This report is a comprehensive study based on a month-long survey of over 2,500 cloud security and DevOps professionals across seven countries and five industries. The survey aimed to identify key decisions that impact cloud-native development and security outcomes. This state of cloud-native security report can be found at `https://packt.link/zpGQi`.

- **CrowdStrike – Global Threat Report**: This comprehensive threat report can be found at `https://packt.link/3jkob`.

- **Wipro – State of Cybersecurity Report**: This report provides comprehensive insights into the latest cybersecurity trends and challenges, as well as practical recommendations for improving cybersecurity posture. This state of cyber security report is available at `https://packt.link/zd2Ad`.

- **Splunk – The State of Security**: This report by Splunk covers challenges faced by the security teams, such as the difficulty of keeping up with security requirements and the prevalence of ransomware attacks, but despite these challenges, there is a growing recognition of the importance of resilience. You can find this report at `https://packt.link/8tIoy`.

- **Accenture – State of Cybersecurity Resilience**: This report is available at `https://packt.link/0vpzS`.

- **Akamai – State of the Internet Report**: This report provides comprehensive insights into the latest trends in internet traffic, connectivity, security, and performance. You can find this report at `https://packt.link/2GK1G`.

- **CompTIA – State of Cybersecurity 2024**: This report can be accessed at `https://packt.link/v1t7k`.

- **Sophos – The State of Cybersecurity**: The report is built upon insights from a survey of 3,000 cybersecurity/IT professionals across 14 countries. It delves into the current landscape of cybersecurity and the evolving strategies employed by adversaries. The report is available at `https://packt.link/y1peR`.

Community and third-party resources

To enrich your understanding and gain additional insights, consider exploring the following communities and resources in the following sections.

Some of the blogs

- Sami Lamppu (`https://packt.link/L2DDz`)

- Harri Jaakkonen (`https://packt.link/Gla3i`)

- *Thomas Naunheim* (`https://packt.link/G8ry3`)

- Rod Trent (https://packt.link/6tevX)
- *Jeffrey Appel* (https://packt.link/PnvaV)
- Ru Campbell (https://packt.link/P6knG)
- *Just do the basics* (https://packt.link/Mqed4)
- Fabian Bader – *Cloudbrothers* (https://packt.link/5G71o)
- Raymond Roethof (https://packt.link/CXGIw)
- Andrew Taylor (https://packt.link/2JHOu)
- Sameh Younis (https://packt.link/i6HHs)
- Truls Dahlsveen (https://packt.link/cqnOA)

Training

- Heike Ritter – Virtual Ninja Training:

  - Microsoft Defender XDR (https://packt.link/krVHh)
  - Microsoft Defender for Cloud (https://packt.link/XoT7j)
  - Microsoft Defender for Endpoint (https://packt.link/TC4Fd)
  - Microsoft Defender for Identity (https://packt.link/vnHzq)
  - Microsoft Defender for Office 365 (https://packt.link/SDVGW)
  - Microsoft Defender for Cloud Apps (https://packt.link/Rsc0k)
  - Microsoft Defender for IoT (https://packt.link/x4S0f)
  - Microsoft Sentinel (https://packt.link/mwQjn)
  - Microsoft Defender Threat Intelligence (https://packt.link/nc1C3)
  - Microsoft Defender Vulnerability Management (https://packt.link/FeEtK)

- Microsoft Sentinel Notebooks (https://packt.link/cjQbr)
- Microsoft Security Webinars (https://packt.link/Oy6vU)
- The Chief Information Security Officer (CISO) Workshop Training (https://packt.link/oE1gw)
- Chief Information Security Officer (CISO) Workshop Training (https://packt.link/3owvG)

- Some of the relevant self-paced Microsoft resources are as follows:

  - SC-100 (`https://packt.link/nI8gt`)

  - SC-200 (`https://packt.link/7vmjk`)

  - SC-300 (`https://packt.link/kIEPh` and `https://packt.link/E2SjJ`)

  - SC-400 (`https://packt.link/WqkEU`)

  - SC-900 (`https://packt.link/EGs9g`)

Community tools and GitHub resources

- Microsoft Sentinel – GitHub (`https://packt.link/JXtB3`)

- *Microsoft 365 roadmap* (`https://packt.link/zzcT8`)

- *Microsoft Cybersecurity Reference Architectures* (`https://packt.link/Cb8Dk`)

- Microsoft Defender XDR – Step by step (`https://packt.link/nZMfJ`)

- Microsoft Defender XDR GitHub Hunting Queries (`https://packt.link/Rg394`)

- *Microsoft Defender XDR Blog* (`https://packt.link/GdsRM`)

- Morten Knudsen – GitHub (`https://packt.link/vQw9a`)

- *Zero Trust deployment plan with Microsoft 365* (`https://packt.link/O6uNY`)

- *Zero Trust adoption framework overview* (`https://packt.link/Q79Gz`)

- *Zero Trust Rapid Modernization Plan* (`https://packt.link/0q0QX`)

- *RaMP checklist — Data protection* (`https://packt.link/aUawb`)

- *RaMP Checklist — Explicitly validate trust for all access requests* (`https://packt.link/VDJq7`)

- *RaMP checklist — Ransomware recovery readiness* (`https://packt.link/D6y1k`)

- *Security Adoption Resources* (`https://packt.link/BUBez`)

- *Step-by-step instructions that are tenant-aware and customized to your organization's needs* (`https://packt.link/UlzTX`)

- *Welcome to the Microsoft Defender for Office 365 step-by-step guides* (`https://packt.link/dEB17`)

- *What's new in Microsoft Defender XDR* (`https://packt.link/NfCOi`)
- GitHub – Azure/Azure-Sentinel: Cloud-native SIEM for intelligent security analytics for your entire enterprise (`https://packt.link/LN8K7`)
- reprise99 · GitHub (`https://packt.link/2P7p1`)
- KQL Search (`https://packt.link/wJi4w`)

Books

- *Mastering Microsoft 365 Defender* by Ru Campbell (Author), Viktor Hedberg (Author), and Heike Ritter (Foreword) – ASIN: B0BYZLJFCR
- *Microsoft Defender for Cloud Cookbook* by Sasha Kranjac (Author) – ASIN: B0B21KXN5C
- *Microsoft Defender for Endpoint in Depth* by Paul Huijbregts (Author), Joe Anich (Author), and Justen Graves (Author) – ASIN: B0BQN5LVWJ
- *Microsoft Security, Compliance, and Identity Fundamentals Exam Ref SC-900* by Dwayne Natwick (Author) and Sonia Cuff (Foreword) – ASIN: B09W9WPP7C
- *Microsoft Sentinel in Action* by Richard Diver (Author), Gary Bushey (Author), and John Perkins (Author) – ISBN-10: 1801815534
- *Must Learn AI Security* by Rod Trent (Author) – ISBN: 979-8870114194
- *Must Learn KQL: Essential Learning for the Cloud* by Rod Trent (Author) – ISBN: 979-8826914960
- *Mastering Microsoft 365 Security and Compliance* by Sasha Kranjac (Author), Omar Kudovic (Author) – ISBN: 978-1837638376
- *Mastering Cloud Security Posture Management (CSPM)* by Qamar Nomani (Author) – ISBN: 978-1837638406
- *The Definitive Guide to Kql*: Using Kusto Query Language for Operations, Defending, and Threat Hunting by Mark Morowczynski (Author), Rod Trent (Author), Matthew Zorich (Author) - ISBN-10: 0138293384
- *Zero Trust Overview and Playbook Introduction*: Guidance for business, security, and technology leaders and practitioners by Mark Simos (Author), Nikhil Kumar (Author), Ann Johnson (Foreword) - ISBN-10: 1800568665

Security shows

- *Microsoft Security* (`https://packt.link/HobzN`)
- *Microsoft Security Insights Show*, hosted by Edward Walton, Andrea Fisher, Rod Trent, and Brodie Cassell (`https://packt.link/cv4Ta`)

LinkedIn groups

- *Microsoft Defender Community* (`https://packt.link/vDHLc`)

- *Microsoft Security Community* (`https://packt.link/Ppqac`)

- *Microsoft Copilot for Security Community* (`https://packt.link/STf2b`)

- *Microsoft Endpoint Manager/Intune Suite Community* (`https://packt.link/KhBeX`)

- *Microsoft Entra Community* (`https://packt.link/JuoCY`)

- *Microsoft Cloud Security Group* (`https://packt.link/0Bvu7`)

- *Copilot, Viva, Office 365 (O365), Microsoft 365 (M365) User Group* (`https://packt.link/nyMde`)

Thank you

We hope you enjoyed reading this book and we trust that you found the book informative. As demonstrated throughout, the synergistic combination of Microsoft Unified XDR and SIEM, supplemented by individual defenders, offers organizations a robust and efficient security ecosystem. By adopting this unified solution, you can anticipate significant improvements in operational efficiency through time saved, while simultaneously witnessing a dramatic enhancement in your overall security posture. This book laid the groundwork, highlighting the core features and benefits, but the true potential lies in embracing and leveraging the full power of this comprehensive solution.

We strongly encourage you to dive in and explore all the features of these tools yourself. This hands-on approach will help you become familiar with their capabilities and unlock their full potential. As Microsoft continuously invests in these products, transforming them into powerful AI-powered solutions, it's important to stay up to date with the latest resources. However, the underlying concepts and foundations will remain constant and crucial to understand, regardless of future updates.

We want to empower the cybersecurity community by making a resource that's accessible to everyone, regardless of their experience level. This book aims to demystify the powerful Microsoft Unified XDR and SIEM solution, positioning it as your one-stop security shop. We're aware the content in this book might not cover everything, but within our limitations, we strived to tackle the most critical aspects of these security platforms. We hope this aligns with your goals and we welcome any feedback the community has to offer. We're eager to learn and improve!

– Raghu and Sami

Index

packtpub.com

Subscribe to our online digital library for full access to over 7,000 books and videos, as well as industry leading tools to help you plan your personal development and advance your career. For more information, please visit our website.

Why subscribe?

- Spend less time learning and more time coding with practical eBooks and Videos from over 4,000 industry professionals

- Improve your learning with Skill Plans built especially for you

- Get a free eBook or video every month

- Fully searchable for easy access to vital information

- Copy and paste, print, and bookmark content

Did you know that Packt offers eBook versions of every book published, with PDF and ePub files available? You can upgrade to the eBook version at packtpub.com and as a print book customer, you are entitled to a discount on the eBook copy. Get in touch with us at customercare@packtpub.com for more details.

At www.packtpub.com, you can also read a collection of free technical articles, sign up for a range of free newsletters, and receive exclusive discounts and offers on Packt books and eBooks.

Other Books You May Enjoy

If you enjoyed this book, you may be interested in these other books by Packt:

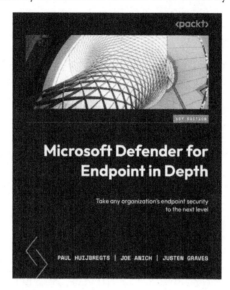

Microsoft Defender for Endpoint in Depth

Paul Huijbregts, Joe Anich, Justen Graves

ISBN: 978-1-80461-546-1

- Understand the backstory of Microsoft Defender for Endpoint
- Discover different features, their applicability, and caveats
- Prepare and plan a rollout within an organization
- Explore tools and methods to successfully operationalize the product
- Implement continuous operations and improvement to your security posture
- Get to grips with the day-to-day of SecOps teams operating the product
- Deal with common issues using various techniques and tools
- Uncover commonly used commands, tips, and tricks

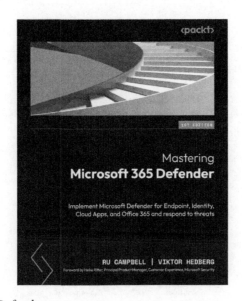

Mastering Microsoft 365 Defender

Ru Campbell, Viktor Hedberg

ISBN: 978-1-80324-170-8

- Understand the Threat Landscape for enterprises
- Effectively implement end-point security
- Manage identity and access management using Microsoft 365 defender
- Protect the productivity suite with Microsoft Defender for Office 365
- Hunting for threats using Microsoft 365 Defender

Packt is searching for authors like you

If you're interested in becoming an author for Packt, please visit authors.packtpub.com and apply today. We have worked with thousands of developers and tech professionals, just like you, to help them share their insight with the global tech community. You can make a general application, apply for a specific hot topic that we are recruiting an author for, or submit your own idea.

Share Your Thoughts

Now you've finished *Microsoft Unified XDR and SIEM Solution Handbook*, we'd love to hear your thoughts! Scan the QR code below to go straight to the Amazon review page for this book and share your feedback or leave a review on the site that you purchased it from.

https://packt.link/r/1835086853

Your review is important to us and the tech community and will help us make sure we're delivering excellent quality content.

Download a free PDF copy of this book

Thanks for purchasing this book!

Do you like to read on the go but are unable to carry your print books everywhere?

Is your eBook purchase not compatible with the device of your choice?

Don't worry, now with every Packt book you get a DRM-free PDF version of that book at no cost.

Read anywhere, any place, on any device. Search, copy, and paste code from your favorite technical books directly into your application.

The perks don't stop there, you can get exclusive access to discounts, newsletters, and great free content in your inbox daily

Follow these simple steps to get the benefits:

1. Scan the QR code or visit the link below

https://packt.link/free-ebook/9781835086858

2. Submit your proof of purchase
3. That's it! We'll send your free PDF and other benefits to your email directly

Printed in Great Britain
by Amazon

42162557R00165